ECOCRITICAL AESTHETICS

ECOCRITICAL AESTHETICS

Language, Beauty, and the Environment

EDITED BY **PETER QUIGLEY** AND **SCOTT SLOVIC**

INDIANA UNIVERSITY PRESS

This book is a publication of

Indiana University Press
Office of Scholarly Publishing
Herman B Wells Library 350
1320 East 10th Street
Bloomington, Indiana 47405 USA

iupress.indiana.edu

© 2018 by Indiana University Press
All rights reserved
No part of this book may be reproduced or utilized in any form or by any means, electronic or mechanical, including photocopying and recording, or by any information storage and retrieval system, without permission in writing from the publisher.

The paper used in this publication meets the minimum requirements of the American National Standard for Information Sciences—Permanence of Paper for Printed Library Materials, ANSI Z39.48–1992.

*Manufactured in the
United States of America*

*Cataloging information is available
from the Library of Congress.*

ISBN 978-0-253-03210-2 (cloth)
ISBN 978-0-253-03212-6 (paperback)
ISBN 978-0-253-03211-9 (ebook)

1 2 3 4 5   23 22 21 20 19 18

CONTENTS

Acknowledgments · *vii*

Introduction / Peter Quigley · *1*

Part 1. The Relevance of Beauty

1 "It Is Out of Fashion to Say So": The Language of Nature and the Rhetoric of Beauty in Robinson Jeffers / Tim Hunt · *23*

2 Thoreau's Poetics of Nature / Arnold Berleant · *41*

3 The Pout's Nest and the Painter's Eye / Frank Stewart · *51*

4 "Yet How Beautiful It Is!": Work, Ethics, and Beauty in Stegner's *Angle of Repose* / Tyler Nickl · *63*

5 Renaissance Aesthetics, Picturesque Beauty, the Natural Landscape: An Essay Examining the Rise and Fall of the Impulse toward Beauty / Mark Luccarelli · *77*

Part 2. Beauty and Engagement

6 Toward an Ecofeminist Aesthetic of Reconnection / Greta Gaard · *97*

7 Beauty and the Body: Toward an Ecofeminist Aesthetic That Includes Loving Our Naked Selves / Janine DeBaise · *115*

8 Dystopia and Utopia in a Nuclear Landscape: Emerging Aesthetics in Satoyama / Yuki Masami · *129*

9 Know Beauty, Know Justice: Why Beauty Matters in
   the Classroom / ShaunAnne Tangney · *143*

Part 3. Materiality, Transcendence, and Aesthetics

10 Nature's Colors: A Prismatic Materiality in the Natural/
    Cultural Realms / Serpil Oppermann · *157*

11 From the Human to the Divine: Nature in the Writings
    of the Tamil Poet-Saints / Cynthia J. Miller · *173*

12 Beauty as Ideological and Material Transcendence / Werner Bigell · *187*

13 Toward Sustainable Aesthetics: The Poetry of Food, Sex, Water,
    Architecture, and Bicycle Riding / Scott Slovic · *201*

Index · *215*

ACKNOWLEDGMENTS

THIS BOOK ORIGINATED with a panel titled "No Beauty, No Peace: Robinson Jeffers and the Politics of Beauty and Justice," which I organized for the 2012 Western Literature Association conference in Lubbock, Texas. The panel was made up of old friends and longtime Jeffers scholars: David C. Morris, David Rothman, and ShaunAnne Tangney. We had a spirited discussion with the audience following the papers, emerging from the session with a shared concern that beauty is being eclipsed in contemporary critical discourse and specifically within the environmental humanities. The four of us from the panel had lunch that day with Barry Lopez and Scott Slovic, and Barry and Scott immediately recognized that our ideas could form the basis of a meaningful book project. Back home in Hawai'i, I received important support from my doctoral student Eric San George and my colleague Frank Stewart, both of whom have helped me plan this project and offered encouragement and advice during the four years it's taken to bring it to fruition.

In acknowledging those who have contributed in major ways to this volume, thanks must first go to all of the contributors to the collection. I appreciate their excellent scholarship, their patience during the editorial and publishing process, and their speedy and careful revisions of their initial manuscripts. I also wish to thank Scott Slovic for his collaborative, informed, friendly, and eclectic approach to the many voices that constitute this volume. Frankly, with his hectic travels all over the world to speak and teach, while holding down teaching and administrative duties in Idaho, I was amazed at his ability to apply studious attention to the editorial details of this project and help propel us toward publication.

Peter Quigley
University of Hawai'i,
Manoa

I HAVE NEVER been blind to the beauty of the literary works I've studied for the past several decades as an ecocritic, but until Peter Quigley and company beckoned Barry and me over to their table in Lubbock, aesthetics had always seemed a somewhat secondary or tertiary dimension of my scholarly preoccupations. Working on this project with Peter has driven home the meaning, the importance, of beauty in all of my work—it will never recede into the background again. I thank Peter for his intensity and enthusiasm, his commitment to the cause—our collaboration has been an exciting one.

Peter and I both appreciate the support of the staff at Indiana University Press and the excellent feedback from our anonymous reviewers. This project has benefited greatly from their contributions.

There is so much to worry about as we consider the prognosis for environmental protection and social justice in the coming years—but there is also much to celebrate. This book is a celebration of cultural engagement with the natural world, and it is also a recognition of how beauty in nature and beauty in human artifacts can inspire attention and activism.

Scott Slovic
University of Idaho

PERMISSIONS

WILLIAM STAFFORD, "Maybe Alone on My Bike," *Smoke's Way: Poems from Limited Editions, 1968–1981*. Originally published in the *New Yorker*, April 4, 1964. Copyright 1964 by William Stafford. Reprinted with the permission of The Permissions Company, Inc., on behalf of Graywolf Press, www.graywolfpress.org.

Ofelia Zepeda, "B 'o e-a:g maṣ 'ab him g ju:kĭ / It Is Going to Rain." Reprinted with the permission of Ofelia Zepeda.

ECOCRITICAL AESTHETICS

INTRODUCTION

PETER QUIGLEY

IN 1996, AT THE DAWN of the contemporary ecocritical enterprise, Sven Birkerts published a review of *The Ecocriticism Reader* in the *Boston Book Review*. It captured the freshness of this new field, the sense of new possibilities as well as the likelihood of some competitive elbowing: "Here is yet another new frontier; a land-rush is underway; critics and thinkers are staking out their fields, their terrain. There is a bit of that excitement of origins that is found when options are still open, before the power brokers have muscled the first orthodoxies into place." Something important has been lost, however, in the inevitable jostling and elbowing that has taken place during the past two decades: a concern for beauty.

Where has interest in the study of beauty gone in ecocritical studies and in critical theory as a whole? One of the reasons Scott Slovic and I collaborated on this project was that we both agreed that, as Scott put it to me in an e-mail, the "beauty of nature and the beautiful renderings of environmental ideas and experience in various media of cultural expression, both of which were among the essential motivations for those who worked to establish ecocriticism as a self-aware scholarly movement in the 1980s and '90s, quickly became subsumed among many other scholarly concerns" ("Latest"). As a numerical indicator of this, I found that the "ASLE Online Bibliography 2000–2010" contains twenty-seven references to "justice" in titles and ninety-four appearances of the word "justice" in the abstracts. For "beauty," however, there were only six appearances in titles and twenty-four in the abstracts. "Aesthetics" turns up three times in titles. I strongly suspect that the upward arc for "social justice" in titles and abstracts has steepened since 2010 and that the mention of beauty or aesthetics has diminished. Similarly, Slovic reported that "in June 2015, the Association for the Study of Literature and Environment (ASLE) hosted at the University of Idaho what may well have been the world's largest gathering of ecocritics to date. Some 900 scholars and writers from thirty countries gathered to talk about literature and the arts in relation to such topics as fracking, global climate change, animal subjectivity, environmental justice, queer ecologies, narrative ethics, acoustic ecologies, humor, the body, activist pedagogy, and many other ideas. Amid the throng, aesthetics was almost nowhere to be found. Only four papers mentioned aesthetics in their titles."

In our correspondence on this issue, Scott wrote that he considers aesthetics to be one of the elephants in the room at eco-conferences, something folks are aware of, thinking about, but for some reason hesitant to engage with: "Scholars hesitate to invoke beauty as an intellectual mechanism for gaining traction on these [environmental] problems. Beauty often feels so private, so complacent, even decadent." I think he's right; I do, of course, think people still experience and think about beauty, but they feel restricted and prohibited due to the options our current critical methodologies allow. In our back-and-forth, I have tended to say that these limiting options have been politically strategic in design, that this erasure of beauty is purposeful, intentional, and not inadvertent. If aesthetics is mentioned at all, it is reduced to a "form of social semiotics . . . in a war of position against All Bad Things" (Bérubé 6–7).[1] Such reductionist treatment diminishes and contorts our lived experience and our intellectual life. Like the seat in the very last row of the airplane, the window has intentionally been removed; I can't see, and it feels odd.

How did we arrive at this contorted and dismissive approach to beauty, and what has it meant for ecocriticism? It might be useful to trace some of the forces of marginalization associated with this issue. In 1985, one year before the publication of *Critical Theory since 1965*, Frederick Turner was talking confidently, in *Natural Classicism: Essays on Literature and Science*, about the return of aesthetics as the result of the collapse of Marxist theory: "The old socioeconomic theories which dismissed aesthetics as merely a superstructure designed to justify and rationalize economic power and social inequality have now largely been exploded" (243). In 1991, however, Turner's tone changed in the first sentence of his book *Beauty: The Value of Values*, where he registers the retreat from beauty as a professional term: "The word *beauty* is a little embarrassing; there is something old-fashioned about it" (1). He follows this confession, however, with a willful insistence on its usage: "It is precisely for this reason that I shall use it rather than the much cooler and more stylish term *the aesthetic*. The aesthetic is often either a euphemism for that coarse and lachrymose old *beauty* or a hard, free, clean and cruel substitute for it, steel flowers for the bride" (1).

So, by the early 1990s, discussing beauty in "serious" circles had become a problem, and "aesthetics" was offered as a device, a more sober-sounding, opaque, albeit sterile substitute.[2] In 1998 Scott Heller, writing in the *Chronicle of Higher Education*, quoted University of California professor of English Emory Elliot admitting this about beauty: "This is the forbidden subject" (qtd. in Heller).[3]

There's a tendency to use these two terms—beauty and aesthetics—interchangeably. Nevertheless, I feel a kind of professional imprecision when I do so. The two terms are notably distinct in theory but possess many related qualities in practice. Aesthetics has generally been thought of as the study of beauty. Originating with the Kantian claim regarding cognitive and moral structures of human perception, aesthetics has historically been applied in the arts as the form, the frame, and the technique by which visions of nature, human relations, or any other artistic themes are represented. Frequently in theory and critical history, these forms or frames were considered to be pleasing, even beautiful, although as Turner suggests, aesthetics and beauty became separated. Walter Pater is credited with introducing aesthetics into Victorian England with an "emphasis on high artifice and stylistic subtlety" along with "his recommendation to crowd one's life with exquisite sensations, and his advocacy of the supreme value of beauty" (Abrams 3). Pater's well-known conclusion to *The Renaissance* has many quotable lines illustrating these issues:

> A counted number of pulses only is given to us of a variegated, dramatic life. How may we see in them all that is to be seen in them by the finest senses? How shall we pass most swiftly from point to point, and be present always at the focus where the greatest number of vital forces unite in their purest energy?
>
> To burn always with this hard, gem-like flame, to maintain this ecstasy, is success in life. (Pater 1105)

It's an important feature of early ecocriticism that it initially returned readers and critics to a strong sense of beauty: beauty as direct engagement with nature as well as a return to an appreciation of language beautifully used to render these engagements.[4] Of course, postmodern theories refigured these forms and frames as well as all language within frameworks as representational elements that were thoroughly ideological, deceptively opaque, and in need of deconstructive analysis, historicizing, and other "interrogations." By the late twentieth century, formalism and beauty no longer figured as stand-alone elements in critical theory. As a result, starting just before and continuing through the first decade of the twenty-first century, the terms "aesthetics" and "beauty" have been oscillating wildly into and out of view, into and out of favor—contemporary ecocriticism was born in the midst of this tumult. A little over a decade after Turner's 1991 confession regarding his struggle over the word "beauty," Allen Carlson and Arnold Berleant, in their introduction to *The Aesthetics of Natural Environments* (2004), documented the fact that "the aesthetic appreciation of the natural world has been . . . marginalized" (12). In 1999, Elaine Scarry, in *On Beauty and Being Just*, also registered protest over the "banishing of beauty from the humanities in the last two decades," which she said "has been carried out by a set of political complaints against it" (57). Nevertheless, in a 2000 essay, "The Return of the Beautiful: Morality, Pleasure, and the Value of Uncertainty," Alexander Nehamas, while reviewing Scarry and other writers on the topic, proclaimed that "beauty is suddenly back. It is impossible to keep up with the books that address it" (393). And Michael Bérubé admitted, "My initial reaction to the late 1998 Return to Beauty was sheer incredulity" (3). It seems the topic had won the high ground for a moment, anyway. The opportunity for a renewed engagement with beauty certainly had presented itself, although it was largely concentrated in fields outside of literary studies. Literary studies berated itself two decades ago for missing the green discussions going on in other humanities disciplines;[5] the question of whether the field has missed this opportunity with aesthetics remains. Though ecocriticism initially entertained opportunities for engaging in this area of beauty and aesthetics, it has since veered away. The present volume is motivated by the possibility that the field of ecocriticism may be missing what several scholars have been proclaiming as a promising "return to beauty."

In his essay, Nehamas makes it clear that the twentieth century was pretty hard on the concept of beauty. Starting with modernism, Nehamas goes on to point out that "Postmodernist authors eventually denounced even the austere satisfactions of Modernism and accused them, too, of *colluding with a corrupt global market*" (393; italics added). Echoing this association between beauty and its capitulation to capitalism, Terry Eagleton has stated that "radical thought has . . . insisted" that considering such things as beauty separately from class issues is designed to sequester art "from all other social practices" in order for it "to become an isolated enclave within which the dominant social order can find an idealized refuge from its own actual values of competiveness, exploitation and material possessiveness" (*Ideology* 9).

To combat this insulated and "idealized refuge" that protects one from dealing with the socioeconomic injustices that saturate daily life, beauty (and one can include here, for ecocritical purposes, nature, place, the individual) must be reined in under the sign of the political. Therefore, as Ian Hunter put it in his contribution to the 1992 anthology *Cultural Studies*,[6] "The cultural studies movement conceives of itself as a critique of aesthetics. . . . The slogan of this project is to 'politicize aesthetics'" (347). Ecocriticism's evolution within these forces has been well described and demonstrated by Lawrence Buell. Initially, Buell embraced the assumptions of the emerging ecocritical field this way: "The prototypical human figure," he observed, is a "solitary human and the experience in question activates a primordial link between human and nonhuman" (*Future* 23). Buell memorializes ecocriticism's exciting breakaway from poststructuralism's gravitational pull by those who had become exhausted and dispirited with those approaches.[7] However, as the field began to take on sociopolitical concerns in the 1990s, this first iteration was left behind and the equation was reformulated: "The prototypical human figure is defined by social category and the 'environment' is artificially constructed" (Buell, *Future* 23). Since beauty and nature are now defined as "universals" that conceal political inequities and thereby serve to defend, cloak, and protect ongoing injustices, ecocriticism's work, following the lead of dominant theoretical trends, must transition to peeling back the layers of this deception.

Readers of Thoreau and Wordsworth in the '60s and '70s found beauty, place, and individual independence powerful players in the critique of "the machine," "the system," "the Apparatus," and the "satanic mills," as well as promising foundational positions for posing alternative lifestyles. These readings became known as a kind of romantic ecology,[8] pitting local, bioregional, aesthetic, and individualist sensibilities against a mechanical and then corporate globalization. And later, with the Buddhist-infused antianthropocentrism of Gary Snyder, the antianthropocentric inhumanism of Robinson Jeffers, and writers such as Terry Tempest Williams, Wendell Berry, Gretel Ehrlich, Edward Abbey, and Leslie Marmon Silko, this interest in place, local lifestyle, beauty, the individual, and, yes, politics was furthered. With the introduction of critical theory, however, most of these writers and the critical methods associated with them were swept aside. What impact has this had on ecocriticism? According to Ira Brooker, there subsequently emerged "a school of thought that casts Thoreau and most of his era's prominent nature writers as naive tools in a massive cover-up of the destructive force of 19th-century America" (138). Reading literature and reading culture then became enormously instrumentalist, creating "politicized forms of criticism that appeared to read right through . . . the text to the layers of ideology underneath" (Bérubé 3). Landscape painting as much as literary texts, for example, could be identified in this way as well: "representation of landscape is . . . intimately bound up with the discourses of imperialism" (Mitchell 9). As Jonathan Sterne has written, cultural studies became "less concerned with the objects in themselves than their existence as means—the uses to which they are put" (84). In ecocriticism, all of this meant an increased pressure on and even erasure of the aesthetic of the individual in place as theory catapulted toward global and political policy.

Although in 2010 Scott Slovic noted a "fruitful tension" between place studies and the global ("Third Wave" 7), Bryon Williams has recently sent up the alarm on this issue, noting that the "very notion of a 'sense of place' finds itself in the crosshairs of intensifying theoretical debates" (162). Specifically, Williams reports that Ursula Heise "aims to dislodge the sense of place from the center of environmental thinking, calling it a 'visionary dead end'" (162).

Of course, the marshaling of aesthetics into the service of politics wasn't invented in the late twentieth century. As Tony Bennett argues in *Formalism and Marxism*, the elements of Russian formalism were conscripted into political service in the 1930s when the Futurists labeled "defamiliarization"—making things strange—as "unmotivated": "The emphasis was shifted from the aesthetic function of the device to its use in the service of a 'social demand.' All the manifestations of the device . . . were now considered in the light of their potential social utility" (26). The devices of defamiliarization—the aesthetic, the beautiful, the disturbing, the strange—were "unmotivated" in that they were not "thought to be motivated by any consideration beyond that of promoting a renewed and sharpened attentiveness" (26). When the aesthetic device is "motivated," its focus is on charting "the effects of culture" rather than self-awareness, attentiveness, elevation of a sense of experience, and "endless and indeterminate possibilities for rereadings" (Juffer 65).[9] This indeterminate quality is what brings the charge of quietism; pluralism of views and approaches irritates those who see a clear vision forward.[10] However, as Bérubé makes clear, it can be argued that insofar as theory's "engagements with the aesthetic have tended to instrumentalize the aesthetic, to see aesthetics as a form of social semiotics that can (and therefore should) be read for its possible use in a war of position, it is plausible to say that cultural studies has simply missed the point" (5–6). For Bérubé, it's not that the political should be jettisoned but that there also has to be a question about whether the "social semiosis is danceable and has a good tune" (6). Moving beyond an instrumentalist approach but avoiding a simplistic return to a naïve pastoralism seems to be a fertile area for ecocritics to move into.

Bérubé's warning notwithstanding, historical moments of urgency or ideologies on a crusade have not treated beauty or aesthetics kindly, but instead focus on the crisis at hand or the crisis being manufactured. In these instances, tools must be deployed to keep one's attention sharp on a movement's *causes célèbre* and to marginalize distractions. To this end, most of the critical energy in the 1980s was focused on deconstructing stealthy and pervasive concepts like beauty or nature—that is, the various linguistic manifestations of "power." Myra Jehlen worried aloud, however, as ideologically charged, crisis-focused criticism was winding its spring and developing such tools. The premise of this new critical approach is that our job as cultural critics is to critique the aesthetic deception of what we read and "expose its misrepresentations and false ideals, to strip away the lie and expose the liar. But this is an ambiguous mission for a literary critic who becomes an adversary of the work he or she analyzes" (5).

Recently, critics have begun to see past this prohibition against thinking and writing about beauty or aesthetics, finding troubling the political assumption of a world where "people no longer need to find solace in the contemplation of beauty" (Scruton 54). This seems to be Wendy Steiner's point in *Venus in Exile: The Rejection of Beauty in Twentieth-Century Art* (2002). Along with Marxist charges of beauty's complicity with capitalism, feminism has had its own set of complaints about beauty's complicity with patriarchy. For Steiner, the rejection of beauty or pleasure is connected to the rejection of the aesthetics of victimization and is largely to be seen as "a history of resistance to the female subject as a symbol of beauty" (xix). Ironically, Steiner notes, the way this equation begins to take shape is troubling: "For many women," resistance to this aesthetic is obvious; however, it comes at a "high price" since rejecting beauty "appears to set freedom and pleasure at odds" (xviii). As a result of the gains achieved in feminist politics, however, Steiner now sees the opportunity to be free of the prohibitions of the past and to reimagine "the female subject as an equal partner in aesthetic pleasure" (xix). She asserts that our abiding interest and need for beauty will not go away "simply by avant-garde or feminist fiat," and adds, "The time has come for a change, and the sudden, widespread fascination with beauty in our day indicates a cultural readiness to move on" (xxv). Janet Wolff also echoes these sentiments in *The Aesthetics of Uncertainty* (2008): "I am one of those who do want to retrieve the possibilities of beauty in contemporary art practice. Feminist critics have had . . . their own difficulties with the mobilization of discourses of beauty in the past. However, I suggest there is no real reason for a feminist distrust either of beauty or of the discourses of beauty" (6).[11]

Wolff underscores that the result of the attacks on beauty and aesthetics have resulted in the erosion of "narratives and principles to live by" (3). Even David Brooks, the *New York Times* columnist, has noted this conversation with concern: "The shift to post-humanism," he argues, "has left the world beauty-poor and meaning-deprived." In one of our exchanges, Scott Slovic cautioned us about the difficulties of returning to a discussion of beauty: "This turn (or re-turn) toward beauty in cultural studies is not without complications and concerns. The dominant narratives within ecocriticism at this time tend to emphasize such themes as justice (environmental justice ecocriticism, postcolonial ecocriticism, queer ecocriticism, environmentalism of the poor, non-human subjectivity and agency) and decentering of the human (posthumanism, new materialism). The human experience of pleasure (beauty) may strike some thinkers as effete or bourgeois, others as reactionary or anti-revolutionary" ("Latest").

In these dominant narratives, therefore, beauty, if mentioned at all, is easily treated as a mask, an ideological film to be stripped away, as opposed to itself being something erased, hidden, distorted to advance a certain politics and ideology. In *Literary Theory* (2003), Eagleton memorialized this new text-based, nonfoundational turn in critical focus by noting that structuralism and other discourse-based strategies offered "a way of refurbishing the literary institution, providing it with a *raison d'être* more respectable and compelling than *gush about sunsets*" (107; italics added). Eagleton's disparaging comments regarding "idealized refuge" and "gush about sunsets" speak directly to issues deemed important to many who originally were working in the new literary environmentalism. Poststructural and deconstructive theory launched a sweeping rejection of so-called universals like beauty and the individual, allowing some Marxists to take advantage of these highly disruptive theoretical interventions to advance a new/old agenda, which aimed at resuscitating the recent theoretical collapse of Marxist theory.

As the assessment of the ASLE bibliography and the ASLE conference paper presentations suggest, ecocritics of late have adopted approaches that parallel the more established critical enterprises within literary studies and the environmental humanities. The impact on beauty, aesthetics, place, and the individual is palpable. For example, ecocritic Simon Estok recently suggested that Leopold's land ethic is problematic on several grounds, including the fact that "it forces us to rehash the problems associated with the term 'beauty'" (209).[12] There is strong evidence, however, that critics today are willing to reinvent a new ecocritical aesthetics. Consider how many contributors to this volume cite Elaine Scarry's *On Beauty and Being Just*, for instance. This alone suggests an interest in finding our way back to the topic of beauty while serving other interests such as social justice. Scarry's description of the way beauty works on the viewer can't help but recall first-wave ecocritical approaches as well as the more political approaches that emerged later. With the perception of an object of beauty, we are transformed, according to Scarry, and in the process an ethical element emerges: "It is not that we cease to stand at the center of the world, for we never stood there. It is that we cease to stand even at the center of our own world. We willingly cede the ground to the thing that stands before us" (57).

In sum, if we return to a more pluralistic framework for our reading and thinking, beauty, or the aesthetic, may serve interests such as enlarging and sustaining our sense of wonder, establishing a heartfelt dedication to other species and the more-than-human world, advancing and drawing attention to sociopolitical issues, and revealing and appreciating diverse human and multiple cultural perspectives and experiences. For Scarry, beauty is the catalyst for caring, which is the fundamental basis for ethics and justice. This is an important issue to several contributors in this volume and points to a return to discussions of aesthetics and beauty. Also, if we are not immovably resolved to seek tight theoretical restrictions—in effect closing ranks around predetermined objectives—we can also seriously engage with those who may reject any claim to sociopolitical utility at all, as does Mary Oliver in her poem "The Summer Day" (1990). Oliver makes no promise of any responsible, secondary benefit related to her appreciation of beauty:

> . . . I don't know exactly what a prayer is.
> I do know how to pay attention, how to fall down
> into the grass, how to kneel down in the grass,
> how to be idle and blessed, how to stroll through the fields,
> which is what I have been doing all day.
> Tell me, what else should I have done?
> . . . Tell me, what is it you plan to do
> with your one wild and precious life? (65)

"What else should I have done?" A provocative question in the context of our discussion here. Slovic talks about the elephant of beauty lurking in every room where ecocritics meet to discuss "agentic capacities and nonhuman narrative perspectives and place attachment and environmental justice" ("Latest"). Our critical focus must always include issues regarding justice and fairness where appropriate. This volume of essays asks how beauty figures into these considerations and how beauty functions as an area, perhaps, unto itself. So the argument here is for a new balance, a new openness. This can't be about winning; it can't be an instrumentalist usage with pre-agreed social or political horizon objectives; it can't be about an either/or: either being willing to close borders around a set of justice issues, or being labeled an irresponsible pluralist. A more open-ended posture seems to be called for. As Raymond Williams generously put it in 1977, "If we are asked to believe that all literature is 'ideology,' in the crude sense that its dominant intention (and then our only response) is the communication or imposition of social or political meanings and values, we can only, in the end, turn away. If we are asked to believe that all literature is 'aesthetic,' in the crude sense that its dominant intention . . . is the beauty of language or form, we may stay a little longer but will still in the end turn away" (qtd. in Bérubé 10).

Or, as John Muir put it in a wonderful and more succinct manner in his 1912 book *The Yosemite*, "Everybody needs beauty as well as bread" (256). And Terry Tempest Williams offers up the beauty and the bread when, in *Refuge* (1991), she declares, "The landscapes we know and return to become places of solace. We are drawn to them because of the stories they tell . . . or simply because of the sheer beauty that calls us back again and again" (244).

Steiner and others are reaching out from previously entrenched positions and have dared to step back into the arena of beauty to see what it may bring. "The time has come for a change," Steiner proclaims, "and the sudden, widespread fascination with beauty in our day indicates a cultural readiness to move on" (xxv). I place much hope in Scott Slovic's seeing a polymorphously activist tendency, and in his noting that scholars and teachers "are finding new and old ways" to work in the field ("Third Wave" 7). I think of this generous intellectual framework as I imagine that beauty might be reconsidered and fresh opportunities for reengagement might go forward. The challenge to move on is before us. The questions remain, "Move on where?" and "What to make of beauty today?" This volume is a start.

Tim Hunt leads off the first section, "The Relevance of Beauty," with "'It Is Out of Fashion to Say So': The Language of Nature and the Rhetoric of Beauty in Robinson Jeffers." As the premier editor of Jeffers's oeuvre as well as a leading critic, Hunt is in an ideal position to clarify where Jeffers is to be situated between Pound and Eliot, but more importantly where Jeffers, as opposed to his fellow modernists, is to be situated on the topic of beauty. Hunt reports Jeffers saying, in an unused preface dated June 1922, "The poet is not to make beauty but to herald beauty; and beauty is everywhere; it needs only senses and intelligence to perceive it" (4: 374). Hunt adds, "This remark helps delineate the fundamental division between Jeffers and his modernist contemporaries." As the chapter's title suggests, Hunt's contribution takes on the central issue for this collection, the same sentiment expressed by Frederick Turner above: the sense that beauty is out of fashion. Hunt's focus is on "The Ocean's Tribute," where Jeffers writes,

> Yesterday's sundown was very beautiful—I know it is out of fashion to say so,
>   I think we are fools
> To turn from the superhuman beauty of the world and dredge our own
>   minds—it built itself up with ceremony
> From the ocean horizon (3: 439)

Hunt demonstrates that the poem is a critique of the modernist poetics of abstraction, the poetics and the criticism that make beauty unfashionable. Hunt's argument goes deeper, however, by claiming that Jeffers's polemic on poetics is only a parenthetical point: "The impulse to polemic," he writes, "is something to be overcome by turning away from 'fashion.'" The poem critiques giving our intellectual, experiential, or artistic lives over to fashion. "We are fools" of fashion to pretend we don't see what we see, don't experience what we experience, since, according to Hunt, "our participation in the natural world . . . is, after all, the basis of our being."

Hunt cuts his nuanced argument even more finely by suggesting that Jeffers's "emphasis on the 'beauty' of nature risks converting the physical world, the environment, into an aesthetic category." The brilliance in the poem, according to Hunt, is that it gives the experience of beauty over to the reader, moving past the critique of modernism and past the temptation to turn the poem into a figurative landscape: "As such," he observes, "the poem is neither a critique of modernism (though such a critique is present) nor a landscape painting in words."

The next two pieces in "The Relevance of Beauty" pay tribute to Henry David Thoreau, in many ways the foundational thinker for American environmental writing and eco-lifestyles. Just as Steiner has challenged us to come out of the bunker and reengage with beauty, so it is time to revisit Thoreau. Arnold Berleant and Frank Stewart wish to rethink the value of Thoreau, however, from several different perspectives.

Berleant, a philosopher, is one of the most prominent voices in the field of environmental aesthetics. He asks the reader to consider the range and the depth of Thoreau's writing, and suggests that the breadth of Thoreau's interests tempts scholars to have to choose one of the many dimensions of Thoreau's work: the literary, the scientific, and the moral. "Moreover," Berleant writes, "these aspects have been taken to represent Thoreau so commonly that they have tended to overshadow other, equally central characteristics. One of these is the author's aesthetic sensibility." Instead of seeing this aesthetic dimension as somehow ancillary to Thoreau's other concerns, Berleant suggests that "the aesthetic reflected in his accounts consists not only in the appreciation of visual beauty but, more broadly, in its multisensory and engaged character. His experience of nature is active, constructive, creative." In the same way Hunt claims that Jeffers uses aesthetics to lead the reader to engage directly with nature, Berleant suggests that Thoreau's aim is to move beyond the sense of the beautiful art object. "To affect the quality of the day," Thoreau writes in *Walden*, "that is the highest of arts." Berleant warns the reader against a quick dismissal of Thoreau's work here: "It would be pure condescension," he says, "to mistake this remarkable passage for mere poetic hyperbole evoked by unrestrained enthusiasm. This is no ordinary encomium to nature's beauties, but a testament to the creative act of nature appreciation: for Thoreau, appreciating nature is comparable to an artistic process."

Frank Stewart is a well-known critic, writer, and editor in the field of environmental literature as well as an accomplished poet. In the spirit of reengagement that has guided us in putting this volume together, Stewart admires Thoreau for his generosity of thought and his unwillingness to be dictated to by what Jeffers called "fashion." As Stewart sees it, Thoreau "believed, for example, that any reductive theory, when held religiously, tended to intrude into the fullness of experience and to become authoritarian; the more authoritarian its intrusion and the more rigid its tenets, the more it excluded generosity and fullness of inquiry." Although his training in scientific thinking "gave Thoreau discipline and a system of classification," it was his poetic vision that "gave him the freedom to make conceptual leaps and uncover analogies." Using the example of Thoreau's experience of discovering a new kind of fish at Walden, Stewart unpacks the relation between the different kinds of thinking that Thoreau deployed and the ways in which Thoreau leveraged them against one another.

Stewart, like Berleant, is interested in Thoreau's thinking process, a process that led to such a robust engagement with the natural world. Thoreau's commitment to the genuine and unconventional is good medicine for today's tendency to see so rigidly and ideologically. Stewart states that Thoreau "knew well that what the eyes see is related not only to who we are but also to what system (or 'institution' or theory) the eye has chosen, or been habituated, to accept." This insistence on freshness and freedom is connected to Thoreau's ability to "see 'with the side of the eye' and hear 'with the side of the ear,' as he said in language reminiscent of Dickinson." Given Thoreau's unwillingness to rest in this or that camp, in this or that perspective, it is a wonder the poststructuralists and other change-oriented critics didn't see him as friend rather than foe. Of course, as Myra Jehlen has pointed out, this was not the thrust of the criticism in the '80s and '90s, a period that forced the reader to become adversarial. And as Sterne reports, the dominant critical methods of cultural studies have been primarily designed "for negative critiques of cultural practices and social relationships . . . some system of relations we oppose" (81).

The relevance of beauty is further advanced by Tyler Nickl's engaging piece, which demonstrates the importance of beauty for issues touching on labor. Nickl examines Wallace Stegner's 1971 novel *Angle of Repose* "with special consideration of beauty's role in nurturing our ethics as it focuses and refocuses the attention we pay to the ordinary experiences of working and living." Nickl argues that Stegner's work operates with a belief that beauty has a special "capacity to engender openness and change," and, following Michael Denning's "labor theory of culture," he discerns that Stegner's—and other writers'—aesthetics "correspond to the real world of work and life." In this correspondence is a rich and meaningful relevance. Ultimately, Nickl documents a "fresh attention to the creation and transmission of aesthetic responses."

Mark Luccarelli, in "Renaissance Aesthetics, Picturesque Beauty, the Natural Landscape," argues that we have a lot to learn by recalling the history of approaches to material theories of beauty in architecture, landscape, painting, literature, and other media. He is concerned that "as in most humanistic discourse today, cutting off the past takes precedence over rereading the past." As a result, criticism no longer talks about beauty because of "two generations of the steady operationalization of literature and culture as instruments of the identity politics of marginal groups." Luccarelli takes considerable pains to trace the complicated origins of some of the arguments and criticism about nature and beauty. He doesn't refer to W. J. T. Mitchell's critique of landscape painting as a thinly disguised apology for imperialism, but he does counter William Cronon and others by stating that natural landscape is not a "uniquely American conceptual confusion." A closer look, he argues, reveals that "the 'natural landscape' is neither a confusion nor uniquely American." Ultimately, Luccarelli wishes to reinsert the importance of art history, or aesthetics, into our conversations about the environment. This focus gives us a more grounded, less politically driven, understanding of writers like Thoreau as well as representations of landscape. Luccarelli takes the reader through the classics, the sublime, the pastoral, the picturesque, and the Gothic, through painting, literature, and architecture, as well as postmodernism. He helps us to see that this long conversation has brought us to a place where "ecocriticism in most, if not all, of its varieties has stripped aesthetics away, remaking environment into a social-ethical sphere; in other words it has created a social geography that replaces both physical geography and the literary imagination. Beauty from this perspective blends effortlessly with power and injustice." Luccarelli thus provides the framework to see another way to proceed.

The title "Beauty and Engagement" captures the thrust of the essays collected in the next section. Leading off is the distinguished ecofeminist Greta Gaard with her piece "Toward an Ecofeminist Aesthetic of Reconnection." In Gaard's creative offering, participation and engagement take on a particularly visceral and dramatic meaning. This chapter provides a reflective narrative of the May-Day Parade in South Minneapolis, Minnesota, which functions as an "enactment of ecofeminist values and ethics." The parade (like Gaard's article, which is written in the form of a dramatic dialogue) has both artistic and political meaning—the distinction between scholarship, art, and activism collapses here, as the "ecofeminist artist" and the "spectator-participant" engage in conversation. Aesthetics, engagement, gender, and politics play off one another in this intriguing performance piece.

Ecocritical writing has frequently been concerned with the individual's radically intimate, bodily, and material connection with topics touching on one's relation with nature. Historian Theodore Roszak made this issue the primary theme of his popular 1978 book *Person/Planet: The Creative Disintegration of Industrial Society*. Gary Snyder's poem "The Bath" (1974) also comes to mind, as do Thoreau's sacred and spiritual "baths" in Walden Pond. This area has accelerated and morphed in recent years to include ecofeminism, queer ecology, ecosexuality, and more. "Beauty and the Body: Toward an Ecofeminist Aesthetic That Includes Loving Our Naked Selves" tells the story of "Project Naked," a playful lark of a scholarly-artistic project that has serious implications for appreciating the beauty of the human body (including the actual, physical bodies of ecocritics). As author Janine DeBaise puts it, "Accepting our bodies as beautiful affects the choices we make, as individuals and as communities." This spills over into larger, nontrivial social and environmental issues. DeBaise has opened a discussion that is rooted in ecocriticism's abiding interest in the borderlands of nature and the body. Her argument is grounded in the deeply personal materiality of our bodies, and she situates it specifically in an "ecofeminist aesthetic," but the implications are relevant to all bodies, not just to women's bodies specifically.

In the next chapter, Yuki Masami invokes the Japanese concept of *satoyama* (homeplace/mountain), an idea akin to bioregionalism in the Western context, in approaching the "language of emergency" displayed in Ishimure Michiko's writing about Minamata disease in the 1960s and more recent Japanese literature, such as Kawakami Hiromi's *Kamisama 2011*, which responds to the March 11, 2011, meltdown of the Fukushima Daiichi nuclear facility. How such writing both "intensifies a sense of 'aliveness'" and motivates political engagement "in an age of global environmental contamination" reveals the complex multidimensionality of ecocritical aesthetics.

In the final chapter in this section, ShaunAnne Tangney provides a helpful overview of how she teaches literary criticism to her university students, correcting her earlier tendency to downplay the importance of beauty and now using beauty ("as a subject, a theme, an obligation") to "drive or undergird all the other critical tactics that might seem to ignore it." In other words, Tangney reveals, in the pedagogical context so relevant to the daily lives of academics, her methods for bringing the sometimes tense relationship between aesthetics and ethics into the experience of her students.

For Luccarelli, what all of this boils down to is the fact that we are "beauty-finding creatures," and this certainly resonates with Serpil Oppermann's chapter, which opens the third section of the book, titled "Materiality, Transcendence, and Aesthetics." Inhabiting the world, as Oppermann explains by way of Jeffrey Jerome Cohen's concept of "prismatic ecology," includes keeping in mind "the material vitality of colors in affecting the cognitive, perceptual, aesthetic, ideational, and cultural experiences of human subjects," as well as "the experiences of nonhuman entities." Oppermann reminds us that the fundamentally human process of seeking beauty also requires us to be cognizant of that which is unbeautiful, even thoroughly unpleasant. Focusing on the narratives of the Turkish writer known as the Fisherman of Halicarnassus, she traces both "the aesthetic appreciation of beautiful landscapes . . . and also the moribund realms of the postnatural that raise questions about moral responsibility in the scenes of waste and rubbish." The idea that positive and negative aesthetic experiences conjure moral imperatives is essential to understanding the utility of beauty in contemporary environmental discourse.

Cynthia J. Miller draws our attention to traditional sacred poetry in South India, where the spiritual and physical dimensions of place-based Tamil culture are deeply intertwined. She writes that "early Tamil notions of beauty—the spectacle of the natural world in all of its many aspects—were not attributed to some unseen entity, but rather located directly in nature, as an essential force." The worldview of these Tamil poet-saints "was characterized by sensuality, deep emotion, and rootedness in the present." This way of being in the world, in other words, was not only grounded in materiality, but thoroughly oriented toward emotional experience in response to beauty. The fact that this sense of deep attention to nature is not so prevalent in contemporary Tamil culture—or in many other contemporary cultures throughout the world—enables us to measure our own detachment from nature by encountering these examples of early Tamil nature writing.

Next, Werner Bigell surveys a striking range of global examples in search of "a vernacular sense of beauty" that will enable us to rehabilitate beauty as a viable, non-elitist concept. The various material and spiritual forms of beauty in Soviet-style housing blocks in Germany and organic farming plots in Thailand illustrate the reality that beauty is a deeply cultural phenomenon—in fact, that one of the basic functions of aesthetics is to represent "a common ideology, in the form of a shared understanding of the world and how it should develop," and thus to foster "a sense of community." Bigell's study of twentieth-century examples of the physical and nonphysical dimensions of the beautiful expands and globalizes the Tamil-based discussion in the preceding chapter.

Scott Slovic's chapter on the literature of sustainability and the aesthetics of engagement uses Berleant's concept of participatory art, in conjunction with W. S. Merwin's plea for a resuscitation of "awe" in order to stem the public's passive unconcern toward environmental destruction, as a way into the aesthetic sensibility of William Stafford's poem "Maybe Alone on My Bike" and other examples of sustainability-oriented poetry, including Gary Snyder's "Song of the Taste" and Nanao Sakaki's "Specification for Mr. Nanao Sakaki's House." By employing certain "technologies," such as bicycles and poems, the critic argues, we might recognize "the splendor" of our lives in the world and act to protect what we come to regard with awe.

Groundlessness and skepticism, so dominant in critical approaches over the last few decades, certainly have a role in our thinking and perhaps in various aspects of our lives, but the impact of postmodern theory, in the last instance, can be said to have taken away more value than has been gained. Beauty is back, it seems, perhaps because living, thinking, and working in a postmodern relativist vacuum isn't ultimately fulfilling, nor does it apparently reflect or connect to what is essential about the human constitution. Relativism is a good way to clear the ground of past concepts but perhaps not a narrative to live by, although this possibility is what Wolff explores in her book.[13] I hope that with this new collection on language, beauty, and the environment, Slovic's elephant in the room has begun to dance a bit. This shouldn't be too hard since so many of our friends in this field of writing and study have testified to beauty as the foundation for their lives and their work. Listen to Rachel Carson on the topic: "Those who contemplate the beauty of the earth find reserves of strength that will endure as long as life lasts. There is symbolic as well as actual beauty in the migration of the birds, the ebb and flow of the tides, the folded bud ready for the spring. There is something infinitely healing in the repeated refrains of nature—the assurance that dawn comes after night, and spring after the winter" (98–100).

Amber Pearson from Michigan State University recently copublished findings connecting a water view with mental health and less stress ("Ocean Views"). Writing in *The Dirt: Uniting the Built and Natural Environments*, Jared Green states that "there has been a boom in studies demonstrating the health benefits of spending time in nature, or even just looking at nature." In addition, during the first two decades of the twenty-first century, there have been many studies of beauty: Denis Donoghue's *Speaking of Beauty* (2004), Roger Scruton's *Beauty: A Very Short Introduction* (2011), David Rothenberg's *Survival of the Beautiful: Art, Science, and Evolution* (2013), Frederick Luis Aldama and Patrick Colm Hogan's *Conversations on Cognitive Cultural Studies: Literature, Language, and Aesthetics* (2014), and physicist Frank Wilczek's *A Beautiful Question: Finding Nature's Deep Design* (2015), among many, many others. As Elaine Scarry has made clear, the opportunity to explore beauty as the basis for justice concerns is upon us. The opportunity to think about beauty and the Anthropocene is also waiting. There are other options as well. As Robinson Jeffers puts it, we could "take a walk, for instance, and admire the landscape: that is better than killing one's brother in war or trying to be superior to one's neighbor in time of peace. We could dig our gardens. . . . We could, according to our abilities, give ourselves to science or art; not to impress somebody, but for love of the beauty each discloses. We could even be quiet occasionally" (4: 419).

In sum, the field of ecocriticism now has a wonderful opportunity to choreograph its future efforts with the current interest in beauty in various humanities disciplines. We refer to this project as "ecocritical aesthetics." Let's see if the elephant can dance.

PETER QUIGLEY is Professor of English at the University of Hawai'i, Manoa, and also Associate Vice President for Academic Affairs for the University of Hawai'i

System. His publications include the edited volume *Coyote in the Maze: Tracking Edward Abbey in a World of Words*, *Housing the Environmental Imagination: Politics, Beauty, and Refuge in American Nature Writing*, and articles on Robinson Jeffers, Gary Snyder, T. S. Eliot, Herman Melville, and environmental philosophy and politics, which have appeared in journals such as *Environmental Ethics*, *CRITIC*, *American Studies in Scandinavia*, and *Jeffers Studies*.

NOTES

I want to begin by thanking my coeditor, Scott Slovic. Scott's eclectic, generous, and welcoming sensibility regarding the critical approaches of colleagues around the nation and around the world is inspiring. He truly represents the best in intellectual forward movement and collegial well-being.

1. "All Bad Things" are enumerated by Bérubé as "racism, patriarchy, homophobia, imperialism, theocracy, and still last and still not least, late capitalism" (7).

2. It is instructive to note issues related to Turner's comments within a six-year period. In the early 1990s he documented that beauty was out of fashion but that aesthetics, as well, was showing questionable usefulness. But it is odd that in 1991, with the theoretical apparatus on the floor that gave rise to the reductionist judgment about aesthetics, his conclusions about the capitulating qualities of aesthetics and beauty nevertheless persisted. In addition, even in 1985, while he was thinking that aesthetics could once again be approached with intellectual freedom and curiosity, he noted, with a welcoming openness, that which had begun to replace the loss of the base/superstructure argument: "In place of the old reductionism" an "extreme cultural-relativist position" had been advanced (243). Turner seemingly didn't see what was coming with this new approach, but he was feeling the effects by 1991.

3. Heller's article indeed documents a professor's being ready for a return to these discussions, but the rest of Elliot's quote is revealing: "I want the best people in the profession to be in charge of taking it to new places." He laments that in the canon wars, the only people talking about aesthetics are the cultural conservatives: "I want my guys leading this direction."

4. Edward Abbey spoke for a legion of early advocates for the environmental movement when he began his iconic *Desert Solitaire* (1968) with this line: "This is the most beautiful place on earth." He was speaking of the wilderness around Moab, Utah, but he quickly qualified this statement by noting that there are many different kinds of beauty: "There are many such places," he writes, and "every man, every woman carries in heart and mind" such a place (1–2). Beauty was the foundational experience that gave rise to much environmental concern in the 1960s and '70s. In *The Ecocriticism Reader* there are many examples of this sentiment, such as Alison Byerly's, "Clearly, environmental groups do agree on one thing: the way to promote nature is to illustrate its picturesque beauty. Our insistence that the natural world should not merely exist but also satisfy our aesthetic sensibilities is . . . difficult to overcome" (Glotfelty and Fromm 64). In the same volume, Paula Gunn Allen (253), Michael P. Branch (291), and others make similar claims about the importance of beauty. Branch, for example, documents the importance of "the feel of being outdoors, the pleasure of looking closely" (277), and Don Scheese

outlines Abbey's interest in the "harsh beauty of the desert landscape" (306). Lawrence Buell discusses pastoral beauty and the simple life as foundations for cultural critique in his 1995 volume *The Environmental Imagination* (41–42), and a quick check of the index in Max Oelschlaeger's *The Idea of Wilderness* (1991) yields a host of references to "beauty," many touching on Aldo Leopold's land ethic, which attempts to synthesize "the ecological, the ethical, and aesthetic" (Oelschlaeger 207). The tradition continues with many writers and critics who followed; Gretel Ehrlich's *The Solace of Open Spaces* (1985) comes to mind.

5. See, for example, Cheryll Glotfelty in *The Ecocriticism Reader*: "If your knowledge of the outside world were limited to what you could infer from the major publications of the literary profession . . . you would never suspect that the earth's life support systems were under stress. Indeed, you might not know that there was an earth at all. . . . Until very recently there has been no sign that the institution of literary studies has even been aware of the environmental crisis" (Glotfelty and Fromm xvi). My 2003 article in *Jeffers Studies* (6.4), "Carrying the Weight: Jeffers's Role in Preparing the Way for Ecocriticism," also discussed this issue.

6. The arguments launched in favor of policy studies and against aesthetics are historically associated with the 1990 cultural studies conference at the University of Illinois, out of which the anthology was published (Juffer 61).

7. In ASLE's online archive, see "Wild Things: Forget Deconstruction—Today's Hippest Literary Critics Have Gone Green," *Utne Reader* (Nov./Dec. 1997).

8. See Jonathan Bate's *Romantic Ecology: Wordsworth and the Environmental Tradition* (London: Routledge, 2014), originally published in 1991.

9. Of course, one of the problems with defamiliarization, understood in this case as the aesthetic, as a means to define literature or art is that defamiliarization assumes a core or center that is "familiar." Nevertheless, David Brooks, in "When Beauty Strikes," makes a case for the defamiliar: "It can be arrestingly beautiful. The unexpected beauty exposes the limitations of the normal, banal streetscape I take for granted every day. But it also reminds me of a worldview, which was more common in eras more romantic than our own." As one knows, "centers" were the main focus of deconstruction, and therefore the notion that there is a "familiar" to "defamiliarize" has been thrown into question. The main goal, however, seems to have been to move away from the perceived paralysis of a position that declares, "A poem shouldn't mean but be" (Archibald MacLeish, "Ars Poetica"). Such a position short-circuits meaningful engagement with political forces afoot and therefore was judged as promoting an ahistorical quietude.

10. According to Eagleton in *Why Marx Was Right* (2011), only by abandoning the talk of an indecisive "phony harmony" perpetrated by those valuing multiple perspectives and pluralistic humanism can we create "a society beyond self-interest" (78).

11. Perhaps this is where Bakhtin's sense of centripetal and centrifugal forces comes into play, as well as his sense of the penultimate word. These centering and decentering forces are clearly a kind of sociopolitical aesthetics. In this case beauty, being marginalized and moved out of the center of discourse, is now capable of new and more interesting engagement.

12. It should be mentioned that Rob Nixon, in *Slow Violence and the Environmentalism of the Poor* (2011), repeats Ursula Heise's condemnation of place-based writers. Timothy Morton, in *Hyperobjects: Philosophy and Ecology after the End of the World*

(2013), takes this global frame to its biological level by proposing hyperobjects that form throughout the geo-climatical environment.

13. After the poststructuralist, postmodernist, and postcolonial attacks on universals, there is a desire to retrieve beauty, but the way forward seems to demand that groundlessness serve as the "foundation." In *The Aesthetics of Uncertainty* Wolff explores a "groundless beauty" (chap. 1).

WORKS CITED

Abbey, Edward. *Desert Solitaire*. 1968. New York: Simon and Schuster, 1990. Print.
Abrams, M. H. *Glossary of Literary Terms*. Boston: Heinle and Heinle, 1999. Print.
Bennett, Tony. *Formalism and Marxism*. London: Routledge, 1986. Print.
Bérubé, Michael, ed. *The Aesthetics of Cultural Studies*. Hoboken, NJ: Wiley-Blackwell, 2004. Print.
Birkerts, Sven. "Only God Can Make a Tree: The Joys and Sorrows of Ecocriticism." *The Boston Book Review* 3.1 (Nov./Dec. 1996): 6+. Web. Nov. 2015.
Brooker, Ira. "Giving the Game Away: Thoreau's Intellectual Imperialism and the Marketing of Walden Pond." *Midwest Quarterly* 45.2 (Winter 2004): 137–54. Web. Sept. 2016.
Brooks, David. "When Beauty Strikes." *New York Times*, 15 Jan. 2016, New York ed.: A31. Web. June 2016.
Buell, Lawrence. *The Environmental Imagination*. Cambridge, MA: Harvard UP, 1995. Print.
———. *The Future of Environmental Criticism*. Malden, MA: Blackwell, 2005. Print.
Carlson, Allen, and Arnold Berleant, eds. *The Aesthetics of Natural Environments*. Peterborough, Ontario: Broadview, 2004. Print.
Carson, Rachel. *The Sense of Wonder: A Celebration of Nature for Parents and Children*. New York: HarperCollins, 1998. Print.
Eagleton, Terry. *The Ideology of the Aesthetic*. Oxford: Basil Blackwell, 1990. Print.
———. *Literary Theory*. Minneapolis: U of Minnesota P, 2003. Print.
———. *Why Marx Was Right*. New Haven, CT: Yale UP, 2005. Print.
Estok, Simon C. "Theorizing in a Space of Ambivalent Openness: Ecocriticism and Ecophobia." *ISLE: Interdisciplinary Studies in Literature and Environment* 16.2 (Spring 2009): 203–25. Print.
Glotfelty, Cheryll, and Harold Fromm, eds. *The Ecocriticism Reader: Landmarks in Literary Ecology*. Athens: U of Georgia P, 1996. Print.
Green, Jared. "What Dose of Nature Do We Need to Feel Better?" *The Dirt: Uniting the Built and Natural Environments*, 3 June 2015. Web. 15 July 2015.
Heller, Scott. "Wearying of Cultural Studies, Some Scholars Rediscover Beauty." *The Chronicle of Higher Education*, 4 Dec. 1998. Web. Nov. 2015.
Hunter, Ian. "Aesthetics and Cultural Studies." *Cultural Studies*. Ed. Lawrence Grossberg, Cary Nelson, and Paula Treichler. London: Routledge, 1991. 347–72. Print.
Jeffers, Robinson. *The Collected Poetry of Robinson Jeffers: Volume Three, 1939–1962*. Ed. Tim Hunt. Stanford, CA: Stanford UP, 1991. Print.
———. *The Collected Poetry of Robinson Jeffers: Volume Four: Poetry 1903–1920, Prose, and Unpublished Writings*. Ed. Tim Hunt. Stanford, CA: Stanford UP, 2000. Print.

Jehlen, Myra. "Introduction: Beyond Transcendence." *Ideology and Classic American Literature*. Ed. Sacvan Berkovitch. New York: Cambridge UP, 1986. 1–18. Print.
Juffer, Jane. "Excessive Practices." *The Aesthetics of Cultural Studies*. Ed. Michael Bérubé. Oxford: Blackwell, 2005. 58–79. Print.
Mitchell, W. J. T. "Imperial Landscape." *Landscape and Power*. Ed. W. J. T. Mitchell. Chicago: U of Chicago P, 1994. Print.
Morton, Timothy. *Hyperobjects: Philosophy and Ecology after the End of the World*. Minneapolis: U of Minnesota P, 2013. Print.
Muir, John. *The Yosemite*. New York: Century, 1912. Print.
Nehamas, Alexander. "The Return of the Beautiful: Morality, Pleasure, and the Value of Uncertainty." *The Journal of Aesthetics and Art Criticism* 58.4 (Autumn 2000): 393–403. Web. Oct. 2015.
"Ocean Views Linked to Better Mental Health." *MSU Today*, 28 Apr. 2016. Web. 10 July 2017.
Oelschlaeger, Max. *The Idea of Wilderness*. New Haven, CT: Yale UP, 1991. Print.
Oliver, Mary. *The Truro Bear and Other Adventures: Poems and Essays*. Boston: Beacon, 2010. Print.
Pater, Walter. Excerpt from *The Renaissance*. *The Oxford Anthology of English Literature*. Vol. 2. Ed. Frank Kermode and John Hollander. London: Oxford UP, 1973. 1099–116. Print.
Scarry, Elaine. *On Beauty and Being Just*. Princeton, NJ: Princeton UP, 1999. Print.
Scruton, Roger. *Beauty: A Very Short Introduction*. New York: Oxford UP, 2011. Print.
Slovic, Scott. "Latest." Received by Peter Quigley, 22 Jan. 2016.
———. "The Third Wave of Ecocriticism: North American Reflections on the Current Phase of the Discipline." *Ecozon@* 1.1 (April 2009): 4–10. Web. 8 July 2017.
Steiner, Wendy. *Venus in Exile: The Rejection of Beauty in Twentieth-Century Art*. Chicago: U of Chicago P, 2002. Print.
Sterne, Jonathan. "The Burden of Culture." *The Aesthetics of Cultural Studies*. Ed. Michael Bérubé. Oxford: Blackwell, 2005. 80–102. Print.
Turner, Frederick. *Beauty: The Value of Values*. Charlottesville: U of Virginia P, 1991. Print.
———. *Natural Classicism: Essays on Literature and Science*. New York: Paragon, 1985. Print.
Williams, Bryon. "Praxis, Gnosis, Poiesis: Inhabitation as Performative Myth in Robin Jeffers." *The Wild That Attracts Us: New Critical Essays on Robinson Jeffers*. Ed. ShaunAnne Tangney. Albuquerque: U of New Mexico P, 2015. 161–92. Print.
Williams, Terry Tempest. *Refuge*. 1991. New York: Vintage, 2001. Print.
Wolff, Janet. *The Aesthetics of Uncertainty*. New York: Columbia UP, 2008. Print.

PART I
THE RELEVANCE OF BEAUTY

CHAPTER 1

"IT IS OUT OF FASHION TO SAY SO"

THE LANGUAGE OF NATURE AND THE RHETORIC OF BEAUTY IN ROBINSON JEFFERS

TIM HUNT

IN HIS 1914 ESSAY "Vorticism," Ezra Pound explains that "In a Station of the Metro" was initially "a thirty-line poem," which he "destroyed . . . because it was what we call a work 'of secondary intensity.'" He then, he notes, "made" from it "a poem half that length" and finally distilled that into the two-line imagist jewel so frequently anthologized. For Pound, "the 'one image poem,'" by setting "one idea . . . on top of another," offered him a way "out of the impasse in which I had been left by my metro emotion" (89).[1] The year and a half that Pound reports that it took him to fashion "In a Station of the Metro" illustrates his meticulous craftsmanship, but what matters for this discussion is how he characterizes his "metro emotion," in these comments, as merely the ore from which the precious metal of the poem is to be smelted: "In a poem of this sort one is trying to record the precise instant when a thing outward and objective transforms itself, or darts into a thing inward and subjective" (89). When this happens, it seems, the dialectic of the merely "objective" (the world out there) and the merely "subjective" (the accidental matters of personality and experience), which are the "being about" that characterizes "secondary intensity," are thereby transcended, transfiguring the referentiality of "secondary intensity" into the primary intensity of the fully aesthetic. To Pound, it seems, "In a Station of the Metro" is neither a beautifully crafted comment on reality nor a beautifully crafted act of self-reflection or self-expression. It is, instead, itself beauty and itself a reality; it has been derived from the initiating experience or its subjective dynamics but is no longer bound to either. For Pound, "In a Station of the Metro" ceases to be a poem of secondary intensity when it is liberated from its occasion and thereby ceases to be a comment on its origin or a mere reflection of it and becomes, instead, through the poet's craft and genius, its own reality—an aesthetic and (thereby?) self-authenticating reality.[2]

Neither Pound nor "In a Station of the Metro" are the focus here, nor are the various critical paradigms of his era and ours that would see his comments as self-evident and synonymous with "poetry." But his comments offer a productive contrast to an early remark of Robinson Jeffers from an unused preface dated "June, 1922": "The poet is not to make beauty but to herald beauty; and beauty is everywhere; it needs only senses and intelligence to perceive it" (4: 374). This remark helps delineate the fundamental division between Jeffers and his modernist contemporaries. For Jeffers, beauty is necessarily outside the poem. The poet, by being able to respond to beauty, is able to construct a poem that "heralds" beauty, and the poem thereby offers the reader a way to "perceive" the beauty to which the poem is witness but which the poem does not and cannot contain. In Jeffers's view the "objective" and the "subjective" are not transformed into the poem, which then both contains and escapes them in transforming them. Instead, the poem provides a means to move from the subjective to a heightened awareness of the redemptive beauty of the objective, which is necessarily prior to, subsequent to, and beyond the poem. The poem enacts a subjective engagement of the world beyond the poet and the poem, and this engagement enables a heightened awareness of nature (an "objective") that is validated by nature's perceived beauty. Jeffers, that is, imagines the poem as, for the poet, an act (even more a process) of witness and thereby as, for the reader, a means of witness. As such, his poems aim at being (and, from Pound's perspective, are necessarily) works of secondary intensity.

That Jeffers's poems can be seen as works of secondary intensity has contributed to his frequent critical dismissal. If his poems are *about* things, if they are comments on them, and if they are (worst of all) discursive and rhetorical, then they have failed to transcend their "objective" and "subjective" origins, and they have, thus, failed as well at being poems—or at least good or significant poems. While it is true that Jeffers "failed" at being Pound (or Eliot, for that matter), what has been insufficiently understood is that he was not concerned with transcending (in the sense of escaping) what Pound would see as the objective and subjective, but was forgoing such transcendence (the transcendence of the aesthetic object, the beauty of the "well-wrought urn") in order to engage the objective and subjective and determine, by exploring the terms of their interplay, the nature of beauty and its meaning for the regarding self. That Jeffers's poems are at least in part reflections on our relationship to nature helps explains why his work has interested those concerned with environmental literature, in spite of the way his emphasis on the beauty of nature risks converting the physical world, the environment, into an aesthetic category.

Jeffers's late lyric "The Ocean's Tribute" (especially if considered in the context of its preliminary workings) helps clarify both his oppositional relationship to his modernist contemporaries and the significance of beauty for his environmental poetics. The poem, I'd also suggest, implicitly functions as an argument for the necessity of secondary intensity if poetry is to matter for our participation in the natural world that is, after all, the basis of our being.

* * *

Published as a broadside by the Grabhorn Press in 1958, "The Ocean's Tribute" is a seemingly casual, even naïve, piece that can be read as little more than a conventional celebration of a conventional scene using the typical details of a sunset—"purple cloud, and the pink rose-petals over all and through all"—to validate the claim of "very beautiful." The poem, though, is both richer and literarily more ambitious than its simple surface suggests. Moreover, it demonstrates something of how Jeffers understood the triad—the trinity?—of art, beauty, and why "beauty" is fundamental to both his aesthetic project and his environmental vision.

The conversational tone and pacing of "The Ocean's Tribute" suggest that it is simply a casual, offhand moment of observation awaiting the better making of an Ezra Pound so that "a thing outward and objective" might be "transform[ed]" into "a thing inward and subjective":

> Yesterday's sundown was very beautiful—I know it is out of fashion to say so, I think we are fools
> To turn from the superhuman beauty of the world and dredge our own minds—it built itself up with ceremony
> From the ocean horizon, smoked amber and tender green, pink and purple and vermilion, great ranks
> Of purple cloud, and the pink rose-petals over all and through all; but the ocean itself, cold slate-color,
> Refused the glory. Then I saw a pink fountain come up from it,
> A whale-spout; there were ten or twelve whales quite near the deep shore, playing together, nuzzling each other,
> Plunging and rising, lifting luminous pink pillars from the flat ocean to the flaming sky. (3: 439)

That this "Tribute" is "out of fashion" is evident both in its occasion (a sunset) and how the rhetorical declaration that bridges the first two lines seemingly casts it as merely an illustration of an abstract proposition. Any self-respecting New Critic of the era would, clearly, dismiss the poem for failing to rise above secondary intensity. However, the sketch from which Jeffers derived the first two-thirds of the poem suggests that this failure to transcend secondary intensity was, in part, the point, and that he was not simply failing to write an imagist masterwork but openly rejecting the aesthetic paradigm of modernism in order to aim at something quite different:

> I was admiring a magnificent sundown—it is not *done* now but I do it, I think we are fools
> If we refuse the inhuman beauty, to chase our own minds and make quotations—or abstractions,
> Which are meaner and easier—it built itself, purple and gold, pink, green and apricot, and the great sculpture,
> Of purple clouds flying northward rank above rank and the pink rose-petals over all, and a scythe moon
> Caught in the glory. But the ocean below, dull slate-color,
> Denied the light. I saw a pink fountain come up,
> A whale-spout (5: 890)

In the completed poem, "it is out of fashion to say so" functions implicitly as a rejection of modernist poetics and the critical orthodoxy of mid-century derived and elaborated from it. The equivalent unit in this initial sketch makes that rejection explicit. The speaker is not merely noticing a sunset, nor simply praising it. He is, instead, actively engaging it. And such "admiring" of nature's "inhuman beauty" stands as the opposite of "mak[ing] quotations" and "abstractions"; it is a rejection of such making. The speaker in this initial draft is the opposite of those who "chase" their "own minds" because they "refuse the inhuman beauty" and end up reduced to the inauthenticity of merely following "fashion."

Were "The Ocean's Tribute" primarily a critique of modernist poetics (or perhaps more specifically the critical "fashion" derived from it, which, at mid-century, had contributed to the eclipse of Jeffers's reputation), the poem would be of some interest as a polemic. But in both the initial sketch and the completed poem, the polemical gesture is a parenthetical that contextualizes what follows rather than being either the poem's central action or its point. The polemical impulse, as an initial reaction to the recognition of beauty in nature, initiates the poem's imaginative and aesthetic action, not because the poem is to celebrate the sunset as a kind of coded criticism of modernism but because the impulse to polemic is something to be overcome by turning away from "fashion" (and the concern with recognition and status it implies) in order to turn to "admiring" the "inhuman" and "superhuman" world—both by means of (through) its "beauty" and for its "beauty." The poem, then, is neither a critique of modernism (though such a critique is present) nor a landscape painting in words—a celebration of a particular sunset. Instead, it is (in spite of its brevity) a dramatic piece in which the tension between the impulse to celebrate the sunset and the recognition that this "is not *done* now" drives the assertion that "I [still] do it," which in turn drives the desire (need) to reconnect the inhuman and the superhuman by "admiring." As such, the admiring is both the action generating the poem and what the poem does. And as such, the dramatic presentation of admiring (engaging through admiring) that follows the parenthetical yields a poem—and a poetics—in which the poem is a record of the process of perceiving, engaging, and responding to an occasion (through aesthetic awareness) rather than an aesthetically crafted object that transcends the engagement that might have occasioned it (and which is validated through the skill of its making and the degree to which the realized work subsumes, even consumes, its occasion and occasioning).

"The Ocean's Tribute" is not, then, a conventional description of a sunset. Rather, it is an enactment of an aesthetic process. And the poem, through this enactment, demonstrates not only that the sunset is "beautiful" but also that actively "admiring" (engaging) such phenomena as sunsets to perceive beauty establishes that beauty is beyond fashion. In the poem, beauty is not merely something decorative the artist ascribes to reality or something the artist fashions through his or her artistry. Instead, beauty is fundamental to the self's relationship to nature, to reality, and it is, and crucially so, redemptive.

* * *

The way the finished version of "The Ocean's Tribute" functions as a dramatized enactment of consciousness is perhaps clearer if one considers why Jeffers might have broken off the initial sketch to start the poem over. In the initial sketch, the speaker is characterizing what he has seen—and admired—in order to support the assertion that "we are fools" if we "chase our own minds" instead of focusing on the "inhuman beauty." The key to how the description functions in this preliminary attempt at the poem is the word "glory" in the fifth line: "a scythe moon / Caught in the glory." Here, "glory" characterizes the details of the sunset which the speaker has been presenting and through which he perceives the "scythe moon." Functioning as a kind of summary or recapitulation, "glory" is more literal (the matrix of light and color) than it is figural (glory as an exalting, a divine splendor). And this literal dimension of "glory" as light, in turn, controls the next sentence: "But the ocean below, dull slate-color, / Denied the light."

In the fragment, the figural possibilities of "glory" are occasioned by the literal features of nature (in this case the lights and colors of the sunset) but are not actually part of nature. The speaker, that is, can cast natural light metaphorically as "glory," but the light of nature is simply light, whatever beauty we may ascribe to it. As such, the ocean can deny neither the actuality of light nor its glory, and this reduces the claim ("the ocean ... Denied the light") to an allegorical construction. It reflects the speaker's efforts to project a significance for nature through the drama he invents for it. The claim reflects the speaker's desire to participate in nature, but the drama exists only in the speaker's "own mind" rather than in (or as) the "inhuman beauty" (Jeffers 5: 890). Having set out to reject "abstractions" as "meaner and easier," the logic of the speaker's relationship to the scene he remembers and constructs for the reader traps him into figuring the "inhuman" as a humanized allegory—an abstraction.

In developing the completed poem from the preliminary draft, Jeffers subtly but decisively alters the speaker's relationship to beauty and nature. Exchanging "inhuman beauty" (in the fragment) for "superhuman beauty" (in the completed poem) is one element of this. Characterizing nature as "inhuman beauty" projects it as a nonhuman object for human contemplation. Characterizing nature as "superhuman" recasts it as a potentially transcendent, comprehensive being, which contains the human as an element within it. As such, nature (here the sunset) shifts from being something that happens to elicit "admiring" to something that is, instead, a dynamic reality that can be contemplated—and implicitly worshipped. In the initial fragment nature is a "great sculpture"—a structure. In the completed poem, it is a "ceremony" enacting itself—a process. The former invites (aesthetic) awareness; the latter invites worshipful participation. In the fragment, that is, affirming the sunset's beauty (and rejecting the modernist paradigm) leads to the more passive (and conventional) act of using the imagination to celebrate nature for its beauty. In the completed poem, rejecting the modernist move of "dredg[ing] our own minds" leads to the more active (and radical) move of using perception, extended through imagination, to recognize nature as process (ceremony) rather than object, and then, through perception and imagination, to participate in the "ceremony" through the parallel (but lesser) process of building up the poem in parallel to nature building up the sunset. In the finished version, the poem, thus, is not only an affirmation of "glory" but also a means by which the speaker (and potentially the reader) participate in it. As such, the poem becomes a part of the celebration. And even though nature necessarily transcends the poem and remains beyond it, the speaker (as actively contemplating awareness) and the reader are drawn into the ceremony through the poem. In "The Ocean's Tribute," then, engaging nature through creative awareness leads to the poem as a record of creative engagement, which in turn the reader can use as a script with which to engage nature.

By casting the sunset as a "ceremony" that nature itself enacts (or that God enacts through nature) instead of treating the sunset as "the great sculpture," Jeffers, in effect, reverses the logic of Pound's operation of distilling the "secondary intensity" of his "metro emotion" into "In a Station of the Metro." Where Pound tries "to record the precise instant when a thing outward transforms itself, or darts into a thing inward and subjective," Jeffers tries to enact (and record) the process by which the contemplating figure of the poet moves beyond the inwardness of the subjective in order to participate in the "superhuman beauty" that contains, but necessarily transcends and outstrips, the perceiving self. In Jeffers, consciousness, "a thing inward," is drawn "outward," and the poem both records that process and provides a script for it. As such, the poem must be of secondary intensity because, for Jeffers, it is most fully and powerfully a poem when it is *about* something rather than when it is *being* something. And this, I'd suggest, further clarifies Jeffers's rejection of the tenets of modernism: In Pound, the procedure of consciousness matters only because a poem has resulted from it, and the poem both embodies and erases that process. In Jeffers, the procedure of consciousness is the poem, and the poem matters not by being an artifact of primary intensity but by enacting—and testifying to—the primary intensity of the "ceremony" that elicits it and to which it points. Because of this, the poem, for Jeffers, is a process moving outward from "our own minds" rather than one of "dredg[ing] our own minds," and the poem must (as the record and result of a process) enact a change in consciousness, which is why the "I" of the speaker necessarily remains present in the poem—but not as a static point of perspective, nor as a didactic authority over the material, but as the locus of consciousness, with consciousness functioning as an evolving process rather than a static awareness, as the three instances of "I" in "The Ocean's Tribute" illustrate.

Although seemingly flat, static, and clearly stylistically unfashionable, "I know" and "I think" (in the opening line) and "I saw" (in the fifth) reflect the speaker's changing relationship to consciousness, nature, and expression that the poem enacts. What the "I" *knows* is the "fashion" of what poems should be—a certainty that functions to impel the poem onward but is of little value in itself. What the "I" *thinks* (a matter involving an element of doubt) is that "we are fools" to regard nature and poetry in this way—a proposition to be tested and one which leads to the initial connection outward to the "sundown" and its beauty, and from there leads to the claim (not as metaphor but as intuitive apprehension) that the sundown "built itself up with ceremony" and the recognition of the interplay of colors—the "great ranks / Of purple cloud" and the "rose-petals over all and through all." What the "I" eventually *sees* (in a kind of visionary moment), then, implicitly counters the hope and doubt of "think" that opens the poem and deepens and intensifies the mere "know[ing]" of the opening line. Jeffers, that is, in the completed version shifts the poem from being an evocation of the sunset's beauty offered as a refutation of current poetic and critical "fashion" to being, instead, an attempt to experience the sunset's beauty and thereby connect the self to nature and understand the self as an element within the "superhuman beauty of the world" and in relationship to it.

The significance—dramatically and thematically—of this progression from "I know" to "I think" to "I saw" becomes clearer, I'd suggest, in the context of the "ocean" seeming to "Refuse[] the glory" of the "ceremony," how this threatens the speaker's affirmation of nature and desired connection to it, and how this also threatens the speaker's attempt to demonstrate the validity of a poetics focused outward on nature rather than inward on the self. This threat is implicit in the seemingly unneeded word "itself." It is the "ocean *itself*" (italics added), not the speaker's perception of the ocean or his imaginative projection of it, that "Refuse[s] the glory" of the "ceremony" by maintaining its "cold slate-color." If the ocean is disconnected from, and impervious to, the "glory" that is seemingly "over all and through all," or if the ocean is, in its "cold[ness]," antithetical or impervious to the ceremony, then the speaker's initial impression of the sunset, of nature, as "ceremony" and "glory" becomes a misapprehension and fails to be a proof of the need to turn from "our own minds" to regard, instead, "the superhuman beauty." If the ocean is a revelation of an absolute nonhuman materiality, then imputing beauty to nature is an act of the mind. If beauty is simply a result of the "dredg[ing] of our own minds" rather than a result of "admiring" the "superhuman beauty of the world," then imputing beauty to nature is delusional. While celebrating the desire for beauty in spite of the reality of perception can be, as Wallace Stevens demonstrates, a validation of the imagination's redemptive power, that is neither the demonstration Jeffers is trying to make nor the position he is attempting to validate.

The dilemma created for the speaker in recognizing that the ocean, as "cold slate-color," seems not to participate in the "ceremony" is the poem's experiential and conceptual crisis. And the "Then I saw" that follows needs to be understood not simply as a continuation of the initial description but as a transformational pivot that reimagines, actually reperceives, the ocean's seeming unresponsiveness to the "glory" as the speaker shifts from observing "the superhuman beauty" that he has been describing to participating in "the superhuman beauty" that he is discovering. As such, this response marks a decisive shift in the poem from what might be termed ordinary observation (the I "admiring" nature) to visionary participation (the I within and of nature, a part of it even as apart from it in the act of observing).

This pivot from ordinary observation to visionary participation is implicit in the shift in the procedure of the description that follows "Then I saw." In the "turn[ing]" to the sundown's beauty in the opening lines, the speaker moves from the general (or categorical) to observed particulars. The recognition of "Yesterday's sundown" as "very beautiful," thus, initiates the catalogue of the particular features of how "it built itself up." Following "Then I saw," the speaker moves in the opposite direction—beginning with perceptual detail, then inductively proceeding to the conceptual or categorical recognition that identifies the detail (but without reducing its figural force):

> Then I saw a pink fountain come up from it,
> A whale-spout;

For the speaker, the spray of water against the horizon is literally pink because of the sundown, and by participating in the "over all and through all" of the "rose-petals," it projects a possible bridge between "cold slate-gray" and the "glory." Moreover, the detail evokes (even as it alters and naturalizes) the conventional Christian figure of the fountain as God's Word and a renewal of faith. For the speaker, through the altered, more participatory, and visionary mode of seeing initiated by "Then I saw," these qualities and implications precede the detail that the fountain is "A whale-spout," which in turn leads to the shift in focus from the sunset's interplay of light and color to the play of the whales, who are enacting nature (rather than, like the speaker, observing it) and "lifting luminous pink-pillars from the flat ocean to the flaming sky."

The centrality of the whales to Jeffers's initial conception of the poem is underscored both by its original title, "Whales at Sunset," and by the lines (discarded) that ended the poem as it was first completed:

> A whale-spout; there were ten or twelve whales quite near the deep shore,
>   playing together,
> Nuzzling each other, spouting rose-color tribute from the dark ocean to the
>   glowing sky, as if
> The whales also were singing glory to God. (5: 890–91)

Here, the whales, through their "tribute," link the "dark ocean" to the "glowing" sunset as if they, too, "were singing glory to God." In this discarded ending, noticing the whales complicates the speaker's sense of the ocean. The "cold" and seemingly blank slate is a feature of the ocean, the appearance of its surface; it is not the ocean as what we might now term an ecosystem. Perceived as an environment for the whales, the ocean becomes a vitalized context rather than inert otherness. As participants capable of "playing together," the whales both enact and represent the ocean's "tribute." While the ocean itself does not sing glory to God, elements within it and of it do.

This original ending of the poem, then, seemingly celebrates the value of turning from "our own minds" in order to turn, instead, to nature. Regarding "superhuman beauty" reveals its "ceremony" and enables one to join in nature's celebration of its "glory." Jeffers's revision to these final lines, though, both complicates and problematizes this affirmation. In the discarded ending, the poem's religious ambition is explicit and its religious affirmation is seemingly unequivocal. Yet the "as if" that ends the penultimate line signals a degree of uncertainty on the speaker's part by casting the detail of the "rose-color tribute" as metaphorical and the whales' "singing glory to God" as the speaker's imaginative projection onto the scene rather than his visionary apprehension of it. While the discarded ending makes the religious desire of the poem overt, the speaker remains separated from nature, even as he regards it and imagines through it, rather than participating in it. He sees nature "as if" it is "very beautiful" and "as if" it is "singing glory to God." Perception (what one actually sees) and imagination (what one constructs from perceptual data) remain different, potentially antithetical matters connected only by the speaker's desire. And if this is the case, then "beauty" is potentially only a construction of "our own minds" rather than an integral feature of "the superhuman," by and through which we know it (or at least recognize that we participate in it).

In the poem as published, Jeffers both simplifies and complicates the discarded ending. He deletes "as if" and cancels the characterization of the whales "singing glory to God" as if they are consciously aware of, and choosing, the religious implications of their actions. Jeffers also converts "dark ocean" (with its overtone of depth and mystery) into "flat ocean," which more nearly parallels the description of the ocean as "cold slate-color" in the fourth line. Most crucially, he shifts the speaker's noticing the whales and their spouts from being the poem's culmination (an occasion for the speaker to cast the whales as the central players in an allegory of nature) to the whales being, instead, a catalyst that occasions the speaker's intensified awareness of the wholeness of "the superhuman beauty," with that being the poem's culmination.

In the discarded ending, perception (noticing the whales as part of the scene) occasions an imaginative projection, and this projection creates a meaning for the scene. However, this meaning is imposed on the scene; it expresses the speaker's desire rather than being drawn from the scene and inherent in it. In revising the ending, Jeffers reimagines this dynamic, so that the poem ends by enacting the primacy of nature (its "superhuman beauty") rather than the power of the imagination to construct beauty from what the self is able to perceive. In the discarded (penultimate) ending, perception is raw material for the imagination to act upon; in the revised ending, perception occasions an intensified awareness of what is observed, and the speaker resists the temptation to overwrite (as in the discarded ending) the scene's nonhuman actuality with human meaning. In the discarded ending, perception generates an enabling fiction that reduces (and partly humanizes) the "superhuman beauty." In the final ending, perception leads to a visionary participation in the observed scene. The speaker is drawn out into a participation in the "superhuman beauty" that contains but vastly exceeds the human.

The two endings, that is, enact different relationships to nature: one a reversion to the romanticism (Wordsworth in particular) that is one source of Jeffers's poetic, the other a move beyond it. In the more traditional or conservative move of the discarded ending, "superhuman beauty" is subsumed into the imagining mind—as if the self is able to possess nature. But this more conventional move involves allegorizing nature, thereby setting the self apart from nature and buffering the self from its extreme otherness ("the nothing that is," as Stevens puts it in "The Snow Man"). In the more modern (though not modernist) move that recasts romanticism (rather than, as in modernism, rejecting it), imagination, subordinated to the "superhuman beauty," deepens participation in nature by intensifying perception. In the discarded ending, imagination subsumes and controls (and thus to a degree erases) perception. In the ending of the completed poem, imagination both draws from and intensifies perception, subsuming the mind into the reality of what is seen in order to achieve a visionary awareness that places the self within the "superhuman beauty." Instead of perception leading to an imaginative construction, a fiction (Supreme or otherwise) that functions as an interpretation, perception enables (and is subsumed into) visionary participation.

The clause that makes up most of the last line of "The Ocean's Tribute"—"lifting luminous pink pillars from the flat ocean to the flaming sky"—exemplifies this participation in nature through perception that is simultaneously literal and visionary, and it also marks the moment when the speaker, in this drama of consciousness, achieves it. The whale spouts seen against the backdrop of the sundown's "pink rose-petals over all and through all" are literally "luminous pink pillars," and the figural dimension of the language intensifies the perception of what is actually present in the scene (in contrast to imagining the whales "singing glory to God" in the discarded ending, where the figural turn moves beyond the actual, converting it into an allegorical tableau). At the same time, perceiving the "pillars" of the whale spouts as an expressive action from within the "flat ocean" links the ocean "to the flaming sky," projects the scene as a whole as implicitly a temple—one that the speaker, by attending to "the superhuman world," enters in what is finally, implicitly, an act of worshipful participation. It is this participation in nature's "glory" within its temple and through its "ceremony" that the speaker declares with the seemingly flat "I saw." What the speaker has come to see through the process the poem records is neither the literal surface of the scene nor how the imagination can aestheticize the scene. Rather, the speaker has discovered (or recovered)—through deliberate attention to the world beyond the self—the possibility of achieving a moment of unreflective participation in the "glory" as an element in its scene.

* * *

For Jeffers, I'd suggest, poetry both derives from and enables a heightened attention to the world—especially the world of natural phenomena beyond the self. The poem is a linguistic construction that records this process of moving outward from the self ("our own mind") in order to engage the "ceremony" nature enacts and thereby achieve moments of visionary awareness of the "glory." And this recording of the speaker's dramatic participation in nature and transformation through it, which is to say the poem, offers the reader a way to imaginatively reenact the process and move toward heightened awareness—an awareness that is necessarily beyond the poem but which authenticates it. The didactic claims and mimetic elements in Jeffers's lyrics, thus, are not ends in themselves but, instead, elements that contribute to the speaker's movement toward engaging the "superhuman beauty" through visionary perception. The disclosure that the poems offer is ultimately not a lesson validated by the poet's authority over the reader but rather the possibility of the reader's own heightened awareness through the poem's dramatic simulation of the speaker's need to "turn" from the self in order to "turn" to what is beyond the self (and as such both the poem and the poet point to an authority neither possesses). The poem as construction of language can be a means to awareness but is necessarily secondary to awareness. It can neither contain nor be awareness, even as it moves toward what is beyond it. As such, the poem is a matter of (what Pound would term) secondary intensity. For Jeffers, the poem enables awareness, which is its justification, its value. For Pound, the poem is a perfected linguistic system that embodies the craft of its making and transcends (by transmuting) both the objectivity of its occasion and the subjectivity of the maker.

Jeffers's insistence that the natural world must be attended to for its own sake rather than culled for impressions that can be converted into aesthetic objects helps explain his relevance for the canon of environmental literature. His advanced training in biology and forestry in his college years and his knowledge of developments in contemporary astronomy contributed to his being a careful observer of the natural world, and across his mature work he consistently acknowledges nature's materiality, assigns it primacy, and stages it as both the domain of ultimate meaning and the context within which human meaning is to be determined. But Jeffers is not, finally, a poet of science. Rather, he is a poet informed by science. In "The Ocean's Tribute," the "cold slate-color" of the ocean and the "glory" of "the flaming sky" are simultaneously engaged (perceived) as natural phenomena and apprehended as a visionary occasion—a dialectic of the literal and the transcendental, in which Jeffers's training in the sciences and his poetic roots in such figures as Wordsworth and Emerson, with their different envisionings of nature as infused with divinity, each play a part.[3]

For Jeffers, a key to his ability to acknowledge nature as the materiality of "the ocean itself, cold slate-color" yet envision it as a "ceremony" enacting a transcendent yet materialistic divinity is the way he understands "beauty" as a mediating term between self and nature and between perception and vision. Beauty links the scientific and the visionary and enables the self to attain moments of vision that include, rather than reject, the actuality of nature. For Jeffers, the purpose of the poem is neither to contain beauty nor to be beautiful.[4] Rather, the purpose of the poem is to enable readers to deploy their "senses and intelligence" and thereby "perceive" what the poem points toward. The poem is a mediation through which the reader engages beauty.

These two moments from Jeffers's career—the early preface of 1922 and the late lyric—both underscore the importance of beauty to his conception of poetry and suggest that the poem should testify to beauty rather than, itself, be beauty. But they do not specifically address the status of beauty, other than to suggest that beauty has to relate in some fashion to the world beyond the self rather than be solely a matter of "our own minds," even as beauty has to be experienced by the perceiving self—must, that is, be available to the self through the process of "I saw." That Jeffers was aware (at least as his career proceeded) of the question of how beauty might be both of the mind and of nature is evident in *Themes in My Poems*, the script he developed for a series of poetry readings he delivered in 1941. To introduce "The Excesses of God" (a lyric from 1920 but one left uncollected until *Be Angry at the Sun* in 1941), he wrote,

> I spoke a moment ago of the beauty of the universe, that calls forth our love and reverence. Beauty, like color, is subjective. It is not in the object but in the mind that regards it. Nevertheless, I believe it corresponds to a reality, a real excellence and nobility in the world; just as the color red corresponds to a reality: certain wave-lengths of light, a certain rhythm of vibrations. It was Plato who defined beauty as the effulgence—the shining forth—of truth. (4: 412–13)

The manuscript from which Jeffers finalized the script shows that he originally further specified "beauty" as "the effulgence of truth—truth shining—like a light from a lamp" (5: 966).[5]

Jeffers senses that beauty is not itself real (an objective aspect of nature) but is instead subjective—a matter of how the self responds to the reality that is not the self but in which the self participates. Yet beauty is not simply a reflection of, or construction from, the self's desire (as if the self's construction of beauty were a transcending of nature); instead, beauty is a kind of action or transaction between self and nature enabled by correspondence. As such, the subjective response Jeffers designates as "beauty" is elicited by the real (in its full materiality and otherness) through the active regarding of the world beyond the self (and self-consciousness) that converts passive perception into "admiring," so that the self experiences beauty both as and through the correspondence that places the self within the "nobility" of the world. In responding to beauty, the self participates in the "universe," experiencing it as simultaneously both material and ideal. And it is beauty (again, more as action or process than state or object) that enables and authenticates the participation and places the self in a position of reverence toward the universe.

Because beauty is a matter of how one relates to the universe (in both its ideal and material dimensions), it is not the poet's task to fashion beauty from nature (in works of what Pound would term primary intensity), nor is it the poet's task to praise nature for its beauty (in what would be works of secondary intensity). It is, instead, the poet's task to engage beauty through dramas of perception and from that process create scripts of engagement, through which the reader can, similarly, look outward from the poem and move beyond it in order to experience correspondence.

For Jeffers, then, beauty is related to aesthetic practice but is, at its most fundamental, related to creation and "reverence" for it. The "effulgence," the "shining forth," is God's expression—an expression through, rather than in, the "object" and one that, when properly regarded, joins the self and God in a "love." None of this is to erase or diminish the conditions of material existence, which include unceasing change and death of the self. Rather, this stands, in Jeffers's work, as the transcendent positive (through beauty to visionary awareness beyond the material self) that is the other side of the coin to the materiality of the self and thereby the self's inevitable absorption back into materiality. In "The Excesses of God" Jeffers celebrates this "superfluousness":

> Is it not by his high superfluousness we know
> Our God? For to equal a need
> Is natural, animal, mineral: but to fling
> Rainbows over the rain
> And beauty above the moon, and secret rainbows
> On the domes of deep sea-shells,
> And make the necessary embrace of breeding
> Beautiful also as fire,
> Not even the weeds to multiply without blossom
> Nor the birds without music:
> There is the great humaneness at the heart of things,

> The extravagant kindness, the fountain
> Humanity can understand, and would flow likewise
> If power and desire were perch-mates. (1: 4)

The materiality of the physical world and its processes do not "need" "beauty." But the "superfluousness," which can be seen by committing to "the great humaneness at the heart of things" rather than to "power and desire," is God's "extravagant kindness"—a gratuitous, inexplicable affirmation, a "fountain" of divine energy and spirit. Similarly, the physical world and its processes have no "need" of the poem. It, too, is "superfluousness"—it "corresponds"; deriving from a recognition of "superhuman beauty," it echoes, and its secondary intensity thereby participates in the primary intensity (rather than being a separate, and as Jeffers would understand it an alienated, intensity).

* * *

Jeffers quite clearly recognized that his understanding of the nature of beauty and the beauty of nature was "out of fashion," and "The Ocean's Tribute" functions as both an acknowledgment of that and a demonstration of a contrary, even oppositional aesthetic. The natural world was not a backdrop for cultural activity; the natural world was the primary reality—the fundamental to which the cultural was a kind of harmonic. Precise observation—geological, biological, astronomical—informed by contemporary science was central to his practice and his aesthetic. In a way that can strike us as prescient of contemporary concerns, he emphasized the natural world (as materiality and material process) as a greater reality than human desire and human production. Yet nature was not, for him, either an ultimate reality or an ultimate meaning. In "The Ocean's Tribute" Jeffers articulates his belief that to turn from the world's "superhuman beauty" to "dredge our own minds" (as he understands the modernists to do) is to be a fool. The contrary failure—suggested in the poem but not explicitly articulated—would be to turn from the world's "superhuman beauty" to dredge only the materiality of nature and natural process.

For Jeffers, knowing nature through the more objective perceptual mechanisms of science is neither an end in itself nor sufficient. The challenge implied in "The Ocean's Tribute" is to move beyond the subjectivity of self within culture (the modernists) and the objectivity of science (in which the self's participation in what is perceived is set aside) and instead to apprehend (through the "shining forth" of "beauty") the "ceremony" that is "built" as nature enacts itself and affirms the "glory" infused through it. In "The Excesses of God," a quite early poem, this "superfluousness" is explicitly God's expression of its own transcendent being. In "The Ocean's Tribute," a very late poem, the use of the passive voice in the crucial "it built" shows Jeffers stopping short of naming the power or agency that generates the "ceremony." In the early poem, beauty derives from, and is our proof of, a more comprehensive reality termed "God." In the later poem, beauty is the nexus of the mystery of our relationship to the natural world and its "ceremony."

When Jeffers wrote "The Ocean's Tribute," its seeming didacticism and discursiveness appeared to mark the poem as a product of secondary intensity—a celebration of beauty rather than itself being beauty. Moreover, its emphasis on the natural world rather than the psychological or cultural world made it even more unfashionable. Ironically, Jeffers's concern with beauty is what now threatens to make him unfashionable, or at least retrograde, in the context of environmental literature, in spite of his emphasis on the reality and primacy of the natural world. The political, ethical, and scientific dimensions of our contemporary environmental crisis will not be understood through beauty nor solved by expressing it. Yet "The Ocean's Tribute," I'd suggest, points to the inadequacy of treating the aesthetic and utilitarian as dichotomous. Beauty was not, is not, a by-product of the aesthetic—and thereby a subjectivity opposite to more objective understandings of nature. For Jeffers, beauty was, and is, the basis of (and product of) engaging the self's participation in nature, in universe—and thereby an "effulgence," a "shining forth," that draws us beyond the inadequate binary of subjective and objective.

TIM HUNT is Professor of English at Illinois State University. He has published many articles on Robinson Jeffers and is editor of five volumes of *The Collected Poetry of Robinson Jeffers*, along with *The Selected Poetry of Robinson Jeffers*. His own collections of poetry include *White Levis* and *Redneck Yoga*, and the newly published *The Tao of Twang*.

NOTES

1. The parallels Pound proposes between mathematics and poets in this same essay further underscore the contrast between his "modernist" aesthetic and Jeffers's modern aesthetic.

2. T. S. Eliot's widely reprinted 1919 essay, "Tradition and the Individual Talent," further develops the modernist rationale for this view.

3. Writing to Jeremy Ingalls on November 9, 1932, Jeffers offers that his "'philosophy'... came, such as it is, from life and prose, science and the like. Perhaps a gleam from Lucretius on one side and Wordsworth on the other." Below his signature, he then adds, "Poe captured me when I was very young; I had almost forgotten. Emerson interested; Whitman never did." In these remarks Jeffers erases, as much as affirms, his interest in Wordsworth and Emerson, but his revision to the introduction to the 1935 Modern Library edition of *Roan Stallion, Tamar and Other Poems* is worth noting in this regard. In the introduction as published, Jeffers notes his interest in Milton and

Shelley in his apprentice years. The manuscript shows that Jeffers originally wrote, "I was still busily imitating Wordsworth," then crossed out "Wordsworth," replacing it with "Shelley and Milton." The revision is, I'd suggest, rich with implication. At the very least it shows that Jeffers could be, in his remarks for publication and his remarks to others, somewhat reticent about his poetic influences and allegiances. See Karman (141), and also Jeffers (5: 941).

 4. The already quoted sentence from the June 1922 preface—"The poet is not to make beauty but to herald beauty; and beauty is everywhere; it needs only senses and intelligence to perceive it"—is worth recalling here.

 5. For the textual history of "The Excesses of God," see Jeffers (5: 314–16).

WORKS CITED

Jeffers, Robinson. *The Collected Poetry of Robinson Jeffers: Volume One, 1920–1928*. Ed. Tim Hunt. Stanford, CA: Stanford UP, 1988. Print.

———. *The Collected Poetry of Robinson Jeffers: Volume Three, 1939–1962*. Ed. Tim Hunt. Stanford, CA: Stanford UP, 1991. Print.

———. *The Collected Poetry of Robinson Jeffers: Volume Four, Poetry 1903–1920, Prose, and Unpublished Writings*. Ed. Tim Hunt. Stanford, CA: Stanford UP, 2000. Print.

———. *The Collected Poetry of Robinson Jeffers: Volume Five, Textual Evidence and Commentary*. Ed. Tim Hunt. Stanford, CA: Stanford UP, 2002. Print.

Karman, James, ed. *The Collected Letters of Robinson Jeffers with Selected Letters of Una Jeffers: Volume 2, 1931–1939*. Stanford, CA: Stanford UP, 2011. Print.

Pound, Ezra. *Gaudier-Brzeska*. New York: New Directions, 1970. Print.

CHAPTER 2

THOREAU'S POETICS OF NATURE

ARNOLD BERLEANT

1.

As an icon for a broad array of political and environmental protest movements, Thoreau's presence and influence are ubiquitous. He has been taken up by passionate and sometimes mutually incompatible advocates, from anarchists, civil rights activists, and environmentalists to novelists, poets, and essayists. His work is well known both in the United States and abroad, and not only in the Western world but in the Far East as well. So much has been written about Thoreau that it is improbable that much can be said that is new. Still, it may refresh our understanding of his deep well of ideas to dip into it from time to time to find clarity and renewal in a fresh draught of his words.

Often associated with environmental concerns, Thoreau's ideas have been used to support values found in the natural world, such as respect for and appreciation of natural processes and of nature not oppressed by human purposes. His mode of life has long been seen as a standard for our unique personal experience of the natural world. But while Thoreau's sojourn at Walden Pond may stand as the epitome of practical independence, it has also served as a model for the scientific organization of community in the interests of economy and efficiency. Its influence continues in the growing effort at sustainable living, both individually and in community.[1]

Few other writers have been so bold or perhaps so foolhardy as to attempt so much. Yet as a result of his range of interests, Thoreau's accomplishments were extraordinary in a milieu of extraordinary people, and his influence has become ubiquitous. He may be said to represent the irreverence and broad competence, as well as the inveterate moralism, of the American character. But because Thoreau's writings encompass such a wide assortment of topics and disciplines, one cannot deal briefly with his work as a whole in a way that avoids laudatory generalities or critical disapproval. Looking over this work, one may be struck by the detail and precision in his descriptions of natural phenomena and see him as a classical naturalist. Or one may take Thoreau as a writer and social critic, considering his writing as a literary enterprise or a nascent political program.[2] But it would not do justice to the full force of its scope to focus a microscopic eye on a single aspect alone.

For there is much to be heard in the range and timbre of Thoreau's voice, unique in American literature. Congenitally critical, his work combines philosophical ruminations, moral adjurations in the tradition of the Hebrew prophets, and social criticism, all informed by wide reading that included distant and past cultures, Eastern ones among them. At the same time, he combines this intellectual scope with an irrepressible scientific curiosity that finds expression in precise descriptions of nature and a perception of detail and nuance characteristic of the best nature writers. The breadth of Thoreau's interests and his moral passion might obscure the vehicle of his words were it not for the irrepressibility of their distinctive eloquence. One commentator has even gone so far as to claim that "Thoreau's chief importance to us [is] his writing," and to proclaim that "at his best, Thoreau wrote the only first-rate prose ever written by an American, with the possible exception of Abraham Lincoln" (Hyman 324, 317). Reactions to Thoreau are characteristically extreme.

Yet the strong moralism and epigrammatic force of Thoreau's literary efforts meld, perhaps improbably, with the care and acuteness of his scientific observations at Walden Pond and on his various excursions. But the literary, the scientific, and the moral are diminished when they are separated. Moreover, these aspects have been taken to represent Thoreau so commonly that they have tended to overshadow other, equally central characteristics. One of these is the author's aesthetic sensibility.

It is easy to overlook how thoroughly the perceptual details in Thoreau's observations are imbued with a sensitive appreciation of natural beauties. Moreover, the aesthetic reflected in his accounts consists not only in the appreciation of visual beauty but, more broadly, in its multisensory and engaged character. His experience of nature is active, constructive, creative. Indeed, Thoreau's practice can tell us much about the aesthetic appreciation of nature. It might respect his intent best to emulate his example of working on a small scale and seize on this theme—Thoreau's poetics of nature. Let us see where it can lead us.

2.

I call this a "poetics" of nature because Thoreau's aesthetic sensibility appears not only in the rich perceptual detail of his observations of nature, but in his active engagement in discerning and activating those sensory details. Here is a striking passage from *Walden*: "It is something to be able to paint a particular picture, or to carve a statue, and so to make a few objects beautiful; but it is far more glorious to carve and paint the very atmosphere and medium through which we look, which morally we can do. To affect the quality of the day, that is the highest of arts" (90).

One may be tempted to dismiss this as romantic excess, but that would be a trifling response. It would be pure condescension to mistake this remarkable passage for mere poetic hyperbole evoked by unrestrained enthusiasm. This is no ordinary encomium to nature's beauties, but a testament to the creative act of nature appreciation: for Thoreau, appreciating nature is comparable to an artistic process.

It would belittle Thoreau not to listen to what he says, for his language is not merely figurative. Indeed, it is revealing to read such comments just as literally as the scientific data he catalogued. They can tell us much about the quality and character of natural experience. This passage, like another in which he describes the earth as "living poetry" (*Walden* 309),[3] is revealing enough in itself. Yet such comments anticipate by more than a century and a half the emergence of an important new interest in the aesthetics of environment. And this, along with the broad scope of Thoreau's sensibility, may be seen as prefiguring contemporary scholarship's increasing attention to urban aesthetics and the aesthetics of everyday life.

The influence of environmental experience on aesthetic theory is perhaps the strongest motive behind the present effort to expand aesthetic appreciation and understanding beyond their customary scope of the fine arts. Writers on aesthetics are now likely to include in their consideration first the practical arts and crafts, and then the various environments as part of which humans carry on their many activities. Thus the range of appreciation has grown from nature to include the urban environment, from the appreciation of natural beauty to the aesthetics of human artifacts, from the enjoyment of works of art to an aesthetic sensibility in engaging the objects and activities of domestic life. Thoreau was one of the first to take us beyond the ultimate and overwhelming in nature and art to the beauty in the prosaics of the world.[4] Sometimes, moreover, Thoreau wrote as if the beauty in nature exceeds that in art: "Art can never match the luxury and superfluity of Nature." Indeed, he added, "Nature is a greater and more perfect art" (*A Week* 318).

In their veracity and minute detail, Thoreau's descriptions of nature prefigure phenomenological description. His account of the scenery at Walden Pond includes the color of the water, which he describes for nearly eight hundred words as it changes from a yellowish tone to green and takes on various shades of blue when seen from different distances and under a changing sky (*Walden* 175–77). Nor is the water taken in isolation, for Thoreau sees the pond in its larger setting, albeit without grandeur, as he describes the shore, the trees that border it, and the hills beyond. This contextual, perceptual appreciation of nature is typical of his descriptions. His eye is not that of the clinician who evaluates things dispassionately or of the anatomist who dissects objects into ever-smaller parts. It is rather the vision of the rhapsodist who carries forward the sweep of his story, or the landscape painter who conveys the quality of an entire scene by what he chooses to place on his canvas.

Reading his detailed descriptions as purely visual observations makes it easy to overlook what I think is a crucial feature of Thoreau the naturalist. One might imagine him looking with scientific detachment at "the cranberries, small waxen gems, pendants of the meadow grass, pearly and red" (*Walden* 238) or examining the bubbles trapped in the ice of the pond. But Thoreau is not an ocular scientist. His engagement with the natural world is, on the contrary, full-bodied. It involves learning, to be sure, but reading alone is never enough. For speaking as if he were a phenomenologist, Thoreau makes the critical observation that "we are in danger of forgetting the language which all things and events speak without metaphor" (*Walden* 111). There were times of cleaning his house when he set even his books, pens, and ink out-of-doors "amid the pines and hickories," as if to balance their abstractions and scholarly associations with nuts and cones. And of course there were the hours spent hoeing beans. These were not dull chores relegated to a mindless routine but, Buddha-like, activities worthy of mindful attention, part of his life and therefore valuable.

Thoreau's world is also filled with sounds, and he devotes an entire chapter in *Walden* to them: the whistle of the locomotive passing within earshot and the varied sights and sounds of the train at different times of the day and season. It is as if this were another natural phenomenon that demanded a description of its cars and cargoes. His aural horizon included animal and bird sounds, rumbling carts and bells, the sound of raindrops, even the soft rustle of the forest growing around him. And if, sitting in his boat, the stillness became too great, he would rap against its side planks and raise up echoes from the surrounding hills and vales (*Walden* 173–74).

3.

Part of the perennial appeal of Thoreau's sensible mentality, if I may identify his distinctive manner of ruminative activity, lies in the ethical insights he discerned in nature, both by simple observation and from scientific inquiry. One might be inclined to dismiss his criticism of the prudential behavior of the local farmers and townspeople as the inverse arrogance of a backwoods moralist, were it not that his judgments were so penetrating and sound in their measure. Calculating the various depths of the pond is a characteristic instance; it led Thoreau to a similar rule for judging the dimensions of a man's character ("The Pond in Winter"). Higher laws include building the temple of one's body ("Higher Laws"). Thoreau lived, too, with the traces of the past on the land and the lore of its former inhabitants: its history was ever present. All this was part of his world, a living present constantly adding a palimpsest of fresh perceptions, literary and historical associations, and personal memories. Is Thoreau being inconsistent here, turning nature into a metaphor for morality? This might seem so, except that the vividness and force of his perceptions of the natural world clearly stand on their own and not as mere crutches for a figurative moralism.

Recognizing in nature a source both of beauty and of moral insight had implications for both. Thoreau's nature is not a passive object of contemplation but a domain of activity: walking in the woods, hoeing his beans, playing his flute while floating on Walden Pond, engaging with full responsiveness in the tasks and pleasures of living in nature. This points to an essential characteristic of Thoreau's poetics of nature. It is not an aesthetics of contemplation but of life lived actively, and constructed, like his house, to his own dimensions. He grasped the beauty in everything, from the tops of the evergreens and the mountain ash to the tree-cranberries in his stew and the wild ground he walked on.[5] His was an active aesthetic, an integral part of the processes of living, an aesthetics of engagement. I call it that advisedly because the prevalence of an aesthetic sensibility in Thoreau's writing is markedly different from the ways in which the aesthetic is usually sequestered and etherealized by separating such appreciative experience from the course of daily life. The concept of aesthetic engagement centers on the unity of aesthetic experience in which active involvement in the aesthetic process involves a unity of perceiver and object in appreciative experience.

This, then, is no disinterested observation of an isolated scene but active participation in the process of appreciation.[6] It reflects both the temper of the man and the temper of the country. For the beauty Thoreau discovered was in relation to an individual person actively engaged, so that we find "as much beauty visible to us in the landscape as we are prepared to appreciate,—not a grain more. The actual objects which one man will see from a particular hill-top are just as different from those which another will see as the beholders are different" ("Autumnal Tints"). Thoreau's writings bring the reader both objects: his actual and our possible ones. Moreover, his words are not of antiquarian interest only, but carry us to the very present, for they stand at the leading edge of an emerging movement called "ecoaesthetics," which "emphasizes the ecological continuity or interrelatedness between the human appreciator and objects" (Cheng).[7]

Thoreau's life, often associated with his stay at Walden Pond, is mistakenly thought of as reclusive and sedentary, but this is misleading. His time there was filled with the many activities of daily life: going to the pond for water, fishing for pickerel, walking about, and occasionally visiting with friends and neighbors. Walking was his transportation of choice, before and beyond his two years at Walden Pond. Working and rambling about, Thoreau was an inveterate pedestrian.[8] He frequently walked around Concord, surveying the land and studying intensively the natural history of the place, putting into practice his adulation of the ordinary and embracing the world from his doorstep. As the bard of the local, Thoreau is unmatched. Yet he was also fascinated by accounts of travels and wrote some of his own.[9]

4.

An idiosyncratic writer, Thoreau cannot be constrained by any school of thought: a transcendentalist by category more than by content, a naturalist who moralized, a loner who valued social relations and was fiercely political. Like Spinoza, another thinker whose originality was disconcerting, Thoreau left no direct descendants. But like that seventeenth-century independent, he continues to be an influence, more as an icon of political individualism and an inspiration for the environmental movement than through any particular doctrine. Thoreau's persistent presence in American culture confirms the continuing allure of living close to nature. The ripples he stirred on Walden Pond have traveled far beyond its shoreline. Without exercising any direct force, their undulations carry us to Dewey's aesthetics, to existential phenomenology, and especially to the growing interest in environmental and everyday aesthetics.[10]

Although Thoreau's aesthetic sensibility is often overlooked, we have seen that it is not only pervasive in his writing but an inseparable part of his life and work. In his appreciation of a natural aesthetic, Thoreau could write with characteristic eloquence, especially in his journal. This passage from his journal is not unique:

> All nature is classic and akin to art. The sumach and pine and hickory which surround my home remind me of the most graceful sculpture. Sometimes their tops, or a single limb or leaf seems to have grown to a

distinct expression as if it were a symbol for me to interpret. Poetry, painting, and sculpture claim at once and associate with themselves those perfect specimens of the art of nature,—leaves, vines, acorns, pine cones, etc. The critic must at last stand as mute though contented before a true poem as before an acorn or a vine leaf. The perfect work of art is received again into the bosom of nature whence its material proceeded, and that criticism which can only detect its unnaturalness has no longer any office to fulfill. The choicest maxims that have come down to us are more beautiful or integrally wise than they are wise to our understandings. This wisdom which we are inclined to pluck from their stalk is the point only of a single association. Every natural form—palm leaves and acorns, oak leaves and sumach and dodder—are [sic] untranslatable aphorisms. (*Journal* 1: 380; 6 Aug. 1845)

Direct engagement with perceptual detail and immersion in intrinsic sensibility are, as I have claimed,[11] at the heart of aesthetic appreciation, and Thoreau was especially responsive to the aesthetic dimension of natural experience. Ralph Waldo Emerson recognized Thoreau's universal sensibility: "His eye was open to beauty, and his ear to music. He found these, not in rare conditions, but wheresoever he went. He thought the best of music was in single strains; and he found poetic suggestion in the humming of the telegraph-wire" (404).

While this discussion of Thoreau's aesthetic has highlighted a feature of his writing that is generally overlooked, it is important not to think of it as a distinct and separate element of Thoreau's unique voice. Emerson observed, after Thoreau's death, that "he was a speaker and actor of the truth" (397). And while this unflinching commitment lay at the core of Thoreau's moral standard, it was equally part of his aesthetic awareness. Thoreau's aesthetic was true to his experience of nature and it pervades his writing as an essential part of his message on how to live. That is a moral message, and his moral call reverberates throughout his writings. More than simply a combination of factors, the moral and the aesthetic are inseparable, and this is nowhere more explicit than in his assertion that "the perception of beauty is a moral test" (*Journal* 4: 126; 21 June 1852).

There is special significance in the coincidence of the moral and the aesthetic. While it is often argued that moral and aesthetic values are separate and must not be confused, Thoreau's moral message is embedded in his aesthetic one. He believed that just as living a moral life demands active attention and resolve, so does the poetics of beauty: "How much of beauty—of color, as well as form—on which our eyes daily rest goes unperceived by us" (*Journal* 14: 3; 1 Aug. 1860), he observed trenchantly. What shall we say of a natural philosopher who has beauty in his heart?

But not only does the aesthetic infuse the moral life, and the moral the aesthetic. One of the most striking things about Thoreau's writing is that its various features fuse into a single stream: scientific naturalism, moral adjuration, personal iconoclasm, political independence, aesthetic sensibility, autobiographical incident. The common penchant for separating and isolating such factors misses their homogeneity, which his writing constantly celebrates. Thoreau wrote about his life as a seamless, active, responsive unity, as living engagement in his immediate world. This is the key feature of engagement: the aesthetic unity of experience. Experience is aesthetic when it is direct, perceptual, undivided, active, lived,[12] and the aesthetic is an inseparable presence in all experience. It is the ever-beating heart of Thoreau's message.

Thoreau stands as a unique figure in the American pantheon. It is gratifying to think of him still beckoning us to move in unaccustomed directions. Like other philosophical beacons in world civilization, such as Lao Tzu, Aristotle, Spinoza, and Marx, Thoreau continues to radiate light.

ARNOLD BERLEANT is Professor Emeritus of Philosophy at Long Island University. His books and articles focus on aesthetics, environmental aesthetics, and ethics. He served as founding editor of *Contemporary Aesthetics*, an international online journal of aesthetic theory, research, and application. His books include *Art and Engagement, The Aesthetics of Environment, Living in the Landscape: Toward an Aesthetics of Environment, Aesthetics and Environment: Variations on a Theme*, and *Aesthetics beyond the Arts: New and Recent Essays*.

NOTES

I want to express my appreciation to Donald Jeweler, from whose suggestion this essay originated.

1. See B. F. Skinner, *Walden Two* (New York: Macmillan, 1948); Kathleen Kinkade, *A Walden Two Experiment: The First Five Years of Twin Oaks Community* (New York: Morrow, 1973). It is probably no exaggeration to regard Thoreau's undertaking as a principal inspiration for the broad array of intentional communities established worldwide beginning in the second half of the twentieth century and continuing into the present.

2. See Stanley Cavell, *The Senses of Walden*, exp. ed. (Chicago: U of Chicago P, 1981); Theodore Baird, "Corn Grows in the Night," in *"Walden" and "Civil Disobedience*,*"* writ. Henry David Thoreau, ed. Owen Thomas (New York: Norton, 1966), 400–409; George Hendrick, "The Influence of Thoreau's 'Civil Disobedience' on Gandhi's *Satyagraha*," ibid., 364–71; Richard Drinnon, "Thoreau's Politics of the Upright Man," ibid., 410–22.

3. The full passage reads, "The earth is not a mere fragment of dead history, stratum upon stratum like the leaves of a book, to be studied by geologists and antiquaries chiefly, but living poetry like the leaves of a tree, which precede flowers and fruit—not a fossil earth, but a living earth; compared with whose great central life all animal and vegetable life is merely parasitic."

4. See Katya Mandoki, *Everyday Aesthetics: Prosaics, the Play of Culture and Social Identities* (Aldershot, UK: Ashgate, 2007).

5. See Thoreau's *The Maine Woods* ("Ktaadn," part 1, and "Chesuncook," parts 2 and 5).

6. See my discussion of aesthetic unity in "Aesthetics and the Unity of Experience," www.academia.edu/3783262/Aesthetics_and_the_Unity_of_Experience.

I have developed the concept of aesthetic engagement in numerous places. A recent statement explains,

> Aesthetic engagement rejects the dualism inherent in traditional accounts of aesthetic appreciation and epitomized in Kantian aesthetics, which treats aesthetic experience as the subjective appreciation of a beautiful object. Instead, aesthetic engagement emphasizes the holistic, contextual character of aesthetic appreciation. Aesthetic engagement involves active participation in the appreciative process, sometimes by overt physical action but always by creative perceptual involvement. Aesthetic engagement also returns aesthetics to its etymological origins by stressing the primacy of sense perception, of sensible experience. It reconfigures perception itself to recognize the mutual activity of all the sense modalities, including kinesthetic and somatic sensibility more generally.
>
> The concept of aesthetic engagement, then, epitomizes a holistic, unified aesthetics in place of the dualism of the traditional account. It rejects the traditional separations between the appreciator and the art object, as well as between the artist and the performer and the audience. It recognizes that all these functions overlap and merge within the aesthetic field, the context of appreciation. The customary separations and oppositions between the functions of artist, object, appreciator, and performer disappear in the reciprocity and continuity of appreciative experience. (Berleant)

Also see Arnold Berleant, *Art and Engagement* (Philadelphia: Temple UP, 1991), *Aesthetics and Environment: Variations on a Theme* (Aldershot, UK: Ashgate, 2005), and *Living in the Landscape: Toward an Aesthetics of Environment* (Lawrence: UP of Kansas, 1997).

7. Cheng defines ecoaesthetics as "the theory of ecological aesthetic appreciation," i.e., environmental aesthetic appreciation construed in the context of a system of interrelated and interdependent natural forces.

8. "I have told many that I walk every day about half the daylight, but I think they do not believe it" (*Journal* 9: 208; 7 Jan. 1857). Also see Thoreau's essay "Walking."

9. These included not only his early expedition down local rivers (*A Week on the Concord and Merrimac Rivers*, 1849), but also a more extended trip to Quebec (*A Yankee in Canada*, 1866), four trips to Cape Cod (*Cape Cod*, 1865), and three excursions in Maine (*The Maine Woods*, 1864). At other times he visited cities including New York, Philadelphia, Chicago, Milwaukee, Detroit, and more.

10. An extensive literature in environmental aesthetics has grown over the past four decades. See the introduction and notes to Allen Carlson and Arnold Berleant, eds., *The Aesthetics of Natural Environments* (Peterborough, ON: Broadview, 2004), and to Arnold Berleant and Allen Carlson, eds., *The Aesthetics of Human Environments* (Peterborough, ON: Broadview, 2007). Everyday aesthetics is a more recent development. In addition to Mandoki's *Everyday Aesthetics*, cited in note 4, see Yuriko Saito, *Everyday Aesthetics* (New York: Oxford University Press, 2007); Thomas Leddy, *The Extraordinary in the Ordinary: The Aesthetics of Everyday Life* (Peterborough, ON: Broadview, 2012); and Thomas Leddy, "Artification," *Contemporary Aesthetics*, special volume 4 (2012).

11. See Arnold Berleant, "Environmental Sensibility," in *Ambiances in Action: Proceedings of the 2nd International Congress on Ambiances*, ed. Jean-Paul Thibeau and Daniel Siret (Grenoble, France: International Ambiances Network, 2012), 53–56.

12. See Berleant, "Aesthetics and the Unity of Experience."

WORKS CITED

Berleant, Arnold. "What Is Aesthetic Engagement?" *Contemporary Aesthetics* 11 (2013). Web. 12 July 2017.

Cheng, Xiangzhan. "Aesthetic Engagement, Ecosophy C, and Ecological Appreciation." *Contemporary Aesthetics* 11 (2013). Web. 12 July 2017.

Emerson, Ralph Waldo. "Thoreau." *"Walden" and "Civil Disobedience."* Writ. Henry David Thoreau. Ed. William Rossi. New York: Norton, 2008. 394–409. Print.

Hyman, Stanley Edgar. *The Promised End: Essays and Reviews, 1942–1962*. Cleveland, OH: World Publishing, 1963. Print.

Thoreau, Henry David. "Autumnal Tints." *The Atlantic Monthly*, October 1862. *American Transcendentalism Web*, n.d. Web. 11 Sept. 2017.

———. *The Journal of Henry D. Thoreau*. Ed. Bradford Torrey and Francis H. Allen. 14 vols. Boston: Houghton Mifflin, 1906. Print.

———. *Walden*. 1854. Princeton, NJ: Princeton University Press, 1971. Print.

———. *A Week on the Concord and Merrimac Rivers*. 1849. Ed. Carl F. Hovde, William L. Howarth, and Elizabeth Hall Witherell. Princeton, NJ: Princeton University Press, 1980. Print.

CHAPTER 3

THE POUT'S NEST AND THE PAINTER'S EYE

FRANK STEWART

On November 26, 1858, Henry David Thoreau took his rowboat onto Walden Pond, as he often did when the weather permitted. Like all the ponds close by—Hubbard's, Goose, and Little Goose—Walden was unusually low this season.

The fallen oak leaves lay like bright, crisp quilts on the muddy shallows. Evergreens had withered and turned reddish, but the red buds of the high-blueberry bushes were swelling. Partially frozen, partially wet, the ground was sugared with snow, the landscape white.

Thoreau was searching for a pout's nest he had seen the previous spring. Underwater then, today it was stranded in the mud and exposed by the receding waterline of the pond. Leaving his boat on the bank, he bent down and dismantled the nest's frozen roof to peer inside. Tiny frogs, hundreds of pollywogs, a few small fish, and minnows struggled in the icy bottom of the muddy nest. From the tracks on the snow, Thoreau observed that otters, mink, and foxes had waded into the shallows and fed on the minnows. He noted that some of the small fish had an unfamiliar coloration, "exceedingly pretty," he wrote in his journal, like old coins (*Journal* 11: 348). Collecting some of them in a jar, he took the most interesting home.

That evening, Thoreau studied the oddly colored minnows. The next day he walked back to the pond for more. He was coming to the tentative conclusion that, hardly a mile from the middle of Concord, in waters familiar to every local fisherman, he had discovered a new species of striped bream, "Very pale golden like a perch, or more bluish, and distinctly shaped, with a single dorsal fin of spiny rays" (*Journal* 11: 346).

Thoreau was cautious about an unlikely finding, so he took careful notes. Finally confident enough, he presented the specimens to the Boston Society of Natural History—whose library he often used for reference—and the society's biologists confirmed his conclusion. Soon afterward, the story appeared as an item of interest in the local newspapers.

The naturalist in Thoreau was justifiably pleased with his discovery, but almost immediately he began to consider its larger meaning. "What is the amount of my discovery to me?" he asked. And then he concluded, "It is not that I have got one in a bottle, that it has got a name in a book" (*Journal* 11: 360). The larger meaning was metaphorical as well as literal. "I can only poise my thought there by its side and try to think like a bream for a moment," he wrote (*Journal* 11: 358–59). To find this new inhabitant so close to his doorstep—like a previously overlooked thought—was, it seemed to him, like discovering that "a poet or an anchorite" had been living in the village undetected for centuries and now revealed himself (*Journal* 11: 359). "How wild it makes the pond and township to find a new fish in it!" he exclaimed (*Journal* 11: 358).

As for the new species' importance to science, Thoreau knew his discovery amounted to little more than a new binomial name added to a very long list. Moreover, he knew that to the natural historians of his day a dead specimen in a jar of alcohol was as good as a living creature, and more convenient for having been removed from its surroundings. In any case, the science of a thing was only part of his lifelong project. As much as he respected scientific thinking, any system of knowledge that excluded sensory and emotional matters—"love, hate, respect, dependency, trust" (Bateson 478)—was not comprehensive enough.

In *Nature*, Emerson had asserted that "every natural fact is a symbol of some spiritual fact" (18). But by the time Thoreau discovered the new species of bream, he was forty-one years old and as skeptical of abstracting the natural world into spiritual symbols as he was of reducing it to concepts and scientific terms. He resisted the notion that the complexity and fullness of the sentient world was merely glyphic (Peck 50). What distinguished him, and the reason he occupies us so profoundly, was his principled, "Spartan-like" determination to "live well" (*eudaimonia*)—as a natural scientist, poet, writer, classicist, practical ethicist, and many other things—and to know the real for himself.[1]

Thoreau was a disciplined polymath. And he resisted the conventional and the orthodox. He believed, for example, that any reductive theory, when held religiously, tended to intrude into the fullness of experience and to become authoritarian; the more authoritarian its intrusion and the more rigid its tenets, the more it excluded generosity and fullness of inquiry. He might have agreed with Paul Feyerabend that a great deal of theory and methodology tends toward the "conquest of abundance"—that is, the abundance of perspectives through which it is possible to understand the boundless multiplicity of our world—and is a hindrance to expansive inquiry.[2]

The most dangerous theories were those that censored the kinds of questions that could be asked about existence, and enforced their untestable claims to being uniquely correct. This mode of thinking, as Gregory Bateson noted, is "in some profound sense immoral or ugly," the opposite of Thoreau's preoccupation with virtue (*arete*) and beauty (*kalon*) (Bateson 264–65).

"Let me not be in haste to detect the *universal law*," Thoreau wrote in his journal; "let me see more clearly a particular instance of it!" (*Journal* 3: 157). Scientific thinking gave Thoreau discipline and a system of classification; his poetic vision gave him the freedom to make conceptual leaps and uncover analogies in structures and relationships; and his nonreligious spiritual vision gave him moral and ethical purpose. The combination of these modes of understanding enabled Thoreau to examine and describe the natural world and human behavior both assiduously and generously.

The majority of his neighbors, Thoreau felt, too often allowed received opinions to limit their thought, ethics, and aesthetic sensibility. They lost faith that their imagination—far from being childish—could be a useful tool alongside pragmatism, science, and spirituality. Creativity, he knew, can be smothered in many ways. "How was it when the youth first discovered fishes?" he wrote as he pondered his new species of bream. "Was it the number of their fin-rays or their arrangement, or the place of the fish in some system that made the boy dream of them? . . . One boy thinks of fishes and goes a-fishing from the same motive that his brother searches the poets for rare lines. It is the poetry of fishes which is their chief use; their flesh is their lowest use." But as the citizen grows up, "generally the boy loses some of his perception and his interest in the fish; he degenerates into a fisherman or an ichthyologist" (*Journal* 11: 360).

Thoreau's contribution to the study of nature, art, ethics, and ecology, as H. Daniel Peck observes, derives chiefly from his stance "between science and art, between 'naturalism' and 'poetry'. . . yet all the while seeking a space of consciousness that lies integrally apart from them and that balances the claims of outer and inner life" (65–66). Peck notes Thoreau's patience in pursing and articulating what was genuine, even if conventional: "Be it life or death, we crave only reality" (Thoreau, *Walden* 97–98). He kept up a sturdy pursuit out of a sense of dissatisfaction with himself.[3] His task was to observe and record his own idiosyncratic thought experiment, not to insist upon it.[4] When Thoreau died, only three years after the autumn day on which he discovered the new bream, his greatest work was the notebooks, comprising about two million words, forty-seven manuscript volumes, which he kept for twenty-four years. This was his "central literary enterprise" (Cameron 3). He recorded phenomena in the field, but also in town, among people of all degrees of stature, status, and sobriety.

Like Emily Dickinson, thirteen years his junior, he was precise and incisive, and could prize wild nights equally with solitude, weeds, words, and snakes; and he could see at dusk as well as in daylight, and could see "with the side of the eye" and hear "with the side of the ear," as he said in language reminiscent of Dickinson (*Journal* 4: 351).[5] Thoreau sought a method of perception that was relational as well as proportionally objective and subjective. He wanted the skill of the taxonomist combined with the analogy-making of a poet. He required in himself an attentiveness that could only be learned over a lifetime of practice until it became a habit of mind, and he valued the solitude needed by any serious literary writer, even if it meant keeping an office in the woods.[6] By profession, he was a manual laborer. In the 1847 Harvard alumni survey, Thoreau listed his professions as "Schoolmaster—a Private Tutor, a Surveyor—a Gardner, a Farmer—a Painter, I mean a House Painter, a Carpenter, a Mason, a Day-laborer, a Pencil-Maker, a Glass-paper Maker, a Writer, and sometimes a Poetaster" (Harding and Bode 196).

He was also a prize-winning melon grower (Harding 89). According to his claim in *Walden*, he was also a bit of a gourmand. "See not with the eye of science, which is barren, nor of youthful poetry, which is impotent," he wrote. "But taste the world and digest it" (*Journal* 3: 85). "Digesting" human and nonhuman life was a metaphor, we can trust, and it would be a literal-minded and humorless scholar who would accuse him of cannibalism or of eating woodchucks raw. "I found in myself, and still find, an instinct toward a higher, or, as it is named, spiritual life, as do most men," he famously wrote in *Walden*, "and another toward a primitive rank and savage one, and I reverence them both. I love the wild not less than the good" (*Walden* 210).

One of the systems that he investigated was visual art: seeing and expressing the exterior world. Thoreau had read Emerson's assertion in *Nature* that "the eye is the best of artists. . . . And as the eye is the best composer, so light is the first of painters" (14). Already, at the age of twenty-three, Thoreau was cultivating the metaphorical similarity and opposition of seeing and science. "We are as much as we see," he wrote. His progress as a writer, he knew, would be measured in large part by how well he could learn to look, and then put the visible, phenomenal world into vivid, poetic language. Seeing came first. "As you *see*, so at length will you *say*," he wrote to himself. As so often, he meant this in more than one way. "When facts are seen superficially," he observed, "they are seen as they lie in relation to certain institutions, perchance. But I would have them expressed as more deeply seen, with deeper references" (*Journal* 3: 85–86).⁷

Thoreau's work, then, is a search for the "deeply seen." But he knew well that what the eyes see is related not only to who we are but also to what system (or "institution" or theory) the eye has chosen, or been habituated, to accept. So, simply to look hard at an object is to see it neither in its fullness nor in its depth. In fact, to look too closely at an object, with a biased eye, can be to overlook it. "I must walk more with free senses," he wrote. "It is as bad to *study* stars and clouds as flowers and stones. I must let my senses wander as my thought, my eyes see without looking" (*Journal* 4: 351).

At age forty, Thoreau remarked in his journal how inadequately most writers described nature. They interpreted too much instead of looking closely, and they lacked an adequate language to render what surrounded them. The "mealy-mouthed enthusiasm of the lover of nature" (*Journal* 1: 237) seemed to him no better than the cool and inexpressive language of scientists and academics. By reading Linnaeus and Darwin, he acquired scientific systems and lexicons to illuminate details and to note distinctions in the nonhuman world, which he would have otherwise overlooked. But he continued to search for a system for seeing and saying aesthetically. On the one hand were the number of fin-rays in the striped bream and their arrangements, and on the other was the mystery and beauty of their existence, and the emotional resonance they evoked. He needed language "to render the highest kind of justice to the visible universe," as Joseph Conrad put it in his preface to *The Nigger of the "Narcissus,"* attending to the physical reality in the curve of the snow flea's eye and the muskrat's claw, as Thoreau would say: things that required "a separate intention of the eye" (*A Week* 40) and that took note of the human preoccupation with the divine.⁸ Visual artists used in their medium what he hoped, in language, to do: to realize the beauty of the experienced world in a replete, sensorial, and nonintellectualized way. Thoreau's fine biographer Robert D. Richardson discusses the array of art available to Thoreau at the Boston Athenaeum (51). Thoreau also read aesthetic theory closely, and followed publications devoted to art (Schneider 69). Writing was able, as Emerson put it, "to pierce this rotten diction and fasten words again to visible things; so that picturesque language is . . . a commanding certificate" (qtd. in Richardson 50).

In fall 1858, when Thoreau discovered the new species of bream, the seasonal colors must have been exceptionally brilliant, or his eyes were particularly acute as he experimented with a language for beauty. Not all his experiments were satisfying to him, of course; being disinclined to romanticize or aestheticize facts, he struggled with his task. He filled his journal with words for the colors of spangled leaves and evening clouds. He tried comparing the luminous atmospheric blue reflected on a white house beside the river to the "transcendent blue" of wildflowers, and the intricately painted feathers of jays and loons to the delicate tints on the skin of a salamander. "In describing the spotted leaves," he wrote, "how often we find ourselves using ineffectually words which merely indicate faintly our good intentions, giving them in our despair a terminal twist toward our mark,—such as reddish, yellowish, purplish, etc. We cannot make a hue of words, for they are not to be compounded like colors, and hence we are obliged to use such ineffectual expressions as reddish brown, etc. They need to be ground together" (*Journal* 11: 255–56).

In the same meditation, he noted "the infinite variety of hues, tints, and shades, for the language affords no names for them, and we must apply the same term monotonously to twenty different things. When the tints are the same they differ so much in purity and delicacy that language, to describe them truly, would have not only to be greatly enriched, but as it were dyed to the same colors herself, and speak to the eye as well as to the ear" (*Journal* 11: 255).

He was drawn for a while to John Ruskin's *Elements of Drawing*, which gave instruction in sketching from nature, the effects of color, and composition. Ruskin demanded of artists that they pay attention to what is in front of the eye—to note details accurately in the moment, and not to rely on memory to reconstruct what has been seen. "The perception of solid Form is entirely a matter of experience. We *see* nothing but flat colours," Ruskin wrote elsewhere. "The whole technical power of painting depends on our recovery of what may be called *the innocence of the eye*: that is to say, of a sort of childish perception of these flat stains of colour, merely as such, without consciousness of what they signify,—as a blind man would see them if suddenly gifted with sight" (qtd. in Richardson 359).

Thoreau learned from Ruskin, just as he had learned from botanists, biologists, and geologists. He appreciated Ruskin's emphasis on accuracy along with his allowance for the obscure and invisible. Years earlier, Thoreau had already noted in his journal the disadvantage of too much detail in writing about landscape—a fault to which even excellent writers were prone. "They express themselves with too great fullness and detail," he complained. "They give the most faithful, natural, and lifelike account of their sensations, mental and physical, but they lack moderation and sententiousness" (*Journal* 2: 418).[9] The corrective instruction that Ruskin offered would have seemed paradoxical to most anyone except Thoreau: "Try to draw a bank of grass with all its blades; or a bush with all its leaves; and you will soon begin to understand under what a universal law of obscurity we live, and perceive that all *distinct* drawing must be *bad* drawing, and that nothing can be right till it is unintelligible" (Ruskin 103). Thoreau must have been reminded of his own observation in *A Week on the Concord and Merri-*

mack Rivers: "The most stupendous scenery ceases to be sublime when it becomes distinct, or in other words limited, and the imagination is no longer encouraged to exaggerate it" (156).

Applying this observation to his prose, he returned to this paradoxical thought in the "Monday" chapter of *A Week*, drawing from a passage in his journal: "I should like to meet the great and serene sentence, which does not reveal itself,—only that it is great,—which I may never with my utmost intelligence pierce through and beyond (more than the earth itself), which no intelligence can understand" (*Journal* 1: 331; *A Week* 122). Similarly, *Walden* concludes, "I do not suppose that I have attained to obscurity, but I should be proud if no more fatal fault were found with my pages on this score than was found with the Walden ice" (325).

For Ruskin, mystery and obscurity were not the result of an inherent inadequacy of the human eye. Instead, like Thoreau, he recognized the presence of the "beautiful invisible"—to borrow a phrase from theoretical physicist Giovanni Vignale—to be a positive quality at the heart of the natural world and of existence.[10] Ruskin's third "law" of landscape drawing, for example, emphasized respect for the way in which mystery participates in the character of plants, rocks, clouds, and waves. In this cloaking mystery he recognized a kinship between natural phenomena and human nature. Just as there is "a perpetual lesson in every serrated point and shining vein which escape or deceive our sight among the forest leaves, how little we may hope to discern clearly, or judge justly, the rents and veins of the human heart; how much of all that is round us, in men's actions or spirits, which we at first think we understand, a closer and more loving watchfulness would show to be full of mystery, never to be either fathomed or withdrawn" (Ruskin 100).

Thoreau did not agree with all of Ruskin's opinions regarding the relation of nature to spirit. He strongly disliked Ruskin's tendency to look at nature through art rather than the other way around. He often found too much art in Ruskin, and not enough of the out-of-doors, not "Nature as Nature, but as Turner painted her" (*Journal* 10: 69). And he dismissed Ruskin's conventional moralizing, the imposition of a Christian conscience on nature's non-Christian truths, and his inclination to transform nature into mere symbols or correspondences—the tendency he also disliked in Emerson.[11] Thoreau nevertheless found Ruskin instructive for training the eye with regard to color and detail, and for conveying a sense of the pictorial qualities in the landscape. As he recorded the colors he saw on Poplar Hill in October, Thoreau attempted, in words, what Ruskin had urged the artist to accomplish with paint. "Now, methinks, the autumnal tints are brightest in our streets and in the woods generally," he wrote in his journal.

> In the streets, the young sugar maples make the most show. The street is never more splendid. As I look up the street from the Mill-Dam, they look like painted screens standing before the houses to celebrate a gala-day. One half of each tree glows with a delicate scarlet. But only one of the large maples on the Common is yet on fire. The butternuts on the street are with, or a little later than, the walnuts. The three-horned acacias have turned (one half) a peculiarly bright and delicate yellow, peculiar also for the smallness of the leaf. Asparagus-beds are a soft mass of yellow and green. Button-woods have no bright colors, but are a brownish yellowish green, somewhat curled and crisp and looking the worse for the wear. Stand where half a dozen large elms droop over a house. It is as if you stood within a ripe pumpkin rind, and you feel as mellow as if you were the pulp. (*Journal* 11: 199–200)

Thoreau revised these language experiments and added them to notes he had made the previous fall for a lecture on the season's colors, which he delivered several times to the Concord Lyceum. He planned to turn his lecture into an extended work to be called "The Fall of the Leaf," but in the months that followed he put his notes aside in favor of larger projects. Not until he lay on his deathbed did he return to them in order to raise money for his family; Thoreau readied four major essays for publication in less than two months. "Autumnal Tints," the first of these, appeared in print in the fall of 1862, five months after his death (Richardson 388).[12]

Like so much of Thoreau's work, "Autumnal Tints" concerns the complex relationship between knowledge expressed by science and imagination, and is about preparing the eye and therefore the mind to see the world as simultaneously ordered, chaotic, and beautiful. "There is just as much beauty visible to us in the landscape as we are prepared to appreciate—not a grain more," Thoreau wrote in this masterful essay. "It requires different intentions of the eye and of the mind to attend to different departments of knowledge! How differently the poet and the naturalist look at objects!" (*Writings* 286).

While he revised "Autumnal Tints" for publication, Thoreau's body was weakening from tuberculosis and respiratory stress. He recalled the many seasons he had struggled with literature, Greek, Latin, Eastern philosophy, science, ethnography, sociology, economics, art, and forestry—until his eyes at last saw them as beauty, a place many learned men considered too trivial (or problematic) to be studied. Speaking metaphorically as well as literally, Thoreau wrote, "I had walked over those Great Fields so many Augusts, and never yet distinctly recognized these purple companions that I had there. I had brushed against them and trodden on them, forsooth; and now, at last, they, as it were, rose up and blessed me. Beauty and true wealth are always thus cheap and despised. Heaven might be defined as the place which men avoid" (*Writings* 257).

Thoreau's journal is indeed, as Sharon Cameron asserts, "the great nineteenth-century American meditation on nature" (3).[13] Written over a period of twenty-four years, and never edited for publication, the journal does not present Thoreau's final theories or conclusions about nature, epistemology, materialism, theology, or how to write about nature. It does not even attempt to define such things and instead questions all systems, especially Thoreau's own. In it he affirms,

> It is only when we forget all our learning that we begin to know. I do not get nearer by a hair's breadth to any natural object so long as I presume that I have an introduction to it from some learned man. To conceive of it with a total apprehension I must for the thousandth time approach it as something totally strange. If you would make acquaintance with the ferns you must forget your botany. You must get rid of what is commonly called knowledge of them. Not a single scientific term or distinction is the least to the purpose, for you would fain perceive something, and you must approach the object totally unprejudiced. You must be aware that *no thing* is what you have taken it to be. (*Journal* 12: 371)

Early in the journal, Thoreau writes, "If he [the reader] would appreciate the true flow that is in these books, he must expect to see [the flow of thought] rise from the page like an exhalation—and wash away the brains of most like burr-millstones" (qtd. in Cameron 108). The journal reveals the mind and spirit of a remarkable man; in the end, we know him better than we know ourselves and are better for it. Those who know how to read poetry and great literature—and to appreciate visual art and music, and appreciate the uncertainty of physics—will not be troubled by a form of cognition that comes alive as an exhalation of thought. The learned professionals with a bone to pick will find an inexhaustible source of observations to be misread.

As he came to the abrupt end of his journal, Thoreau's desire for a "true and absolute account of things—of the evening & the morning & all the phenomena between them" brought him back to the conviction that beauty had a "high use" that must always be part of a true account of existence (*Journal* 3: 103). In "Autumnal Tints" he praised the glory of the fall colors for no other reason than that they "address our taste for beauty alone" (*Writings* 244). He asked,

> In what book is this world and its beauty described? Who has plotted the steps toward the discovery of beauty? You have got to be in a different state from common. Your greatest success will be simply to perceive that such things are, and you will have no communication to make to the Royal Society. If it were required to know the position of the fruit-dots or the character of the indusium, nothing could be easier than to ascertain it; but if it is required that you be affected by ferns, that they amount to anything, signify

anything, to you, that they be another sacred scripture and revelation to you, helping to redeem your life, this end is not so surely accomplished. (*Journal* 12: 371–72).

Thoreau's genius was that he was affected by the ferns, saw them, and painted them in beautiful, precise language. In his posthumously published essay "Walking," he lamented, "We have to be told that the Greeks called the world *Kosmos*, Beauty, or Order, but we do not see clearly why they did so, and we esteem it at best only a curious philological fact" (115). Accounting for nature immersed in the literary form he perfected, Thoreau meant to demonstrate the reasons that beauty and order are the true names of this world.

FRANK STEWART is Professor of English at the University of Hawai'i, Manoa. He is author of six books, including *A Natural History of Nature Writing*. His edited books of environmental writing include *Wao Akua: The Sacred Source*, *The Presence of Whales: Contemporary Writings on the Whale*, and *A World between the Waves*. He has edited over fifty volumes of *Manoa: A Pacific Journal of International Writing*, in addition to numerous collections of literature and natural history from the Pacific, Asia, and the Americas.

NOTES

1. It's useful to understand Thoreau's life and mind as an experiment in Stoicism. He was not a follower of any system, but his moral, ascetic, ethical, skeptical life, along with the metaphors "self-cultivation" and "flourishing," are evidence of the Stoic ideal. See, for example, Philip Cafaro, *Thoreau's Living Ethics: Walden and the Pursuit of Virtue* (Athens: University of Georgia Press, 2000); and Robert D. Richardson Jr., *Henry Thoreau: A Life of the Mind* (Berkeley: University of California Press, 1986). That some of Thoreau's neighbors didn't get what he was attempting to do ("But all this is very selfish"; *Walden* 16) is not surprising; the scholars who complain about his mother's cookies are also bafflingly literal-minded.

2. Feyerabend's assessment is that "the only principle that does not inhibit progress is: *anything goes*" (*Conquest* 23). Feyerabend's book is, in his own words, "intended to show how specialists and common people reduce the abundance that surrounds and confuses them, and the consequences of their actions" (viii). He believes that that is okay, but only when it assumes its infallibility and does not become rigidly authoritarian. In his book *Against Method*, he argues that "theorizing in any field should be anarchic" (23). He is thinking of the history of science, but his suggestion applies to other disciplines.

3. "The man who is dissatisfied with himself—what can he not do?" (*Journal* 2: 109).

4. Thoreau can sound crusty and scolding, particularly in *Walden*, where it's hard to get his jokes and irony; one should compare Socrates and others. Diogenes ("Socrates gone mad," according to Plato) famously said, "Other dogs bite their enemies, but I bite my friends."

5. See Peck (53). Those who fault Thoreau for not showing enough carnality might equally fault Dickinson, Socrates, and many others until it becomes obviously absurd.

6. See ibid.

7. For a discussion of "seeing" among nineteenth-century American writers see, for example, F. O. Matthiessen, *American Renaissance: Art and Expression in the Age of Emerson and Whitman* (New York: Oxford UP, 1941).

8. See Joel Porte, *Emerson and Thoreau: Transcendentalists in Conflict* (Middletown, CT: Wesleyan UP, 1966); Porte, "Emerson, Thoreau, and the Double Consciousness," *New England Quarterly* 41 (1968): 40–50; and Edward Wagenknecht, *Henry David Thoreau: What Manner of Man?* (Amherst: U of Massachusetts P, 1981), 123–54.

9. William Gilpin was also important to Thoreau's exploration of art theory; he read eleven volumes of Gilpin's work and made more notes in his journal about Gilpin than he did about nearly any other writer. There is not room in this chapter to discuss Gilpin. See William D. Templeman, "Thoreau, Moralist of the Picturesque," *PMLA* 47 (1932): 864–89; Gordon V. Boudreau, "Henry David Thoreau, William Gilpin, and the Metaphysical Ground of the Picturesque," *American Literature* 45 (1973): 357–69; Norman Foerster, "Thoreau as Artist," *Sewanee Review* 29.l (1921): 2–13; and Walter John Hipple Jr., *The Beautiful, the Sublime, and the Picturesque in Eighteenth-Century British Aesthetic Theory* (Carbondale: Southern Illinois University Press, 1957), 186.

10. Giovanni Vignale, *The Beautiful Invisible: Creativity, Imagination, and Theoretical Physics* (New York: Oxford UP, 2011). Also see Frank Wilczek, *A Beautiful Question: Finding Nature's Deep Design* (New York: Penguin, 2015). Vignale and Wilczek are but two recent examples of mathematicians, physicists, biologists, et al., who affirm and integrate into their professions the presence and importance of "beauty," "elegance," and so forth.

11. See Laura Dassow Walls, *Henry David Thoreau: A Life* (Chicago: U of Chicago P, 2017), 276. While Thoreau was at first inspired by Emerson's assertion, in his essay *Nature*, that "nature is the symbol of the spirit," Thoreau came to think this was a mistaken idea; he believed instead that nature and spirit were essentially the same. Walls goes further, suggesting that Thoreau may have had, on at least two occasions, a mystical vision brought about by his intimacy with the natural world.

12. The other essays were "Life without Principles," "Walking," and "Wild Apples."

13. Cameron notes the vastness of the journal, which makes it inaccessible to the general reader as well as to critics who are not Thoreau specialists.

WORKS CITED

Bateson, Gregory. *Steps to an Ecology of Mind*. Chicago: U of Chicago P, 1972. Print.

Cameron, Sharon. *Writing Nature: Henry Thoreau's Journal*. New York: Oxford UP, 1985. Print.

Emerson, Ralph Waldo. *The Collected Works of Ralph Waldo Emerson: Volume 1, "Nature," Addresses, and Lectures*. Ed. Robert E. Spiller and Alfred R. Ferguson. Cambridge, MA: Belknap Press of Harvard UP, 1971. Print.

Feyerabend, Paul. *Against Method*. New York: Verso, 2010. Print.

———. *Conquest of Abundance: A Tale of Abstraction versus the Richness of Being*. Chicago: U of Chicago P, 1999. Print.

Harding, Walter. *The Days of Henry Thoreau*. New York: Dover, 1982. Print.
Harding, Walter, and Carl Bode, eds. *The Correspondence of Henry David Thoreau*. New York: New York UP, 1958. Print.
Peck, H. Daniel. *Thoreau's Morning Work*. New Haven, CT: Yale UP, 1990. Print.
Richardson, Robert D., Jr. *Henry Thoreau: A Life of the Mind*. Berkeley: U of California P, 1986. Print.
Ruskin, John. *The Elements of Drawing and the Elements of Perspective*. 1857. London: Dutton, 1907. Print.
Schneider, Richard J. *Thoreau's Sense of Place: Essays in American Environmental Writing*. Iowa City: U of Iowa P, 2000. Print.
Thoreau, Henry David. *The Journal of Henry D. Thoreau*. Ed. Bradford Torrey and Francis H. Allen. 14 vols. Boston: Houghton Mifflin, 1906. Print.
———. *Walden*. 1854. Princeton, NJ: Princeton UP, 1971. Print.
———. "Walking." *"Nature" and "Walking."* Writ. Ralph Waldo Emerson and Henry David Thoreau. 1862. Boston: Beacon, 1991. 3–68. Print.
———. *"A Week on the Concord and Merrimack Rivers"; "Walden, or, Life in the Woods"; "The Maine Woods"; "Cape Cod."* New York: Library Classics of the United States, 1985. Print.
———. *The Writings of Henry David Thoreau: Volume 5, Excursions and Poems*. Ed. Bradford Torrey. Boston: Houghton Mifflin, 1906. Print.

CHAPTER 4

"YET HOW BEAUTIFUL IT IS!"

WORK, ETHICS, AND BEAUTY IN STEGNER'S *ANGLE OF REPOSE*

TYLER NICKL

To WRITE ABOUT WALLACE STEGNER must strike some readers as terribly passé. The "dean of Western letters" has received more than his fair share of critical attention from at least two generations of scholars. The first generation noted his important contributions to conservation and the environmental literary tradition, and its successors have refigured Stegner's legacy as an environmental activist in the light of poststructural critiques and theories of social difference. This follows a more general trend in the environmental humanities. Whereas authors once were to be celebrated for their views on stewardship or the spiritual majesty of wilderness, environmental humanists now tend to put texts about nature under the knife of critical scrutiny to excise the ideologies lying just under the skin. Discussions about Stegner's views of American history and western regionalism have developed similarly. While Stegner's contemporaries lauded his clear-eyed view of historical continuity and his rejection of western myth, other critics have more recently identified vestiges of national allegory, nostalgia, and romance in his writing. In short, Stegner's "geography of hope" has been remapped as a highly provisional and mutable landscape, one that, to some scholars, may seem fully described and undeserving of further study for all the attention it has already had.

However, whether they celebrate Stegner's politics or deconstruct them, the arguments mentioned above work from the common assumption that culture is a political instrument, that Stegner's work deserves our attention only for its effects in the real world. Stegner scholarship tracks the turns from social to cultural history, from preservationism to global environmentalism and environmental justice, but despite these changes, it all tends to treat his writing as a cultural vehicle in the service of something else. Obviously, writers do write to have an effect on the world—Stegner not excepted—and this fact warrants the study of literature's relation to power. But some humanists have begun to worry that our methods have ossified into an unreflexive and reductive emphasis on the politics of culture that can only ever engage its objects defensively. Rita Felski notes that "relentless interrogation" by resisting readers has come to feel "choreographed rather than chosen" (*Uses* 4); Eve Sedgwick similarly diagnoses literary critics as infected by a "hermeneutics of suspicion" that renders them paranoid and hypervigilant (4). Many are beginning to prescribe aesthetics as the antidote that will cure us of our negative faith. Elaine Scarry, Michael P. Clark, Marjorie Perloff, and other proponents of this "return to beauty" have pushed cultural studies critics and others to qualify their arguments in interesting and important ways that help us to understand aesthetics as embedded in the political and social world without reducing the variety and complexity of our aesthetic experiences. Stegner scholars have not yet incorporated these debates into their research.

I propose jump-starting the conversation about the humanist values *and* politics of Stegner's aesthetics by rereading *Angle of Repose* (1971) with special consideration of beauty's role in nurturing our ethics as it focuses and refocuses the attention we pay to the ordinary experiences of working and living. Implicit in Stegner's Pulitzer Prize–winning novel is a philosophy of aesthetics that views beauty in terms of its capacity to engender openness and change, that understands beauty as both cultural product and a personal visceral reaction to the experience of life. Working from these premises refigures the novel's denouement to render its protagonist, Susan Burling Ward, an ethical exemplar.

To discover this philosophy of ethics and beauty in *Angle of Repose*, I draw upon a rich and developing conversation among literary theorists and cultural studies critics. Though at times these two groups have talked past each other,[1] the debate between them has over time revealed more differences in emphasis than in principles. In his collection responding to criticisms from proponents of the new aesthetic turn, Michael Bérubé concedes that "insofar as cultural studies' engagements with the aesthetic have tended to instrumentalize the aesthetic . . . it is plausible to say that cultural studies has been simply missing the point," and he encourages scholars to consider "the varieties of evaluative mechanisms" by which people experience beauty and other pleasures in cultural objects (5–6, 7).

Rita Felski defended cultural studies against mischaracterization by Perloff and others, but her recent work finds common ground with the aesthetic turn as she laments "what is lost when we [as scholars and theorists] deny a work any capacity to bite back,. . . to challenge or change our own beliefs and commitments" in creating impactful, even beautiful, experiences (*Uses* 7).

The renewed interest in beauty is no call for a return to the canon or some reactionary nostalgia for simpler times in literary criticism and teaching. Even a relatively conservative critic like Perloff says that the "study of specific literatures comes and goes," and she is perfectly happy to admit study of "a new field such as video art" into literature departments (B5). What we are witnessing, rather, is a fresh attention to the creation and transmission of aesthetic responses. Cultural studies scholars' reconsiderations of aesthetics and beauty recognize the great variety and complexity exhibited in human responses to cultural objects without separating those objects from the conditions of their production and consumption. In so doing, they synthesize the sociopolitical insights of poststructuralism with a richer description and celebration of aesthetics and questions of value, seeking a critical method that neither aestheticizes away a writer's political complicity nor misreads writing as mere propaganda.

Two critical dimensions of cultural studies' contribution to the aesthetic turn are the consumption and the production of culture. These two dimensions, when given their full measure and not reduced to economic or ideological function, allow me to rescue *Angle of Repose* and Susan Burling Ward from disrepute. My analysis draws in particular on two important critics who have updated cultural theory on these two points, and so it is worth briefly discussing each in turn before proceeding. Michael Denning offers a "labor theory of culture" that expands the field of cultural production to make more room for human agency in what has commonly been called the culture industries (431). Denning sympathizes with Perloff and her colleagues when he says that cultural studies and poststructural literary scholarship have exhibited a "tendency to see all of culture as first and foremost a weapon, a tool for constructing subjects of one sort or another," and he acknowledges that cultural production "always goes beyond the ideological function emphasized in the political definitions of culture" (435). He also remains committed to the political import of culture because he observes that culture requires work and work is economic. Like other forms of labor, cultural work may be specialized and socially divided by capital or it may yet be uncommodified and performed to meet our own personal or communal needs (433). Recognizing the diverse circumstances under which cultural products are created, Denning admits a greater number of participants in beauty's production and considers the diverse meanings and motivations people bring to that participation. He emphasizes the unities between pop culture, folk art, and highbrow literature by reminding us that all of these are produced by people who need to both make a living and cope with that life. A labor theory of culture integrates the cultural work of artists and writers with the rest of their working lives. Rather than imagine the solipsistic genius toiling alone, we can remember that artists live in the world and are laborers; we can remember that they, like us, are accountable to employers and audiences in their cultural work, but that they are never fully captured by those influences. The point is this: a writer's aesthetics correspond to the real world of work and life, however subjectively perceived and rendered that world is.

Just as cultural studies helps us to broaden the aesthetic turn's stance on cultural production, it also broadens the stance on cultural consumption. Rita Felski argues that a broader definition of literature's usefulness accommodates instrumental/ideological concepts of cultural consumption without foreclosing other possibilities. "'Use' is not always strategic or purposeful, manipulative or grasping," she reminds us, adding that a consideration of literature's various affective and material uses "opens up for investigation a vast terrain of practices, expectations, emotions, hopes, dreams, and interpretations" (*Uses* 8). To actually examine beautiful experiences and the affective registers of culture would entail reckoning more seriously with the remarkable capacity of human subjectivity for self-reflection and change, which has been muted in scholarship today by "the off-hand references to persons as bundles of signifiers or textual effects that engenders a singularly flimsy and unsatisfying model of the self" (*Uses* 46). We need a different relationship to reading and criticism, one that abides with its objects long enough to observe the "complex interplay of individualized predispositions, deep cultural influences, and reflexive practices of self-interpretation and adjustment that is poorly captured by the often anodyne rhetoric of social construction" (*Uses* 47). Felski proposes that we adopt a neophenomenology of reading, defining it as "phenomenology after the linguistic turn, cognizant that cultural mediation renders consciousness neither self-contained nor self-evident.... What it borrows from phenomenology is the willingness to be patient rather than impatient, to describe rather than prescribe, to look carefully at rather than through appearances, to respect rather than to reject what is in plain view. It presumes, in other words, the irreducible complexity of everyday structures of experience" ("After Suspicion" 31).

When combined, Denning's and Felski's ideas paint a picture of aesthetic experience as a dynamic system of participation that harmonizes with some of Stegner's biography and his own thoughts on society. Consider, for example, how Denning's integrative take on cultural work invites a reappraisal of Stegner's teaching career and its importance to his writing. The twenty-five years he spent at the head of Stanford's creative writing program cannot be wholly separated from his artistic career. Recalling his years under Stegner's tutelage, Wendell Berry compared Stegner to "a really good foreman" on a jobsite because "he gave you good technical criticism" and showed "how an able workman made use of a form" (qtd. in Benson 262). Berry's reminiscence accords with Denning's insistence on the unity of labor with cultural labor as it recasts Stegner's students as apprentices and realizes writing seminars as "workshops" in the fullest sense of the word. The volume of professional attention and effort Stegner paid to form and aesthetics as a teacher (read laborer) begs our reconsideration of these features in his writing. Stegner himself, speaking through his narrator Lyman Ward, corroborates Denning's point when he refers to art and literature as "by-products of living" (*Angle* 42).

One imagines, too, Stegner agreeing with how Felski frames her support of phenomenology. By insisting that the world is always the world from our own perspective, "phenomenology encourages us to zoom in and look closely at what this condition of being-a-self involves"; because "we cannot vault outside our own vantage point," we need an "attentiveness to first-person perspective" (*Uses* 17). Stegner made a similar point when he said, "I know no way to look at the world, settled or wild, except through my own eyes. . . . I am the only instrument that I have access to by which I can enjoy the world and try to understand it" (qtd. in MacDonald 279). Stegner's thought and writing, emphasizing knowledge as a process derived from the gradual experience of working and living, is well served by an aesthetic reading guided by Felski's and Denning's theories.

Angle of Repose provides a particularly rich example of how beauty and experience inflect each other in Stegner's thought. Arguably Stegner's most complex novel, the book relates the struggles of Susan and Oliver Ward, a pioneering couple in Victorian America, as narrated by their grandson Lyman, a professional historian. Lyman's interest in his grandparents' lives helps him to escape the disappointment and loss from his wife's desertion, his retirement from the academy, and the physical disability of a crippling bone disease. Combing the family archive for facts, Lyman recounts—and at times invents—his family's history.

Many critics have focused on the novel's obvious concern for western history, but the book's aesthetic dimensions have received far less attention. William Handley explores the multiple and unstable meanings that Oliver and Susan Ward's marriage brings to bear on history, nostalgia, and national identity, but that focus leads him to dismiss Susan's artistic and literary talents as "ephemeral comforts they reach for in difficult circumstances" of their married life. Susan's interest in the arts brings "a soothing sense of eastern culture to the West and provides an aesthetic stay against constant change" (193). There is some truth to Handley's point. After all, Felski's conception of aesthetics' usefulness certainly admits distraction and escape as possible uses. But she reminds us that beauty may also be made of sturdier stuff. What I think Handley forgets is that Susan is a professional artist, one who more than once supports her family by her craft. As Denning would suggest, we must remember the importance that her artistic sensibilities bring to bear on her work as a homemaker and a pioneer. If, as Felski suggests, we can attentively listen to Susan's first-person accounts, we hear that her aesthetic sensibility—her taste for the beautiful—is more dynamic and challenging than we have yet acknowledged.

Witness the ways in which her affinity for the picturesque helps her to begin adapting to the life she has chosen. Susan's courtship to Oliver was brief, and Lyman infers from some catty letters that his grandmother's engagement to Oliver was at least partly motivated by her feelings of betrayal aroused by her best friend, Augusta, abandoning her to marry another of her dear friends. Susan's artistic training helps her at times to overcome these naïve and inauspicious beginnings. Riding into New Almaden, California, to establish her first mutual home with Oliver, she cannot help but be offended at the haphazard look of the mining camp: "The whole place had the air of having been dumped down the hillside," and "vacant lots were littered with cans and trash, dogs prowled and children screamed" (72). Susan's training and tastes as an artist—which Lyman describes as "incorrigibly Hudson River school"—predispose her to dislike New Almaden and its people (49). Yet her training and tastes also give her the capacity for close attention and self-reflection, and they necessarily change and mature as Susan does the same. Moments after seeing the unkempt camp, Susan's artistic eye finds something to appreciate, noting that the New Almaden residents "made sharp pictures, too: a boy hoisting a water yoke with a pail at each end, the pails sloshing silver over their rims" (73). Here Stegner's affection for ordinary scenes of life comes off the page. The trochaic alliteration of "sloshing silver over" translates the clumsy gait of the boy and his buckets into an aural effect, and this sort of detail illustrates the danger of assuming that Susan's eye for beauty is fixed in any one direction. Yes, Susan has aesthetic predilections that correlate to her class, gender, and race, but, as Stegner writes her, she remains open to experience's instruction as she learns to see and appreciate the new things and people with whom she must reckon.

But no matter how carefully Susan attends to her adopted home, new neighbors, and husband, her history necessarily mediates her perception of them and leads her to error. The "sharp pictures" she makes at New Almaden imply a romanticism that easily deconstructs, but stopping there impedes our understanding of beauty developing in process. Rita Felski cautions us not to fall for such absolutist thinking. Our understanding of the world and Others we encounter in it may lead us to recognize and identify them erroneously, but "misrecognition presumes and enfolds its antithesis" because "it implies that a less flawed perception can be attained, that our assessments can be scrutinized and found wanting. If self-deception is hailed as the inescapable ground of subjectivity, however, it is evacuated of all critical purchase and diagnostic force, leaving us with no means of making distinctions or of gauging incremental changes in understanding" (*Uses* 28). Susan cannot know the truth about the boy with his buckets or the mining camp, but observing the "incremental changes" in her perception rescues the beauty in Stegner's novel from a mob trial by a jury of our presentist ethics.

Elaine Scarry argues that errors in our appreciation of beauty actually assist our ethical judgments. Arising out of the interplay between attention and its objects, beauty arouses our senses but in a way that "prompts one to judgments that one then continues to scrutinize, and that one frequently discovers to be in error" (29). The very attention that elicits our rapture with the beautiful object opens our judgment of that object to redaction by virtue of its intensity. Similarly, repulsion and disgust for something unbeautiful may double back on themselves to prompt a reexamination of the object, since even these negative types of attention are not merely ignorant or indifferent to their objects. Scarry values beauty for these dialogical tendencies, which are always "hurtling us forward and back, requiring us to break new ground, but obliging us also to bridge back not only to the ground we just left but to still earlier, even ancient, ground" (46).

Susan commits plenty of errors as she and Oliver make a life in the West. Toward the end of the couple's time in New Almaden, Oliver's on-the-job political situation becomes contentious, and he fears some retribution from Kendall, the mine manager. Susan overhears Oliver warning another mine employee, Hernandez, about Kendall's treachery. Alerted to the instability of Hernandez's livelihood, Susan regrets the romantic and picturesque way she imagined his family:

> Her drawings of Hernandez's two sisters for Mr. Howells and the *Atlantic* had shown them languid, slim, domestic, offering figs and native wine to a visitor, herself. She had dwelt not on the harsh life at whose insecure edge they lived, but on their grace, their dark and speaking eyes, the elegance of their dancing, the attractiveness of *rebozo* or *mantilla* over their hair, the feminine gentleness of their gestures and postures. In her indignation she almost wished those blocks back, so that she could send in their place something closer to the truth of mining camp lives. Yet how would she get close to those lives to draw them? She had lived in New Almaden nearly a year and had seen only its picturesque surface. (140–41)

In this passage, the catalogue of reductive and aestheticizing observations about the Hernandez sisters provides the attentive force that enables Susan's indignation on their behalf and her embarrassment at having been so wrong. Still, she must balance her realization against the constraints of her profession as an illustrator. That she "*almost* wished those blocks back" and fantasizes about sending "something *closer* to the truth" voices a hesitancy that recalls Denning's assertion that culture workers both obey and resist their employers' directions. Susan is obliged to continue working for Howells and trying to please him, but her art is also deeply personal. The cultural products she creates are never wholly evacuated of her own feelings and motivations just because they are brought to market by capital, nor are those products a perfect reflection of her preferences and opinions. The beauty Susan is commissioned to produce for those who read the *Atlantic* is a complex blend of eastern artistic expectations and Susan's own developing conscience as a westerner.

The tension between professional duties and personal aesthetics vibrates intensely during the Wards' journey to Mexico. Dispatched by his eastern employers to survey a Mexican mine for development or sale, Oliver brings Susan to Michoacán. Always quick to make the best of her family's transience, Susan earns a commission to chronicle and illustrate her travel south of the border. She filters her experience of the trip through a picturesque lens, and the reports she gives of the trip lead Lyman to say that the ports of Mexico "wore the patina of romantic time" and that her journey there was "an interlude of magic between a chapter of defeats" (306, 307). Yet the difficulty of life in New Almaden for herself and others has peeled some of the veneer off her sense of the beautiful by revealing the raw skin of human labor underneath. Perhaps generalizing what she learned from the Hernandez sisters in New Almaden, Susan confronts the grinding effort of daily subsistence as she rides through the villages. She notices women preparing meals and wares for sale, "sandaled Indians bent under hundred-pound bundles," and "swineherds driving herds of black pigs" to market (308). The struggling poor look to her like "people waiting for their souls" for the desperate expressions of weariness they wear. Still, she admires the grandeur of Old World society emblematized by the cathedrals and hacienda estates. Lyman suggests the difficulty Susan had reconciling these feelings: "She had a heart as well as an eye, and they were sometimes at war," and though she was "ashamed of the delight she took in a picturesqueness created out of so much driven human labor," she "got her sketches just the same" (308).

This scene tempts us to convict beauty as an accomplice to Susan's refusal to fully acknowledge sociopolitical realities. "Aha!" we may say. "At the very moment when Susan peeks behind the veil of reification to view the labor that creates her privilege, she retreats into the lofty ideologies of romantic idealism!" I believe the transaction is more complex than that. Behind Lyman's glib comment that she "got her sketches just the same" lies not an ethical refusal but an acknowledgment that Susan is a worker like anyone else, and that she lacks complete control over what and how she will write and illustrate for her employer. A beautiful object, if it is to be brought to market—as most paintings, movies, books, and poems are in our time—it will happen through culture workers who are obliged to sell their labor for their living. Accusing Susan in this moment of an ethical failure to fully sympathize with the Mexican peasants treats her only as a culture consumer, as one imbibing the picturesque to become drunk on her own visual pleasure. Remembering that Susan is also a cultural laborer acknowledges the constraints she works under and helps us better understand and describe the decisions she makes to render the beauty she sees in the world saleable for her employers. This is a highly individualized process that theories of the culture industries or culture hegemonies flatten out. As Denning argues, cultural studies has valorized the efforts of resisting readers and consumers while homogenizing the scene of cultural labor. In truth, "if no reading is uncontested, neither is any composition or performance" (435). Susan's position in the culture industry ought to acquit her of ethical failure by reminding us of the constraints under which she works; instead, we can appreciate how she achieves the "incremental changes in understanding" that Felski says become visible when we wait with beauty long enough to see its true effects (*Uses* 28).

Susan repeats this process of aesthetic reconsideration throughout the novel. When the couple eventually relocates to Leadville, Colorado, Susan writes Augusta about Oliver's new employees. She describes Pricey, Oliver's clerk, as awkward and unhandsome, as though "his flesh seems to have been put on his bones by the lumpy handful" (235). Though Susan enjoys his bookishness, she writes off the possibility of developing a real friendship with him. She does not feel an affinity for Pricey like she does for Frank Sargent (who it, it must be remembered, develops a lifelong affection for Susan that may have become an extramarital romance). But a visit through the mountain meadows of Leadville one day with Pricey changes the situation. Her artistic training renders the landscape a painterly enchantment, with "stirrup-high grass" that "flowed and flawed in the wind," revealing "streaks and splashes of flowers" tended by the "bare peaks patched with snow" (237). Reveling in the sunlight, Susan is oblivious to Pricey beside her until he quotes a couplet from Ralph Waldo Emerson, "in his fine cultivated Oxonian voice, strongly, without the trace of a stammer": *Oh, tenderly the haughty day / Fills his blue urn with fire* (237). Lyman relates his grandmother's shock at Pricey's eloquence, musing, "Who but Pricey? Where but Leadville?"

Susan's rapture in the meadow and her surprised delight at sharing a connection with Pricey match Felski's description of enchantment, one of the "uses" for literature that she identifies by her neophenomenology of reading. "Enchantment," Felski writes, "is soaked through with an unusual intensity of perception and affect" akin to "the condition of being intoxicated, drugged, or dreaming" as you are "sucked in, swept up, spirited away" (*Uses* 55). Modern criticism, rallying under the banner of demystification, shies away from enchantment, seeing it as an aesthetic mode that signals a lapse in intellectual judgment. But to condemn our enchantment with beauty reads aesthetic experience in a narrow, moralistic way and ignores that critics and theorists have also at times been enraptured lay readers. Jonathan Sterne considers the variety of personal attachments, passions, and interests that lead people into careers as humanists and critics to argue that the politics of culture are "rarely enough to draw or sustain the passion of cultural studies scholars" and that "politics sometimes comes secondarily" since scholars often "begin with aspects of culture for which they have an affinity and then seek to discover their political content," at times justifying "their personal pleasures in political terms" (81). Susan Ward's example here, as imagined by Lyman, justifies some of the pleasure we take in enchantment by showing how even the solipsistic pleasures beauty affords can quickly transform into shared moments that help us to realize connections to people and things we had imagined as fundamentally different from ourselves.

Perhaps the most important arenas in which Susan struggles to see beauty are her relationships to her husband and her adopted home in the American West. As Graulich and Handley have separately demonstrated, the two concerns are intimately tied. Since the Wards' marriage metonymically represents the Turnerian drama of settlement, "writing about a marriage . . . *is* writing western history" (Graulich 88). What interests Graulich are the ways in which Lyman struggles to make the confounding and complicated biographical facts of Susan and Oliver Ward's marriage conform to gender myths that structure our imagination of the frontier. She questions Lyman's reliability as a narrator, since his own personal hurt inflects his views on marriage and his reactionary politics partly motivate his retreat to nineteenth-century history, "where the problems and the people are less messy" (*Angle* 158).

Though this chapter is not overtly concerned with frontier history, Graulich's effort to excise Lyman's interpretations and interjections from Susan Ward's story allows me to boast more for beauty's capacity to enlarge and enrich our sympathies and wisdom. My claims rely on a view of beauty that is at least amenable to personal and social progress even if it is not wholly devoted to it. Susan, as I have argued, progresses—however haltingly and imperfectly—from ignorance to knowledge, from distance and difference to familiarity and friendship. The novel's conclusion, at least as Lyman tells it, poses a serious challenge to this view. Having invoked Hester Prynne, Eve, and other types representing mythic femininity's dangerous affiliation with uncivilized nature, Lyman labels Susan's ambiguous relationship to Frank Sargent as infidelity and attributes the Wards' fall from grace to her actions. Susan is responsible for "breaking something she couldn't mend" in her husband's heart, which sent the detritus of their marriage tumbling downhill until it nearly reached rock bottom—which is the more colloquial definition for "angle of repose" (551). But Graulich argues that the extensive narrative space and quotation Stegner gives Susan Ward offer us "alternative readings of her motives and behavior" (98). I would add that Lyman's near silence on the last fifty years of Susan's life ignores the many signs that imply the Wards' full and happy reconciliation. What are we to make of Oliver building the beautiful home Susan had yearned for once they arrive in Grass Valley? Did he tear up the Idaho rose garden in anguish for his dead daughter or jealousy for his wife's indiscretion? What feelings motivated his replanting it at the Zodiac Cottage?

I prefer to see Susan and Oliver dancing around their differences—the pull of infatuation and admiration yielding at times to the push of frustration and conflict—as they come to better know themselves and each other with the aid of beautiful experiences. We may agree with Lyman that his grandmother struggled at times to fully appreciate Oliver—struggled to find the beauty in him—because she "wanted more for him, and better, than he apparently wanted for himself," but that cannot negate the evidence of the efforts she made to overcome that feeling (251). Her openness to her husband's differences shine through in the excitement she is able to muster for each of their successive moves and the beauty she is able to find even in uncomfortable places. Preparing to leave her parents' picturesque farm to follow Oliver out west for a second time, she suddenly feels excited to "make a home in that wild beautiful place" (269). Moving to Idaho especially challenges Susan, but even here, her taste for beautiful landscapes helps her to see the best in her husband and her place. She at first describes the land to Augusta as sublime but unwelcoming, but she soon retracts her first impressions:

> It is a place where silence closes about you after the bustle of the train, where a soft, dry wind from great distances hums through the telephone wires and a stage road goes out of sight in one direction and a new railroad track in another. There is not a tree, nothing but sage. As moonlight unto sunlight is that desert sage to other greens. The wind has magic in it, and the air is full of birds and birdsong.... Not a house, windmill, hill, only that jade-gray plain with lilac mountains on every distant horizon.... And yet how beautiful it is! For the first time I understood Oliver's enthusiasm. We went softly on that sandy trail among the sage, and that dry magical wind from the west blew across us. (364–65)

Witness how Susan's first impersonal gaze upon the land soon yields an appreciation of it and of her husband's differences from herself. Mutual understanding results from Susan's taste in landscape, and possibly from her own act of description. Processing the raw sensory detail of her ride into the valley into prose for an intimate friend may have worked its own beguiling magic to help Susan reappraise unfamiliar and perhaps unwelcomed people and things. If we consider the role that Susan's writing played in courting an affection for the place, we may well marvel with Felski at the power of text to create and distill experience: "How is it that black squiggles on a page can conjure up such vivid simulacra of persons, things, actions, places; that readers can experience such powerful sensations and emotions as we react to these shadows and phantasms?" (61). Beauty, even when it is being described for a friend who questions Susan's choices and marriage, pushes Susan to bridge differences and appreciate others.

For these reasons, I view Susan's contrite letter to Augusta as the novel's triumph rather than as its denouement following a tragic climax. "Behind all this anguish," she says, "has been my refusal to *submit*. I do not mean to my husband only. I have held myself above my chosen life, with results that I must repent and grieve for the rest of my days" (518). Certainly Susan's anguish leads her to exaggerate by forecasting her sadness indefinitely into the future, and we secular, modern readers balk at the conservative marriage politics Susan embraces and the Christian morality that provides her apologetic vocabulary and structures her remorse. But to stop there is to commit the error of presentism that causes Lyman to misunderstand his grandparents: "present your subject in his own terms, judge him in yours" (463). To say Susan is forced into a life of penance denies her recognition for what could be construed as a supreme ethical achievement. We must acknowledge that the institution of marriage and discourses of gender constrain Susan's choice, but we deny her talent for openness and self-censure if we remove her volition from the calculus by which human subjectivity determines its obligations to and boundaries between Self and Other.

We would be wrong to deny the possibility, at least, that the Wards found happiness together and that Susan and Oliver learned to see each other in more compassionate, appreciative ways. In the novel's final scene, Lyman's estranged wife, Ellen, intrudes upon his exile at Zodiac Cottage to ask for their reconciliation. After hearing Lyman's bitter and biased conclusions about his grandparents' lives, she is incredulous: "Living death? Fifty years of it? No rest till they lay down? There must have been something . . . short of that. She couldn't have been doing penance for fifty years" (550). Lyman only shrugs in reply, an oddly diffident gesture from someone who spoke with vehement certainty just moments before.

The theory of beauty applied here emphasizes the complex process of personal perception and social conditioning that accounts for our aesthetic experiences and ethical choices. Stegner conceived of the balance and play between internal and external forces similarly when he once said that "if Newton, Darwin, Marx, and Freud constitute a grammar of living, our actual daily lives are the usage" (qtd. in Robinson and Robinson 71). Beauty—far from being a platonic ideal to which we must aspire—arises out of those "actual daily lives," punctuating the rhythm of ordinary workaday life. It finds us where we stand, and we put it to use as it suits us; in return, it may suit us to its own uses. Stegner's oeuvre—rich in biographical allusion and imbricated in Stegner's political commitments to the natural and social world—provides the perfect forum to begin exploring the variety and complexity of our aesthetic encounters, an exploration that sheds new light on an author who I hope will enjoy a renewed popular interest.

TYLER NICKL is a PhD candidate at the University of Nevada, Reno, where he specializes in ecocritical approaches to western American literature. He has published articles and reviews in *Southwestern American Literature*, *ISLE: Interdisciplinary Studies in Literature and Environment*, and *American Literature*.

NOTES

1. I refer here to arguments in *The Chronicle of Higher Education* in which literary critics, especially Marjorie Perloff and Elaine Scarry, flippantly labeled all political scholarship as "cultural studies"; cultural studies scholars responded impatiently as they clarified the aims and concerns of their subfield. See Perloff, "A Passion for Content"; Heller, "Wearying of Cultural Studies"; Felski, "Those Who Disdain."

WORKS CITED

Benson, Jackson J. *Wallace Stegner: His Life and Work*. Lincoln: U of Nebraska P, 1996. Print.
Bérubé, Michael. "Introduction: Engaging the Aesthetic." *The Aesthetics of Cultural Studies*. Ed. Michael Bérubé. Oxford: Blackwell, 2005. 1–27. Print.
Denning, Michael. "Work and Culture in American Studies." *The Futures of American Studies*. Ed. Donald E. Pease and Robyn Wiegman. Durham, NC: Duke UP, 2002. 419–40. Print.
Felski, Rita. "After Suspicion." *Profession 2009*: 28–35. JSTOR. Web. 26 Mar. 2014.
———. "Those Who Disdain Cultural Studies Don't Know What They're Talking About." *The Chronicle of Higher Education*, 23 July 1999: B6–B7. ProQuest Social Sciences Premium Collection. Web. 14 Aug. 2017.
———. *Uses of Literature*. Oxford: Blackwell, 2008. Print.
Graulich, Melody. "The Guides to Conduct that a Tradition Offers." *South Dakota Review* 23.4 (1985): 87–106. Print.
Handley, William R. *Marriage, Violence, and the Nation in the American Literary West*. New York: Cambridge UP, 2009. Print.
Heller, Scott. "Wearying of Cultural Studies, Some Scholars Rediscover Beauty." *The Chronicle of Higher Education*, 4 Dec. 1998: A15–A16. ProQuest Social Sciences Premium Collection. Web. 14 Aug. 2017.
MacDonald, Bonney. "Authoring an Authentic Place: Environmental and Literary Stewardship in Stegner and Kittredge." *True West: Authenticity and the American West*. Ed. William R. Handley and Nathaniel Lewis. Lincoln: U of Nebraska P, 2004. 275–89. Print.

Perloff, Marjorie. "A Passion for Content: Restoring 'Literary Literacy' to the English Curriculum." *The Chronicle of Higher Education*, 9 May 1997: B4–B5. *ProQuest Social Sciences Premium Collection*. Web. 14 Aug. 2017.

Robinson, Forrest G., and Margaret G. Robinson. *Wallace Stegner*. Boston: Twayne, 1977. Print.

Scarry, Elaine. *On Beauty and Being Just*. Princeton, NJ: Princeton UP, 1999. Print.

Sedgwick, Eve Kosofsky. "Paranoid Reading and Reparative Reading: Or, You're So Paranoid, You Probably Think This Introduction Is About You." *Novel Gazing: Queer Readings in Fiction*. Ed. Eve Kosofsky Sedgwick. Chapel Hill: U of North Carolina P, 1997. 1–37. Print.

Stegner, Wallace. *Angle of Repose*. 1971. New York: Penguin, 2000. Print.

Sterne, Jonathan. "The Burden of Culture." *The Aesthetics of Cultural Studies*. Ed. Michael Bérubé. Oxford: Blackwell, 2005. 80–102. Print.

CHAPTER 5

RENAISSANCE AESTHETICS, PICTURESQUE BEAUTY, THE NATURAL LANDSCAPE
AN ESSAY EXAMINING THE RISE AND FALL OF THE IMPULSE TOWARD BEAUTY

MARK LUCCARELLI

CONSIDERING BEAUTY IN RELATION to ecocriticism raises a question I've long been interested in as a cultural historian operating on the borders of literary study: If literature is to be seen as meta-aesthetic, read largely to take on the tasks of the political, what is the purpose of reading it? After all, we already have social and political history, sociology, anthropology, and political science. Specifically, what do literature and literary study actually contribute to environmental awareness and politics? Could the acknowledgment of beauty in the surround be part of the answer?

The need to rediscover beauty owes much to the trajectory of the humanities since the rise of abstract expressionism after World War II. Beauty's devolution is reflected in the claim that all spaces are equally aesthetic and nonaesthetic at the same time, that aesthetic meaning is found in randomness, repetition, and convergence (Wolin 22). This attempt to converge the ordinary with the aesthetic, to claim a completed revolution of perception in a world of capitalist production and consumption, rejects the life-shaping conception of art inherited from the

Renaissance and manifest in Romantic conceptions of the artist as interlocutor of genius locus, of the poetic reawakening to the rhythms and demands of nature. The prewar interest of continental philosophy in the lifeworld of special places—the phenomenology of place-awareness in pastoral settings linking human destiny to that of the land, to ecology, to community; the idea of culture in and through nature—this philosophical push toward nature breathed life into postwar American ecocriticism, but it proved to be a temporary respite. Postmodernism has completed the abstract modernist revolution away from the sources of western art and literature: "Post-modernism behaves as if the radical transformation of material life sought by the [modernist] avant-garde has already been achieved. But since this is not the case, what results instead is the false sublation of autonomous art. The new marriage between art and facticity can be seen in the choice of artistic subject matter for pop: the detritus of everyday life reemerges, transfigured, glorified, literally larger than life in Warhol's silk screens, which become indistinguishable from an ad campaign" (Wolin 23).

This "sublation" of art to everyday life in a world of commercial banality has been freshened a bit since Warhol by bringing forth the themes of whimsy and frivolity—as, for example, in the celebration of the "carnivalesque" amidst most degraded commercial spaces of the capitalist city. Ironically this quest for playfulness, while expressed against high culture, against beauty, and against bourgeois normativity, has actually led aesthetics and social theory back to the trivialization of beauty as decor noted in nineteenth-century Victorian culture, even to the point of unwillingly falling back into the preclassical narcissistic sensual beauty that modernism had once rejected: "If beauty is a subjective pleasure, it would seem to have no higher status than anything that entertains, amuses, or distracts; it seems odd or ridiculous to regard it as being comparable in importance to truth or justice, for example. And the twentieth century also abandoned beauty as the dominant goal of the arts, again possibly in part because its trivialization in theory led artists to believe that they ought to pursue more real and more serious projects" (Sartwell).

In this general picture of decline, one could say that nature writing was a holdout in favor of beauty; nature as a cultural margin, picturesque tourism, the sublimity of the national parks, as well as the more sophisticated redefinitions of the compelling attraction to wildness—all were manifestations of finding an aesthetics that pointed to the life-shaping qualities of nature and culture, including art and literature. In addition, beauty became a protest against unthinking and relentless modernization, an attempt to locate value in a world increasingly defined by raw political and technological power, but the history of beauty, and specifically the attempt to work out a relation of beauty to spatial and geographic structures, is even older.

American literary criticism in the first half of the twentieth century was embroiled in a great debate over the aesthetics of American pastoralism. The New Humanists defended Thoreau along classical lines, while modernists tended to see pastoral aesthetics as various expressions of the genius loci, linked to the promises of the new—from the "New World" to new urbanisms. In both classical and modern narratives, aesthetic expression was seen as essential to the authenticity of the literary work. After the Great Depression and World War II, there was a generally shared understanding that nature writing, like other genres, expressed authenticity through its documentary quality. According to Thomas Lyon, "the main burden" of nature writing "is to convey pointed instruction in the facts of nature," and it served as a source for interpretation through the "writer's experience" (5). First-wave ecocriticism focused on the latter, interpreted in the context of ecological theory. But already with the arrival of the new historicism, both documentation and aesthetic authenticity were to be sacrificed to radical reinterpretation of society. According to Lawrence Buell, Annette Kolodny's reinterpretation of the settlement and symbolic meaning of the American West in *The Lay of the Land* (1975) was particularly relevant for the history of ecocriticism. Hers was one of a number of efforts that aimed at demythologizing the nation-state and all of its cultural apparatuses. Aesthetic experience of various sorts was seen as a ploy to cover the exertion of power by "heroic" male figures and by the state itself. Much of contemporary ecocriticism is now driven by an attempt to compensate for the perceived political weaknesses of the nature writing tradition and earlier ecocriticism, a process undertaken through a deconstruction of the "pastoral ideology" and the assertion of a multiplicity of readings (Buell, *Environmental Imagination* 31–52). A parenthetical question is to what extent, if at all, does postecological ecocriticism (Gifford; Buell; Garrard), for all its claims of relevancy, respond to the political crisis of mainstream environmentalism? Critics like Mark Dowie, Michael Shellenberger, and Ted Nordhaus suggest that environmentalism is hampered by its failure to speak to the techno-environmental sphere. One could rightly ask, then, what has been gained by the postmodern political approaches of recent ecocritics, but this chapter will subordinate that question to focus on what has been lost aesthetically by such approaches.

One might wish that the teaching and presentation of environmental literatures would make an effective case for why nature matters to the human spirit. Instead, the prevailing direction seems to have been put forth by William Cronon in his oft-cited 1995 essay aimed at getting us back to another kind of nature: the interpretation of nature writing and first-wave ecocriticism as a displacement of the "myth of a fallen humanity in a fallen world" ("Trouble with Wilderness" 4). The rhetorical device suggested in the phrase "another kind of nature" implies that somehow "nature" in the American tradition is a simple-minded pastoralism or, more sinisterly, a pastoral ideology that has been one of the biggest obstacles to environmental reform. This observation has become commonplace in environmental criticism and historical writing: countless conferences, including one of my own, begin with this formulation. As in most humanistic discourse today, cutting off the past takes precedence over rereading the past. Displacement of the guilt generated by reading nature writers who don't share the cosmopolitan dream is part of the program as well. (See, for instance, Buell's discussion of the "metropolitan dream" in *The Environmental Imagination* [82].)

One missing alternative comes from the radical environmental tradition in the sciences and social sciences that built on resource conservation—dating back to Marsh, but including a series of writers such as MacKaye, Mumford, and Commoner, among others. Environmental criticism may think it is moving toward developing a larger socioenvironmental and political narrative, but other versions of "social justice environmentalism"—broader and better grounded in the political—have generated significant new political frames often missing in the humanities (for example, in the fields of urban geography and political ecology). My concern here is narrower and may be framed in a single question: What, if anything, do environmental literature and ecocriticism have to contribute to a faltering environmental consciousness? Criticism once appreciated beauty; sure, this was associated with the New Criticism's formalism and its attempt to carve an aesthetic sphere apart from life, but it also carried over into cultural criticism as practiced by American studies scholars at midcentury.[1] Is it possible to resurrect those concerns in the face of two generations of the steady operationalization of literature and culture as instruments of the identity politics of marginal groups?

BEAUTY AND ORDER

Ernest Flagg was an American architectural reformer active in the early twentieth century. I came across his name many years ago when reading Scott and Helen Nearing's account of homesteading in Maine right after World War I. Facing the need to build solid and pleasing structures cheaply, they turned to Flagg's writings; he had worked out a method for building simple, attractive, and functional structures of fieldstone. For Flagg attractiveness and usefulness could be brought into relation. If economy means the avoidance of waste (overconsumption) and the efficient distribution of goods, and if beauty reflects on good economy, then what we desire (beauty) is what we need (efficiency) and we have arrived at the foundation of environmental governance.

Furthermore, we have returned to a classical formulation: Plato and Aristotle understood beauty as an objective characteristic of the world that could be expressed in terms of the values of order and proportion. In architectural practice, the human body measured beauty, not sensually or imaginatively, but functionally, through scale. To the extent that beauty is still relevant to architecture and city planning, it is precisely the question of scale and the relation of movement to scale that remains most relevant to these discourses. Arguably beauty in this restrictive spatial sense has much to do with our problem of environment. It is a problem of space, that is, it reflects our inability to contain the bursting of our cities over the land and to organize structures that support conservation, better organize mobility, and promote the distribution of productivity.

One of the most important historical frameworks for the discussion of beauty and structure is the Italian Renaissance, specifically the discourse of the ideal city, which became the basis for the development of European urbanism. The function and beauty of buildings was largely determined by human scale in relation to public spaces, which led to the interpretation of urbanism as "humanist space" (Cosgrove, *Social Formation* 64) defined by the cityscape of structured prospects around public and ecclesiastical buildings. This "idea of landscape" (92) harnessed geometries of space to organize perspective in creating an all-seeing observer for whom everything is in perfect focus (see figure 5.1). Thus we arrive at a neoclassical principle of order, whereby a comprehensive view is achieved through a mastery of the external dynamics of space. Beauty is wed to Logos—the ordered and coded space of the ideal city.

Other aesthetic expressions, such as those rooted in sensuality, were seen, at least for the architect, as misleading, a potential threat to truth ascertained through Logos and therefore as the opposite of the beautiful. But with the rise of neo-Platonism in the late classical period, beauty became an expression of the soul, which opened the door to subjectivity and sanctified aspects of the sensual as divine. Here beauty becomes autonomous, freed of classical aesthetic codes, though, as we shall see, bound by mythic narrative. In figure 5.2, beauty manifests itself in the human body, an organic form, albeit sitting in poses of tranquility and equanimity within a pastoral setting. There can be little doubt of the importance of the organic, that the curvilinear body invokes the curvilinear earth. The organic is linked to the imagination, particularly through the transfiguration of sexual desire into sensual beauty, upon which an understanding of human origin depends. While sensuous beauty and classical proportionality is synthesized through the human form, the threat of sexual desire to public order remains a concern. Lurking beneath the surface of the classical trope of ideal beauty is the potential of Eros, represented by Paris's attraction to Venus, to undermine order, thereby plunging his people into war. The painting takes the form of a landscape, embodying a narrative drawn from a well-known myth of classical antiquity that generates rhetorical power as a cautionary tale. Like the landscapes of many Italian Renaissance paintings, Marcantonio and Raphael's was drawn from myth,

82 | ECOCRITICAL AESTHETICS

FIGURE 5.1. *Scuola di Atene* (The school of Athens), 1509–1511, fresco by Raphael (Apostolic Palace, Vatican, Rome). A building is a microcosm of the city. What it shares with Renaissance city planning is the visual projecting of single-point perspective (here focused on the figures at the center, Plato and Aristotle). The entire scene is focused and arranged to lead the eye to the central point. The visual organization of space, as well as the content of the scene, literally creates the public perspective and public space. Source: Wikipedia Commons.

rendered as a means to indulge our thirst for passion, while simultaneously sustaining the social (if not visual) order against the destabilizing effects of beauty by associating sensuous beauty with tragedy of Promethean proportion. Standing in the background is the tragic and (for us) hidden history of the democratic uprisings, guild communalism, and civic egalitarianism that was crushed during the period of transition from the late Middle Ages to the Renaissance. Raphael's invocation of mythos—encompassing earthly and heavenly, ideal and material, history and nature—is powerful, but leaves us with the question of beauty and order unresolved.

LANDSCAPE: MEDIATIONS OF BEAUTY AND STRUCTURE

The Judgment of Paris (figure 5.2) can stand for one mode of landscape representation in the Italian Renaissance: a stage for metaphorical encounters with

FIGURE 5.2. *Das Urteil des Paris*, or *Giudizio di Paride* (The judgment of Paris), ca. 1515, engraving by Marcantonio Raimondi, drawing attributed to Raphael (Staatsgalerie Stuttgart). Classic attributes of beauty as identified by Uvedale Price—smoothness of surfaces, curvilinear forms, repose—are given sculptural expression in this print's strong lines, making it seem like a depiction of a landscape-world. Ironically, as a representation of the beautiful, it is based on a myth telling us of the danger of beauty to the social order: the Trojan prince Paris is asked to choose the most beautiful goddess, and his choosing Venus (Aphrodite) will have tragic consequences for the Trojan people. Source: Wikipedia Commons.

ancient myth. It is a humanist landscape, that is, it is scholarly and autonomous, and it reflects the rise of humanist learning shaped specifically for the "humanist space" of the emerging European culture—a culture expressed spatially in the development of European urbanism. Thus the unstated and assumed spatial dimension of humanism was what Denis Cosgrove calls "the idea of landscape," encompassing ideal cities, perfect geometries, and harmonic spaces (*Social Formation* 63–64, 84, 92, 97). At the same time, *The Judgment of Paris* also stands more generally for the dilemma of making nature an object of desire and hope: at the very least, it acknowledges what contemporary environmental discourse of the ecocentric varieties often fail to admit, namely, that nature as object becomes a landscape humanized, which is to say it is concerned with human values, from which, historically and discursively speaking, beauty emerges as one of the chief concerns. "Topophilia," Tuan tells us, begins with attraction. But even a deep humanism cannot escape the dilemma that as soon as we look at nature it becomes an object, an externality (the surround). For even if and as we are open to the imaginative association between culture and nature, between human and other forms of life, we have also made nature into environment. I call it "structure," and all relations we achieve are ultimately predicated and mediated by it. The power of the surround is such that it brackets the social world, requiring our imaginative commitment.

Until recently, for Americans the answer to these dilemmas was simple enough: the humanist landscapes of classical myth and European urbanism, which hardly made sense in the colonial period, much less after the Revolutionary War, were supplanted by the "natural landscape." Among other problems, this fails to account for the effect the Amerindians had on the land before Euro-American settlement. Consequently "natural landscape" is seen as a uniquely American conceptual confusion of the term "landscape," which refers either to the representation of terrain in painting or more directly to the geographical process of human occupation of and adaptation to specific landforms. On deeper examination, however, the "natural landscape" is neither a confusion nor uniquely American. The term derives from the naturalist tradition in landscape painting that began in the 1820s with the Hudson River school. "Landscape" in this context refers to nature, and the juxtaposition of nature and culture is actually a reworking of the medieval binary (predating modern European conceptions) between all that was cultivated and inhabited (the profane), on the one hand, and the splendor of the forests and oceans (the sacred), on the other (Le Goff, *Medieval Imagination* 58). These conceptions also reflected developments in the material world: the structure of space. British North America, huddled along the Eastern Seaboard, with relatively isolated populations linked only by trade routes, loosely shared a spatial structure with the towns of the late Middle Ages on the continent (Bridenbaugh). Populations were small (Europe was just recovering from the Black Death, while in North America Amerindian populations were still shrinking under the impact of new diseases brought by a relatively small number of European settlers), and as a consequence territory was relatively abundant. Under such circumstances, emphasizing the difference between settled and unsettled areas makes sense. Identifying nature with wilderness (or lack of settlement) is therefore a consequence of practical reason, but there was something else at play.

Nature had already become identified in Catholic humanism with God's immanence, an accompaniment to reason as a guide to human behavior (Le Goff, *Birth of Europe* 80). Initially the emphasis on reason and nature envisioned compatible attributes of the Creation. The blending of Aristotelian reason, Christian cosmology, and the emergence of the public sphere has produced "spaces in-between," helping to create Catholic humanism as against formalist scholasticism and doctrinal Catholicism. Humanist Christianity opened the door to naturalism through a deepening place sensibility predicated in part on encounters with natural and cultural landscapes (Luccarelli, "Medieval Green Cities"). By the early nineteenth century, natural landscape could be rearticulated in North America, though the cultural context had shifted. Formalism, no longer the province of the Church, had become secularized, implicit in the development of the state and the capital city, reflecting the association of reason with the formal structures and infrastructures of European urban-centered life.

The idea of the natural took aesthetic form in the picturesque, first evident in gardening and landscape architecture and later in the landscape as object of tourism and art. The most important picturesque aesthetician in the Anglophone world was Uvedale Price. Writing at the end of the eighteenth century, Price developed the picturesque into an idea and practice of landscape interpretation. Picturesque is defined as a visual means of seeing landscape—one sees through the "eyes of painters" (Price xiii). The word is derived from the Italian *pitteresco*, or picture-like, but it is also a means of developing a sensibility of place. Attraction to the landscape is conceived in terms of "curiosity" and arises from observation of what Price terms the "natural intricacy of the ground" (23, 24). This attention to detail requires moving beyond the pictorial to the experiential and back again to the pictorial. The motion is back and forth, for experience loses significance over time without a grounding in the empirical foundation on which the image rests.

The picturesque helped to develop the idea of a "natural landscape" understood as a sphere apart—the "natural world"—from humankind, a world in which the observer takes his place merely as a visitor. It is this understanding that has supported the charge that the origins of American environmental discourse are mere idealizations. But in the case of the picturesque, as I have suggested, there was a strong empirical orientation. One indication of this lies with Price's discourse against an environmentally destructive behavior of his day, namely, the gentrification of the countryside, through which "picturesque circumstances . . . are so frequently and irrecoverably destroyed" (xi). In this formulation Price follows William Gilpin's lead as exemplified in his travel guide to the River Wye, written in 1782, by completing a shift in the picturesque from the design of aristocratic estates to the appreciation of publicly accessible landscapes. As such, the picturesque became a middle-class discourse and was oriented toward public space imbued with a sense of the beautiful—a point missed by John Barrell in his seminal work, *The Idea of Landscape and the Sense of Place* (1972), which has landscape opposed to place and the picturesque little more than an adjunct to the aristocratic enclosure of the English countryside. By the end of the eighteenth century, the picturesque had identified the beauty of nature with informality and the curvilinear forms found in landscapes generally. Indeed Gilpin, ever the didact, had worked out a rather supercilious set of criteria (rules) to teach the reader/viewer how to see the picturesque and distinguish it from less attractive landscapes and landscape features. Though the picturesque had many limitations, at the birth of nineteenth-century environmental movements, picturesque beauty and the cause of environmental reform lived side by side. By the twentieth century the picturesque could be taken as an invitation to rethink urbanism and public space.

The sublime was the second landscape aesthetic to attempt to mediate beauty and order. In *A Philosophical Enquiry into the Origin of Our Ideas of the Sublime and Beautiful* (1757), Burke contrasted an aesthetic of the beautiful with that of the sublime, seeing the former as far less dramatic and significant to the human psyche's contact with the natural world. But it was Schopenhauer, in *The World as Will and Representation*, who came closest to understanding the strange dynamic of culture destruction and creation inherent in the motif of the sublime: "[A person] perceives himself, on the one hand, as an individual, as the frail phenomenon of will, which the slightest touch of these forces can utterly destroy, helpless against powerful nature, dependent, the victim of chance, a vanishing nothing in the presence of stupendous might; and, on the other hand, as the eternal, peaceful, knowing subject. . . . Here he obtains a glimpse of a power beyond all comparison superior to the individual, threatening it with annihilation" (204–5). But he also points out that the sublime could be applied to any scene in which converted danger was remote enough to be converted to attraction. Sublimity was thus an attempt to escape the problem of making natural beauty a mere reflection of our desires and hopes by making it unreachable, transcendent in its power over us, a clear danger to the present culture of human assertion. In this it succeeded; however, its limitation in creating a new spatial order was soon apparent. The very formulation of the sublime, unlike the picturesque, lent itself to landscapes of extraordinary power and scale. There was nothing subtle, no inherent visual rules of nature one need discover, no aesthetic to cultivate, as in the picturesque. It was the sublime, far more than wilderness, that led to the framing of national parks as "wonderlands," unique formations set far apart from the everyday, transcendent rather than immanent manifestations of the divine. Here one could speak of the difficulty of nature constructed as a "realm apart," but also of the power of nature to move us.

The gothic was a third and perhaps the most fecund version of natural landscape. It was northern European in general and British in particular. The architecture of the European North inspired Ruskin's equation of rudeness and wildness with landscape—an ambiance redolent of the rough lands of the North and supportive of attention to everyday life and to the principle of social equality. North America was even further removed from the seat of European culture; there the "natural landscape" was wild and both difficult and an opportunity. As Lewis Mumford puts it, to develop "the culture of the mind through the land" requires reworking the linkages between landscape and agriculture/horticulture, urban layout and architecture, and works of infrastructural engineering (101–2). In this reiteration, the "natural landscape" implicitly critiques capitalism by applying a holistic vision of the land against the ravages of private property. But the fundamental point in our context is that the rediscovery and rearticulation of beauty as simple, rough, direct, and unmediated became essential to the further development of the concept of the natural landscape in the direction of social and cultural criticism. Indeed it makes us look at the concept of wildness differently than do contemporary environmental critics who see in wilderness only the spatial dimension of isolated and marginal lands.

Reading *Walden*, written in the same midcentury period, one must think in terms of the gothic landscape when Thoreau appeals to the prospect of an original relation to the natural world: "I take infinite pains to know all phenomena of the spring, for instance, thinking that I have here the entire poem, and then, to my chagrin, I hear that it is but an imperfect copy that I possess and have read, that my ancestors have torn out many of the first leaves and grandest passages, and mutilated it in many places" (qtd. in Cronon, "Trouble with Wilderness" 15). For Cronon, who according to Lawrence Buell (Statement in discussion) has acknowledged and apologized for his "mistakes," but whose "mistakes" have nonetheless been instrumental in setting the current tone of skepticism, we must be firm in our rejection of Thoreau's flights of fancy, of his imaginative possession of nature as worthy of preservation. Cronon argues, "Our project must be to locate a nature which is within rather than without history, for only by doing so can we find human communities which are inside rather than outside nature" ("Trouble with Wilderness" 15).

Cronon says he speaks for "history," but what he means is that he wishes to entrench the development of the present configuration of liberal capitalist societies as the only conceivable result of western historical development. For what his magnum opus, *Nature's Metropolis* (1991), makes clear is that history means the rise of global capitalist markets through which nature is transformed into commodity. This process becomes the "practical" environmental context Cronon advances. We ought instead to consider the question of whether Thoreau is recalling an Arcadia outside of time or beginning a discussion of how to employ history to a different end. No doubt there are many Arcadian moments in Thoreau where we are invited to imaginatively restore what has been lost—for instance,

"Perchance after a few thousands of years, if the fishes will be patient, and pass their summers elsewhere meanwhile, nature will have leveled the Billerica dam, and the Lowell factories, and the Grass-ground river [the Musketaquid, renamed the Concord] run clear again, to be explored by new migratory shoals, even as far as Hopkinton pond and Westborough swamp" (32). Surely Thoreau gives us, to put it in Northrop Frye's terms, history as a romance, but is Thoreau's undoubted "drama of self-identification" in truth "symbolized by the hero's transcendence of the world of experience, his victory over it, and his final liberation from it" (White 8)? Or is Thoreau struggling to open experience to a broader and truer understanding of beauty and thus resuscitate the imagination on which all true political and cultural change is predicated?

In discussing Thoreau, a nature writer, in the context of landscape, I am not denying the significance of the specific cultural experience that gave rise to American nature writing, or its literary/scientific origins in the English nature essay with its roots in both the Arcadian vision and Christian pastoralism.[2] But the development of the American picturesque, the "natural landscape," was also critically important as Thoreau came to realize that his observations required a reference in art. In "Autumnal Hints," Thoreau's description of an oak leaf reflects what he learned from Ruskin about visual detail and color (Richardson 360). Color, light/shade, mountain/forest: these visuals and visual binaries frame what we see. It is how we see it rather than the object itself (363) that begins to concern Thoreau here. I suppose this perspectival view was always there regarding matters of subjectivity—the inner eye—but Thoreau came to realize the importance of understanding how these are reproduced by the artist in framing the visible world. Thus he became interested in art, despite his protestations to the contrary. Furthermore, "the Turnerian visual grandeur of landscape . . . evident in Thoreau's late landscape writing" comes from Ruskin (360); here is Thoreau in 1857 in his journal: "I steadily ascended along a rocky ridge half clad with stinted trees, where wild beasts haunted, till I lost myself in the upper air and clouds . . . into a superterranean grandeur and sublimity" (qtd. in Richardson 362). This makes an interesting contrast with the famous Katahdin passage in which Thoreau confronts the emptiness of the material universe and the insignificance of humankind; evidently rough-and-ready contact with the archaic earth is not enough.

THE RISE AND RISE OF NEOFORMALISM AND THE FALL OF BEAUTY

When one looks at the critics of the environmental imagination, one can't help but agree with what Peter Quigley states in the introduction to this book: the rise of theory and its project includes a "sweeping rejection of so-called universals like beauty and the individual," assuming these to be distractions from important political causes. It amounts to a graceless attack on art and literature. Constructivism becomes a tool for formulating a bottomless set of demands in absolute terms, thereby misunderstanding the conditional nature of the political world as well as denying, by overlooking, the instrumentality of practical reason as it actually operates in the real world. Thus, rather than understanding the broader conditions of urbanization and industrialization that have preceded environmental degradation, the Foucauldians imagine that idealized landscapes construct polluted ones; wilderness parks construct degraded cities; and garden cities construct highway strip development. Yes, we might well acknowledge that aesthetic ideals can and do function as a means of escape. But Foucauldians want more: they wish to argue that by its nature language constructs binaries that defeat meaning and the capacity to construct alternatives. Hiding behind radicalism does not obscure the formalist quality of this form of thinking. The satisfaction attained is purely intellectual. The first set of solutions that is entertained, struggle at the micro-level of society, which is presented as an imperative to link environmentalism with the struggles of marginal groups, has been ineffectual. Post-Marxist formulations that link aesthetics to class formations are often heavy-handed (as in the case of Barrell's, mentioned earlier) and in any case blend seamlessly with constructivist formulations, sacrificing one of the valuable frames of Marxist thinking.

The bottom line is that the public sees environmentalism as another special-interest lobby. In one sense it no longer matters—no point in worrying about a strategy that is in full retreat anyway. Nonetheless we feel compelled to "interrogate" Thoreau, for we cannot permit beauty to stand independently, even for a moment, for fear that the self-deceptive nature of our rhetoric would be concealed to all eyes. Is this critical impulse so different from that of orthodox Catholicism in suppressing humanist openings to the beauty of the natural world? Ecocriticism in most, if not all, of its varieties has stripped aesthetics away, remaking environment into a social-ethical sphere; in other words it has created a social geography that replaces both physical geography and the literary imagination. Beauty from this perspective blends effortlessly with power and injustice.

The irony is that while the attack against "Thoreau the imperialist" has been at least partly successful in chastising a writer of great integrity and insight according to cannons of political correctness, the politics of the current social order are proceeding toward a global imperialism of unprecedented scale and scope that goes virtually unopposed. Many of the critics of "settler imperialism" seem to fail to understand that the globalization they countenance in the name of cosmopolitanism has been set in motion by an even greater imperialism of capital.

One does not choose among "globalizations," a conceit which reflects the liberalistic ideology of choice. Much of the discourse of cultural studies confuses structural and cultural issues, pretending that fundamental political choices exist at a micro–social scale or within the realm of representation of value. Beautiful landscapes, representations of spaces in-between, green imaginaries: all certainly have discursive implications, but they are not political discourses and certainly fail as politics.

The double irony of the attack on nineteenth-century ideas of nature and landscape beauty is that they contributed to making changes in the way lands were treated. In the nineteenth century, conservation was as much an attitude as a set of policies, and it was linked to appreciation of nature as well as utilization of natural resources. Another important point is that unlike the response to "environmentalism" today, the "natural landscape" was popular. One reason was that the eighteenth- and nineteenth-century aestheticians (from Burke to Gilpin) understood that landscape is about perception in the eyes of the individual beholders and began in effect what became empirical studies of how different landscapes affect human beings, a discourse that took different directions, including the concern with human health in workplaces and built environments. True, the objects of the nineteenth-century landscape discourse based on picturesque beauty were Victorian and post-Victorian concerns—especially with bourgeois identity in a mass society and the destruction of civility under the impact of urbanization. Art, very much like ideas, is subject to appropriation. But significantly, as I suggested earlier, picturesque aesthetics were reinvented in the 1890–1930 period, beginning a process of reinventing the structure of landscape by establishing design criteria and wielding influence in parks and city planning, but also through the maturation of the gothic conception of returning to cultural roots to formulate demands for social justice (Ruskin/Morris) and to find the greater meaning of modernist functionalism (the Goodmans). Though halted in the 1960s, it offered the possibility of altering the hideous course of urban modernization, which was destroying the environment of the modern world. Why is this all so forgotten in favor of creating an undifferentiated past and glorious present?

SURVIVAL

The picturesque landscape lost its hold largely because it stood in the way of the capitalist urbanization and industrialization that swept American life in the twentieth century, making the American romance implausible. Modernism preferred the aestheticization of the urban industrial world common as the only authentic expression. The harsh aesthetics of urban scenes is a more significant response than the genteel concern with beauty (and propriety). One can find interesting angles, use particular combinations of black-and-white film and developers to create a gritty look or create a dark, shadowy ambiance. Twentieth-century modernism is all about creating such aesthetics: dark and gritty, as in Paul Strand's view of Wall Street in his photograph of the same name, with deep black and shadowy lights anticipating film noir. Authenticity requires a tragic view of life that borders on despair, increasingly so harsh that it becomes the dystopian visions of our time (as in the oft-cited work of Cormac McCarthy).

Finding beauty in nature can survive as a gesture toward life over death; it could be a statement of the primitive impulse but no longer a culture in itself. Santayana speaks to the young Californian living in a "thriving society" and aware of the existence of a "virgin and prodigious world." Because of the lack of an archaic tradition of land use as well as a history of experimentation with converting natural resources to various uses, the Californian does not assume "that nature was made by you or for you." Rather, we are simply "one brave little force among her immense forces." Consequently, nature freed from our power and control is beautiful and inspirational:

> When you escape, as you love to do, to your forests and your Sierras, I am sure again that you do not feel you made them, or that they were made for you. They have grown as you have grown, only more massively and more slowly. In their non-human beauty and peace they stir the sub-human depths and the super-human possibilities of your own spirit. It is no transcendental logic that they teach; and they give no sign of any deliberate morality seated in the world. It is rather the vanity and superficiality of all logic, the needlessness of argument, the finitude of morals, the strength of time, the fertility of matter, the variety, the unspeakable variety, of possible life.... Everywhere is an incipient beauty and nowhere permanence, everywhere an incipient harmony, nowhere an intention, nor a responsibility, nor a plan. (62–63)

Santayana understands that the appeal is not abstraction, which implies distance, but immediacy, something akin to what we wish to recover from the sense of the primitive. But we are also left with the fact that the industrial sphere mentioned by Santayana as a benign experimentation with natural "forces" (62) grows all the more dangerous. What lay ahead was the oil revolution, the chemical revolution, the atomic revolution—and several phases of industrialization moving us further and further along the path of ecological destruction. Is it so surprising, then, that "green urbanism" and green-energy policies have become emptied out and become the agent of the urban booster (Luccarelli and Røe)? I've consistently taken the view that it is possible to create a new politics of vision and planning, but since 1985 when I first completed my dissertation on Lewis Mumford, regionalism, and the vision of early environmental planning, humanists have taken very little notice; I've had better luck with planners and sociologists.

Van Wyck Brooks criticized the residual genteel ethos of the late Victorian age as an ineffective idealism. The power of such analysis, however, should be context specific. We seem to accept a mentalist (culturalist) interpretation where picturesque is a static ideality, where beauty equals ideality equals stasis. The search for beauty, however, is not essentially an appropriation of transcendent ideality; actually at bottom it is more the search for confirmation that we humans, who are after all beauty-finding creatures, matter, and that as such creatures it is possible to shape the material world we inhabit. And only when we rediscover beauty and find a way to symbolize it and apply it can we tackle the job of environmental reform.

MARK LUCCARELLI is Associate Professor of British and North American literature at the University of Oslo in Norway. In addition to many articles in the environmental humanities, his publications include *Lewis Mumford and the Ecological Region: The Politics of Planning*, *Green Oslo: Visions, Planning and Discourse*, and *Spaces In-Between: Cultural and Political Perspectives on Environmental Discourse*.

NOTES

1. For instance, Leo Marx, in "American Studies: A Defense of an Unscientific Method," argues that pastoral imagery as represented and interpreted in literary texts from the nineteenth century onward frames a tragic sensibility necessary to the critique of raw technological power. But this very formulation, Marx admits, requires a "concept of 'high' culture [and] marks a crucial distinction between the methods of the humanist and the social scientist" (80).

2. Important works here are Lyon, *This Incomparable Land*; and Worster, *Nature's Economy*.

WORKS CITED OR CONSULTED

Barrell, John. *The Idea of Landscape and the Sense of Place*. Cambridge: Cambridge UP, 1972. Print.
Bridenbaugh, Carl. *Cities in the Wilderness: The First Century of Urban Life in America, 1625–1742*. 1938. New York: Oxford UP, 1971. Print.
Buell, Lawrence. *The Environmental Imagination: Thoreau, Nature Writing, and the Formation of American Culture*. Cambridge, MA: Harvard UP, 1995. Print.
———. *The Future of Environmental Criticism: Environmental Crisis and Literary Imagination*. Malden, MA: Blackwell. 2005. Print.
———. Statement in discussion. Counter-Natures Symposium. Nordic Network for Interdisciplinary Environmental Studies conference, Uppsala, Sweden. 20–22 Nov. 2009.

———. *Writing for an Endangered World: Literature, Culture and Environment in the U.S. and Beyond*. Cambridge, MA: Belknap Press of Harvard UP, 2001. Print.
Commoner, Barry. *The Closing Circle: Nature, Man and Technology*. New York: Knopf, 1971. Print.
———. *The Poverty of Power: Energy and the Economic Crisis*. New York: Random House, 1976. Print.
Cosgrove, Denis E. *Social Formation and Symbolic Landscape*. 1984. Madison: U of Wisconsin P, 1998. Print.
Cronon, William. *Changes in the Land: Indians, Colonists, and the Ecology of New England*. New York: Hill and Wang, 1983. Print.
———. *Nature's Metropolis*. New York: Norton, 1991. Print.
———. "The Trouble with Wilderness; or, Getting Back to the Wrong Nature." *Uncommon Ground: Rethinking the Human Place in Nature*. Ed. William Cronon. New York: Norton, 1996. 69–90. Print.
Douglass, Ann. *The Feminization of American Culture*. 1977. New York: Farrar, Straus and Giroux, 1998. Print.
Dowie, Mark. *Losing Ground: American Environmentalism at the Close of the Twentieth Century*. Cambridge, MA: MIT P, 1995. Print.
Flagg, Ernest. *Small Houses: Their Economic Design and Construction*. 1921. New York: Dover, 2006. Print.
Garrard, Greg. *Ecocriticism*. London: Routledge, 2004. Print.
Gifford, Terry. *Pastoral*. London: Routledge, 1999. Print.
Gilpin, William. *Observations on the River Wye*. 1782. London: Pallas Athene, 2005. Print.
Jamison, Andrew. "Ecology and the Environmental Movement." *Ecology Revisited: Reflecting on Concepts, Advancing Science*. Ed. Astrid Schwartz and Kurt Jax. London: Springer, 2011. 195–204. Print.
Kolodny, Annette. *The Lay of the Land: Metaphor as Experience and History in American Life and Letters*. Chapel Hill: U of North Carolina P, 1975. Print.
Le Goff, Jacques. *The Birth of Europe*. Trans. Janet Lloyd. Oxford: Wiley-Blackwell, 2005. Print.
———. *The Medieval Imagination*. Trans. Arthur Goldhammer. Chicago: U of Chicago P, 1992. Print.
Luccarelli, Mark. "Landscape, Anti-landscape and the Western Political Imagination: J. B. Jackson's Challenge to Environmentalism." *The Anti-landscape*. Ed. David E. Nye and Sarah Elkind. Amsterdam: Rodopi, 2014. 61–76. Print.
———. *Lewis Mumford and the Ecological Region*. New York: Guilford, 1995. Print.
———. "Medieval Green Cities: Third Space and the Challenge of History." *Spaces In-Between: Cultural and Political Perspectives on Environmental Discourse*. Ed. Mark Luccarelli and Sigurd Bergmann. Leiden: Brill/Rodopi, 2015. 179–201. Print.
Luccarelli, Mark, and Per Gunnar Røe. "Introduction: Nature, Urbanism and Liveability." *Green Oslo: Visions, Planning and Discourse*. Ed. Mark Luccarelli and Per Gunnar Røe. Farnham: Ashgate, 2012. Print.
Lyon, Thomas J. *This Incomparable Land: A Guide to American Nature Writing*. New York: Penguin, 1989. Print.
Martin, Richard. "Nature's Nature/Nature's Art: Responses to the 'Natural' World." *"Nature's Nation" Revisited: American Concepts of Nature from Wonder to Ecologi-*

cal Crisis. Ed. Hans Bak and Walter W. Hölbling, Amsterdam: VU UP, 2003. 60–77. Print.

Marx, Leo. "American Studies: A Defense of an Unscientific Method." *New Literary History* 1.1 (October 1969): 75–90. Print.

Mumford, Lewis. "Frederick Law Olmsted's Contribution." *Roots of Contemporary American Architecture*. 1952. Ed. Lewis Mumford. New York: Dover, 1972. Print.

Nordhaus, Ted, and Michael Shellenberger. "The Death of Environmentalism: Global Warming Politics in a Post-Environmental World." *Grist*, 14 Jan. 2005. Web. 30 June 2015.

Price, Uvedale. *An Essay on the Picturesque*. London: Robson, 1796. Print.

Richardson, Robert D., Jr. *Henry Thoreau: A Life of the Mind*. Berkeley: U of California P, 1988. Print.

Ruskin, John. "The Nature of Gothic." *The Stones of Venice*. 1851–1853. Ed. J. G. Links. New York: Da Capo, 2003. 157–90. Print.

Santayana, George. "The Genteel Tradition in American Philosophy." *The Genteel Tradition: Nine Essays by George Santayana*. Ed. Douglas L. Wilson. Lincoln: U of Nebraska P, 1998. 37–64. Print.

Sartwell, Crispin. "Beauty." *Stanford Encyclopedia of Philosophy*, 4 Sept. 2012 (rev. 5 Oct. 2016). Web. 7 Dec. 2015.

Schopenhauer, Arthur. *The World as Will and Representation*. Trans. E. F. J. Payne. Vol. 1. New York: Dover, 1966. Print.

Thoreau, Henry David. *A Week on the Concord and Merrimac Rivers*. 1849. Boston: Houghton Mifflin, 1961. Print.

Tuan, Yi-Fu. *Topophilia*. New York: Columbia UP, 1990. Print.

White, Hayden. *Metahistory: The Historical Imagination in Nineteenth-Century Europe*. 1973. Baltimore: John Hopkins UP, 2014. Print.

Wolin, Richard. *Labyrinths: Explorations in the Critical History of Ideas*. Amherst: U of Massachusetts P, 1995. Print.

Worster, Donald. *Nature's Economy: A History of Ecological Ideas*. 1977. New York: Cambridge UP, 1985. Print.

PART 2
BEAUTY AND ENGAGEMENT

CHAPTER 6

TOWARD AN ECOFEMINIST AESTHETIC OF RECONNECTION

GRETA GAARD

Act I. Late summer afternoon at Hidden Falls Regional Park in St. Paul, Minnesota, in an oak forest savanna with a natural amphitheater, on the banks of the Mississippi River.

Enter two humans, walking upright together.

GG (looking up at the tree canopy): Wouldn't an ecofeminist aesthetic be beautiful?

URHere: Can't say. Define "ecofeminist" and "beauty." We know a bit about aesthetics already; this isn't the first chapter in the volume. And, who are you? Have we met?

GG: Fair enough. In this narrative performance, I'm the ecofeminist artist, and you are the spectator-participant. (These roles are temporary; in another narrative, we might trade places, occupy similar locations, or invent new ones.) Although it sounds like you've read other chapters in this book, in my chapter you don't exist at the time of my writing, since the narrative is just now unfolding, and I'm actively anticipating your presence. When you pick up this narrative and begin reading, both of us will come into being through that relationship. You might be thinking, "Oh, reader-response theory, that's so 1960s; Wolfgang Iser and Stanley Fish"—but that's not my only frame of reference.

URHere (unnerved): Oh gosh, I don't exist yet. Existentialism, right?

GG (nods): Yes and no, but not here: it's feminism, and let me explain why. Both our identities are shaped as we enter this conversation together. As scholars in feminist ethics and feminist psychology have argued, in western cultures, women's sense of self is crafted through relationships—not that men's selfhood isn't similarly crafted, but that men aren't as aware of their relational selves, so they make behavioral and ethical choices differently, based more on liberalism's concept of autonomous individualism rather than on a relational and contextual selfhood. This autonomous individualism—which can be traced back to Greek philosophy and politics, incidentally—is most frequently associated with the Enlightenment philosophy of Immanuel Kant and the mind/body dualisms of René Descartes. That era formed the groundwork for today's mechanist views of nature as mindless and inert, a view that has legitimated eco-exploitations from colonialism to capitalism.

Instead, I'm talking about the relational self, described in feminist psychologist Carol Gilligan's study of girls' moral development, where Gilligan observed girls making ethical decisions based on care ethics—considering every affected person's needs and interests in the ethical decision—rather than on masculinized and autonomous individuals' rights. Gilligan's work, though groundbreaking, inspired critiques of gender essentialism which in turn prompted more nuanced and contextual approaches, such as Evelyn Fox Keller's "dynamic autonomy," a sense of self that is both differentiated from and associated with others, and Marilyn Friedman's definition of autonomy as "socially rooted."

Today, the feminist notion of "relational autonomy" (Freeman) describes a standpoint and selfhood that emerge contextually, through relationships, and compares favorably with Martin Heidegger's concept of Mitsein (being-with). For our purposes, though, it's Freya Mathews's notion of panpsychism that's most relevant: this view recognizes matter and place as alive, as subjects, as protagonists along with humans in this drama of material existence. Mathews's panpsychism takes feminism's relational self to its eco-logical conclusions, understanding that we cannot recognize a selfhood apart from the world in which all selves are nested—rather, self is realized through this world. This is a selfhood described by most indigenous communities: a selfhood cultivated through relations with place, other animals, plants, insects, water, stone, and all the inhabitants of place.

URHere: Do you really talk this way to your friends? Reader-response, feminist psychology, phenomenology—what does this have to do with ecofeminism?

GG: It's a quick literature review, a prologue to the present; and yes, I actually talk this way. Here we are, emerging through a contextual relationship that—on the ground of the preceding scholarship—can be described through even more contemporary philosophies of material feminism, ecofeminism, and Buddhist philosophy.

From material feminism, we get the conceptual tools of "transcorporeality, in which the human is always intermeshed with the more-than-human world" (Alaimo 238), and intra-action, defined by Karen Barad as the mutual constitution of all objects and agencies in an undivided field of existence (133). With Jane Bennett's work on "vibrant matter," material feminism draws on feminist science studies, ecology, and new materialisms to argue for the agency of all matter—in other words, every part of this world, every part of "nature," is alive with intention, purpose, and action. This view effectively displaces humanism, or the idea that we humans are the only figures capable of agency and meaningful action, performing on and against a background of others—other less-than-human humans, other animals, and other beings such as plants, hills, rivers, stones, air.

URHere: I'm seeing the ecofeminist connection here too, particularly since "backgrounding" is one of the five operations that maintains the Master Model, described by Val Plumwood (*Feminism*) as the "Man of Reason" that is the dominant construction of humanist identity in western cultures. But you and I are the only ones talking here (gestures around the oak savanna).

GG (gestures to the oaks, mirroring *URHere*): We're the only ones talking in human language—there are other languages going on here, just as there are many languages among human cultures. We are talking, but that doesn't mean the plants here aren't also communicating—with each other, with other beings like insects, birds, and bacteria, and maybe with us too, but we're not listening very carefully to them right now (Chamovitz; Hall; Pollan).

URHere (skeptical): Is this animism, or ecofeminism?

GG: Both! And do you notice how the very term "animism" carries the taint of a pejorative, as if there's no intelligence behind such a view, when in fact plant studies is now confirming through science the views that animist cultures have held for millennia? Though not a scientist herself, Val Plumwood's ecofeminist philosophy anticipated the insights of material feminism and plant studies by over a decade (notices *URHere* looking doubtful).

How? She listened to and studied indigenous perspectives—aboriginal Australian writers like Bill Neidjie—to develop her concept of earthothers

("Animals and Ecology"), a relational description of all beings on earth that includes humans too. One of many significant differences between material feminisms and Plumwood's ecofeminism is her emphasis on praxis, the inseparability of socially engaged action and philosophical or scholarly practice. Plumwood's philosophy returns again and again to the values and viewpoints of indigenous cultures, and to the critical importance of standing in solidarity with indigenous communities and their sovereign right to land and self-determination.

URHere: So we've coproduced—listening is half the conversation, remember—this ecofeminist, relational, intra-active selfhood, which I now see you couldn't have theorized without me. But the aesthetic connection still needs development.

GG: It might be helpful to look at an example. In a nutshell (bends down to pick up an acorn that has fallen from the oak trees, hands it to human companion), an ecological and feminist theory of self-in-relation grounds any theory of social relations, such as a political theory and an aesthetic theory. And aesthetics is all about relations—between and among artists, creativity, creations, viewer-audience-participants, histories and cultures, social and ecological texts and contexts. Such a theory of self-in-relation also grounds any theory of ethics, so my hunch is that an ecofeminist aesthetic theory is enmeshed—intra-active, if you will—with the ecofeminist relational self, the selfhood of earthothers, and with ecofeminist ethics (cf. Wolosky). In short, an ecofeminist aesthetic would find beauty in the enactment of ecofeminist values and ethics.

URHere: Ugh (flicks the acorn away). So goody-two-shoes.

GG (raises eyebrows, expressing astonishment): You just threw away the point! Perhaps you haven't heard about Audre Lorde's "Uses of the Erotic" or Chaia Heller's theory of the socioerotic, and the five fingers of social desire.

URHere (amused): Much better: aesthetics, saved from ethics by the erotic!

GG: Can't aesthetics be both ethical and erotic? Clearly we need to define the erotic too, so let's check out an example of ecofeminist aesthetics: the MayDay Parade.

Act II. MayDay Parade. Bloomington Avenue in South Minneapolis. High noon on a sunny spring Sunday, the first of May.

The parade winds through a diverse neighborhood populated by Latino American, African American, Nordic American, Native American, and GLBTQ families and individuals, largely working class to bohemian middle class. In a community where winter arrives early in November and can last through April, people line the parade route, eager for this annual ritual welcoming the spring.

Scene 1: Consider this

The 2012 parade begins with the "mud people," a group of eco-anarchists who don't organize with the regular MayDay Parade yet precede it, riding in black on their tall bicycles, or covered in mud, walking, embodying the material experience of spring. Then the parade banner appears, announcing the start of the parade, and the theme: "It's the End of the World as We Know It." Puppets and performers dressed in repurposed fabric, cardboard, and papier mâché silently perform the message: we are entangled in a vast network of manufacturing and consumption that provides convenience at the cost of depleting our limited fossil-fuel resources. A long Pipeline and shrouded figures using modern technologies symbolize our dependence on these resources. Energy Gremlins make sure everyone stays plugged in, as the Wounded Earth suffers. Cranes dance behind, mourning and absorbing the grief of the Wounded Earth.

Scene 2: Break the spell

The overconsumption of the earth is breaking our hearts, and we are under a spell of delusion, believing that we have no alternative. Puppeteers show that we can break the spell that divides us from each other. As humans, we live very separate, isolated lives.

Whirling Deer Hearts urge us to awaken and open our hearts, while keeping rooted to the earth. Deer Spirits urge us to love and give unconditionally. Sacred Spirit Shirts honor those who have passed from this earth.

Earth's Heart sleeps, worn down by the drudge of our daily life.

The Goddess of Compassion reminds us that genuine compassion is the source of change—let your heart open to embrace change. Here we turn toward the root problem, our isolation from one another, and begin seeking strength in community.

Scene 3: Make do

Puppeteers perform and celebrate the work being done to change our communities. This change requires a combination of old and new ideas, and reaching out to neighbors. Sweepers reclaim the streets, clearing out the old ways so new ones can enter. Busy beavers with tools are resourceful! The

FIGURE 6.1. *Two Sloths*. Courtesy of In the Heart of the Beast Puppet and Mask Theatre.

Town Square and Maypoles offer a place for dancing and meeting our neighbors. Human Libraries honor the wisdom of our elders and the knowledge held in our communities.

Sloths on bicycles remind us to slow down and enjoy the little things in life. Clotheslines are carried too, reminding us of ways to cut down on energy use.

Scene 4: Surround of light

We are surrounded by light, which embraces us all as we journey around the sun through the seasons.

The Four Horses from the four directions—north, south, east, and west—gather to await the message from the Forest. The thirty-eight trees of the Forest warn us of a colonialist history we do not want to repeat: the 150th anniversary of the hanging of thirty-eight Dakota men in Mankato, Minnesota.

Aztec dancers remind us that we stand on stolen land. The people, the traditions, and the knowledge of indigenous people are still alive, still showing how to live in this place.

The Sun calls for us to move and grow. Performers carry Seed Arks to symbolize the new beginnings, along with Vegetable Beds and Compost Toilets to remind us that we are a part of a larger cycle of life.

FIGURE 6.2. *Tree of Life Resurrected at Pageant.* Courtesy of In the Heart of the Beast Puppet and Mask Theatre.

Zumba Bees energize and celebrate the changes occurring.

Dance! Remembering the history of people and place, and honoring the bees, we can grow these seeds of food justice, and feed one another!

A puppeted Ouroboros marches to symbolize the eternal cycle of life, death, and rebirth. Dragons bring auspicious energy to these new beginnings.

The puppeted parade ends here, and is followed by the Free Speech section, where community groups offering political, ecological, and social pathways toward sustainability and eco-justice carry banners, bicycle, skateboard, push baby strollers, and inspire parade-goers with tangible actions for bringing the parade's message into their lives.

Scene 5: Tree of Life ceremony in Powderhorn Park

After the parade, performers gather at the west end of Powderhorn Lake to reenact the narrative of the parade. Although we have experienced a dark winter of disconnection, we can change, and with our changes we can revive the great Tree of Life.

In the words of MayDay founder Sandy Spieler, "Behold the curious wonder of an end, which unleashes a beginning, the wonder of tiny beings having a big impact in the world, the wonder of human-powered work, the wonder of common sense, the foreboding wonder of the wounded Mother Earth, the radiant wonder of the medicine of recognizing each other; of coming together O eternal wonder of Prairie, Woods, Sky, and River; the sustaining energy of the Sun, the Tree of Life!"

Act III. Oak savanna, later in the day, near evening.

GG and *URHere*, walking.

URHere: Beautiful indeed! How do they do it?

GG (nods): Well, a call goes out through a variety of networks, targeting diverse communities, and people show up in January to plan the theme of the parade. A few community discussions are held, and everyone has a chance to speak; there are signers and translators to make sure everyone can speak and understand. Even children speak and are listened to respectfully—their ideas and images can be the most creative! Then the story is formulated and presented, and people get to work!

Each section of the parade has a leader who has made a drawing of all the puppets, masks, and props that need to be created for that section. Through dumpster diving, thrift shops, and donations, the materials for the parade are assembled: all reusable and recyclable water, flour, newspaper, cardboard, fabric, boards, and paint. People bring sewing machines and create the costumes from old sheets, curtains, and discarded clothing. The months of March and April are the busiest, with children and families and artists working together two nights a week and all day on Saturdays.

URHere: Where do I sign up? (Laughs.) Seriously, this sounds like a lot of work. Where's the money coming from?

GG (scowls): Good question. There's some money from arts grants, which have to be renewed and reapplied in cycles. But the parade, like the theater, is entirely a nonprofit and largely volunteer-driven. There are very few paid (and only part-time) artists on staff. Even the artistic director, Sandy Spieler, is hired on contract. This is why at the front and back of the parade, puppeteers hold out barrels they can pound on, drumming up donations from the crowd! Some folks are regular donors to the Beast, and—

URHere (interrupts): "The Beast"?

GG: Right. The MayDay Parade is produced by In the Heart of the Beast Puppet and Mask Theatre, or just "the Beast"! Spieler led the conversion of the theater from pornography to puppetry over forty years ago, but the erotic arts continue in a more consensual and community-centered format, and the parade is the Beast's most popular production. The city doesn't support the parade at all—though the city found $150 million to give to building the new Vikings stadium! You could say it's a case of environmental classism, since the stadium is expected to generate corporate profits, whereas the MayDay Parade operates on a gift economy and donations from a low-income community.

URHere: Careful—I like football. But it does seem your parade is a better topic for radical democracy than for aesthetics.

GG: In fact, ecofeminists have written at length about the importance of ecological citizenship in a radical democracy (Plumwood, Feminism; Gaard; Sandilands; Shiva; MacGregor). And there's real beauty in the practice of participatory democracy!

URHere: Okay, then what makes the parade feminist? Or ecofeminist? Is everyone in the parade a feminist?

GG (laughs): People are not screened for their political ideology before being handed the cardboard and paste for their masks!

URHere: I should hope not! So where's the feminist aesthetic, and the erotics you promised?

GG: Right here! Feminist aesthetics are visible in the parade's eco-justice orientation, and in its multicultural and intergenerational actors and themes. Eco-aesthetics appear in the reused materials, the absence of corporate sponsors, the clear agency of trees and animal species in the parade, and the presence of community involvement. But the erotic—surely you remember Audre Lorde's definition of the erotic as power, as a life force inclusive of but larger than sexuality. "We have been raised to fear the yes within ourselves," she wrote, arguing that "in order to perpetuate itself, every oppression must corrupt or distort those various sources of power within the culture of the oppressed that can provide energy for change" (57, 53).

MayDay is all about reconnecting people with their ecosocial connections to place, community, and creativity, so that they will have the energy to make changes in their lives and in their communities: this is beauty. But when we live our lives in accordance with external directives—make money, work more, buy more—we are tricked into trading away the leisure that allows us to reflect on our condition and to join the multivocal conversation of plants with other species and communities of insects, birds, and elements. We become alienated from our bodily emotions, from our own knowledge, creativity, and needs. The parade wakes us up! As Lorde explains,

When we begin to live from within outward, in touch with the power of the erotic within ourselves, and allowing that power to inform and illuminate our actions upon the world around us, then we begin to be responsible to ourselves in the deepest sense. For as we begin to recognize our deepest feelings, we begin to give up, of necessity, being satisfied with suffering and self-negation, and with the numbness which so often seems like their only alternative in our society. Our acts against oppression become integral with self.... Recognizing the power of the erotic within our lives can give us the energy to pursue genuine change within our world, rather than merely settling for a shift of characters in the same weary drama. (58–59)

URHere: Now I'm remembering the sloths on bicycles with signs reading "Take Your Time," and all the groups that were dancing. Certainly our system of extractive economics has co-opted people's sense of time, slicing life up into marketable segments, valued only for their ability to produce and consume more goods for capital. And there's no "enough" to that system, only "more"—more work, more money, more consumption.

GG: Fortunately, the antidote to endless production for capital is creative play! Play is crucial to our well-being, but it's almost written out of western culture except in organized sports. There's not enough randomness, spontaneity, and creativity in the ways we play—and MayDay invites us to join the play!

URHere (jokingly): But will this creative play really challenge multinational corporations, get the oil money out of politics, stop wolf massacres, and end climate racism?

GG: You're such a cynic. In fact, this kind of creativity and artistry might be more effective than handing out political flyers! Our parade gives people a different narrative, a different way of seeing eco-justice problems and our own relational identities in ways that make activist responses more visible. There's a huge blossoming of interest in environmental art around the country, because young people believe that art can carry the message in a way that is more appealing and more likely to be understood (Westervelt). There's even a new Center for Artistic Activism in New York.

URHere: So Eros and creativity generate energy for all sorts of activism. Where does this Eros come from, exactly? And what about its evil twin, Thanatos?

GG: Remember Greek mythology? Eros was born from Chaos, and both forces are at work in this next example of ecofeminist aesthetics. Your pal Thanatos will be there too.

FIGURE 6.3. BareBones entrance. Courtesy of Jayme Halbritter.

Act IV. BareBones Halloween Pageant 2012: Chicka-BOOM! Hidden Falls Park, St. Paul.

It is twilight on a late October weekend. The performance area sits at the base of a natural amphitheater, in an oak savanna next to the Mississippi River. Rows of hay bales form an arc facing the stage, and stretch up the hill. Next to the performance stage is the orchestra stage, where musicians in skeleton-face are warming up. A path of lights glimmers from the ground, winding from the entry arch at the parking lot through the oak forest and out to the hay bale seating.

Before and after the performance, people visit the Hungry Ghost Altar, an ofrenda set up around a tree at the edge of the pageant site, where people can light candles and leave photos or notes to those who have died. The altar invites sacred grieving, and is hosted by priestesses in white shrouds. As people file into the rows of hay bales and find their seats, they are entertained by the dance of skeletons large and small, for people in all stages of life are among the dead.

Scene 1: Creation

Once upon a time, 13.75 billion years ago, out of the immeasurable, life began. Our universe, the size of a grapefruit, was a fireball containing all energy, matter, and light. This chaos is personified as the Great Mother. She called together her sisters to focus their energy, matter, and light, and then—

Chicka-BOOM!

Galaxies burst into existence! In the blink of an eye, our Mother Star was born, exploded into a Supernova, and cooled down . . . to stardust . . . the same stardust that has formed, exactly, each one of us.

Everything made of this same star stuff exploded out of that grapefruit-sized ball. Life on earth began. Inscriptions on the cave walls help us understand and remember our origins in these orbs of light, these eggs from which new life is born.

Scene 2: Life begins

Ancient animals, wooly mammoths, and later, humans emerge from these eggs of creation. They dance! They are alive!

But the dancers are having so much fun, they do not notice the passage of time. They think their dance will last forever.

Scene 3: Death arrives, separating the dancers

Stilted skeletons with swords enter the dance, reminding the dancers that their time is up. Singly and in groups, they herd us to our common destination.

Animals and other dancers are pushed through the portal of death, separating the twin sisters, and leaving one alive to grieve.

Scene 4: Grief

The surviving sister rides on the back of a skeleton, and calls out her sister's name to the skies. The women in white, priestesses of grief, silently bring incense and walk among the spirits of the dead, reminding us of the sacredness in this universal experience, death.

Mourners invite the audience to call out the names of family and friends who have passed through the veil of death. Voices call out names from around the amphitheater, joining performers and audience in a ritual of grief and remembrance.

Scene 5: The cycle of life

Grieving performers begin the chant, "We remember," repeated until the audience has joined in and the song swells and subsides. The surviving twin sees that the worms have returned to reclaim life.

Joined by the worms, performers begin the concluding song, written by feminist eco-activist Starhawk:

When we are gone they will remain
The wind and rock, the fire and rain
They will remain when we return
The wind will blow and the fire will burn

Chaos returns, and hands to the surviving twin the ball of matter and energy that is the stuff of creation, and together they begin the spiral dance, with all the performers joining in, singing.

Act V. Oak savanna, later that same day, at twilight

GG and ***URHere***, walking.

URHere: Wow. How did this group get started?

GG: Artist and puppeteer Alison Heimstead founded BareBones's Halloween performance as her senior thesis at the University of Minnesota in 1994. For more than twenty years, this annual outdoor performance of larger-than-life puppetry, drama, stilting, dance, fire, music, and song has reminded us of Halloween's deeper significance, honoring impermanence in the cycles of life by celebrating the arc of death. Since 1994, the show has grown from one performance to five each year, with a combined audience that has mushroomed from around 100 to over 6,500 (Beckstrom; Regan).

The pageant is not merely spectacle; it is participatory too, as you saw. And after the performance, the audience joins the cast and crew in sharing hot food and drink served by Sisters' Camelot, Minneapolis's free organic food distribution collective, and in raucous dancing with live music performed by local bands.

URHere: It sounds a lot like MayDay: community based, volunteer energy, repurposed materials. I see the "eco" part right away, but where's the feminism?

GG: BareBones is ecological in its use of materials and in its theme of death as an integral part of life to be celebrated; it is feminist in its inclusion of community, in its pay-what-you-can donations at the gate, and in its attentiveness to emotions—a clear blow to the humanist Master Model of Reason. As

Joanna Macy's work has shown, the other side of eco-justice involves confronting the inevitability of death, grief, and letting go (Macy and Brown). Our activist sustainability requires cultivating this ability to grieve.

As you know, some of our work—political, activist, creative, interpersonal—well, some of it doesn't succeed. We lose political battles, waterways, family members. Right now, according to Elizabeth Kolbert, we are witnessing the earth's Sixth Extinction. How do we make the space for grieving, for turning toward Thanatos, toward loss and despair, working through (rather than around) these feelings, so that we can continue doing the work of the erotic and eco-erotic, our activism and art? There's a lot of life and creativity that goes into these BareBones productions, as well as a lot of digging deep into our own losses, both individually and collectively, as performers collaborate to produce the narrative for each year's performance.

URHere: Hey—the performance happens right here, where we are walking! (They pause to look around the oak trees and shadows surrounding the grassy amphitheater.) But what happened to the Buddhist ethics and aesthetics? Remember? When we first started walking, you mentioned material feminism, ecofeminism, and Buddhism. Did you forget?

GG: I did not forget; I wanted us to step back from theorizing to look at artistic examples, a parade and a performance. Both spectacles exemplify an ecofeminist aesthetic in the ways they involve community participation, create playfulness, narrate and respond to eco-justice ethical problems, and perform a ritual aimed at dissolving Cartesian, humanist dualisms by reconnecting humans with our erotic selves in communion with earthothers. We've covered that!

So here's the Buddhist connection, and it's compatible with material feminism, ecofeminism, and indigenous worldviews as well: it has to do with impermanence. From a Buddhist perspective, the three characteristics of existence are its unavoidable suffering (dukkha), its impermanence (anicca), and the fact of no-self (anatta). Material feminism's concept of transcorporeality fits nicely with no-self, in that both illuminate our material continuity and inseparability from other "flows" of life—from our parents, to our social and ecological relations, to our corporeal bodies and their numerous microscopic inhabitants.

Impermanence fits well with indigenous views of time as defined by seasonal cycles of birth, life, death, and rebirth. Western cultures view time as linear, and consequently we celebrate birth but fear death; in contrast, Buddhist and indigenous cultures understand the impermanence, flow, and cyclical character of life and death as interconnected. And here's where

Plumwood's ecofeminism fits so nicely. After her near-death experience with a crocodile ("Human Vulnerability"), Plumwood's thinking expanded to challenge human exceptionalism by placing humans in the food chain both as "eaters" and as edible, integrating human death into her ecological feminism: "The recognition of life as a circulation and of our death as an opportunity for other life can discourage the human greediness and ingratitude that tries to grasp for eternal youth through transcendence, privilege and technological mastery. At the individual level, death confirms transience, but on the level of the ecological community, it can affirm an enduring, resilient cycle or process" ("Cemetery Wars" 67). Instead of cemeteries that are barren of plant and animal life, Plumwood argued for practices that "revere the burial place as a site of union with the prior sacred presences of earth. . . and honour the dissolution of the human into the more-than-human flux" (68).

URHere: Ecological death as composting. Hmm. Aren't you forgetting the suffering, the dukkha?

GG: Well, the suffering comes from not understanding the inevitability and impersonal character of the cycle, and from clinging to certain parts of the cycle—birth, life, and pleasant experiences—while rejecting the other parts—old age, sickness, death, and other unpleasant experiences. You know about the three poisons (kleshas)—the unsuccessful strategies we use to "seek refuge" from experiences, instead of being fully present in our lives just as they are. These unsuccessful strategies are what cause suffering: clinging (lobha) to pleasant experiences, along with pushing unpleasant experiences away (dosa), are two such strategies. Together with delusion (moha), they make us unaware of—or in denial about—our clinging and aversion, and thus we perpetuate our own suffering (dukkha). This is not lovely, eh? The beautiful solution is cultivating the ability to show up, to be fully present in your life, without placing conditions on how life has to be, and in recognizing our interbeing with all matter.

URHere: So in an ecofeminist aesthetic, beauty emerges through a ritual—a narrative, a performance, an art form—that reminds human viewers of our material, emotional, psychological, even spiritual embeddedness with all earthothers. The beauty emerges through our shift in perspective, freeing us from the suffering produced by antiecological humanism, and shifting to an unconditional attentiveness, to an eco-justice panpsychism and interbeing—and orienting our actions accordingly.

GG: You're fast! Look how long it took me to say all that, and you just summed it up.

URHere: That's lucky, because our walk has ended. What's next?

(They stand at the edge of the Mississippi River, looking at the water. It is almost night. They look at each other, and some understanding passes between them. Immediately they begin peeling off their clothes, then they race each other and dive into the river, where they are submerged.)

GRETA GAARD is Professor of English and Coordinator of the Sustainability Faculty Fellows at the University of Wisconsin–River Falls. She is author or editor of six books, including *International Perspectives in Feminist Ecocriticism*, edited with Simon Estok and Serpil Oppermann, and most recently *Critical Ecofeminism* (2017). Her creative nonfiction eco-memoir, *The Nature of Home*, has been translated into Chinese and Portuguese.

WORKS CITED OR CONSULTED

Alaimo, Stacy. "Trans-Corporeal Feminisms and the Ethical Space of Nature." *Material Feminisms*. Ed. Stacy Alaimo and Susan Hekman. Bloomington: Indiana UP, 2008. 237–64. Print.

Barad, Karen. "Posthumanist Performativity: Toward an Understanding of How Matter Comes to Matter." *Material Feminisms*. Ed. Stacy Alaimo and Susan Hekman. Bloomington: Indiana UP, 2008. 120–54. Print.

BareBones Productions. "BareBones Halloween Outdoor Puppet Extravaganza." 2017. Web. 2 Sept. 2017.

Beckstrom, Maja. "BareBones Productions' Annual Halloween Pageant Reflects on Cycle of Life." *TwinCities.com*, 21 Oct. 2013. Web. 18 July 2017.

Bennett, Jane. *Vibrant Matter: A Political Ecology of Things*. Chapel Hill, NC: Duke UP, 2010. Print.

Bigwood, Carol. *Earth Muse: Feminism, Nature, and Art*. Philadelphia: Temple UP, 1993. Print.

Brady, Emily. "Animals in Environmental Art: Relationship and Aesthetic Regard." *Journal of Visual Art Practice* 9.1 (2010): 47–58. Print.

Chamovitz, Daniel. *What a Plant Knows: A Field Guide to the Senses*. New York: Farrar, Straus and Giroux, 2012. Print.

Freeman, Lauren. "Reconsidering Relational Autonomy: A Feminist Approach to Selfhood and the Other in the Thinking of Martin Heidegger." *Inquiry* 54.4 (2011): 361–83. Print.

Friedman, Marilyn. *Autonomy, Gender, Politics*. Oxford: Oxford UP, 2003. Print.

Gaard, Greta. *Ecological Politics: Ecofeminists and the Greens*. Philadelphia: Temple UP, 1998. Print.

Gilligan, Carol. *In a Different Voice: Psychological Theory and Women's Moral Development*. Cambridge, MA: Harvard UP, 1982. Print.

Hall, Matthew. *Plants as Persons: A Philosophical Botany*. Albany: SUNY P, 2011. Print.

Heller, Chaia. *Ecology of Everyday Life: Rethinking the Desire for Nature*. Montreal: Black Rose, 1999. Print.

Keller, Evelyn Fox. *Refiguring Life: Metaphors of Twentieth-Century Biology*. New York: Columbia UP, 1995. Print.
Kolbert, Elizabeth. *The Sixth Extinction: An Unnatural History*. New York: Henry Holt, 2014. Print.
Lorde, Audre. "Uses of the Erotic: The Erotic as Power." *Sister Outsider*. Trumansburg, NY: Crossing, 1984. 53–59. Print.
MacGregor, Sherilyn. *Beyond Mothering Earth: Ecological Citizenship and the Politics of Care*. Vancouver, BC: U of British Columbia P, 2007. Print.
Macy, Joanna, and Molly Brown. *Coming Back to Life: Practices to Reconnect Our Lives, Our World*. 1998. Gabriola, BC: New Society, 2014. Print.
Mathews, Freya. *For Love of Matter: A Contemporary Panpsychism*. Albany: SUNY P, 2003. Print.
MayDay Parade 2012. "The End of the World as We Know It." In the Heart of the Beast Puppet and Mask Theatre, n.d. Web. 18 July 2017.
Moore, Catriona. "The More Things Change: Feminist Aesthetics, Then and Now." *Artlink* 33.3 (2013): 20–22. Web. 18 July 2017.
Plumwood, Val. "Animals and Ecology: Toward a Better Integration." *Food for Thought: The Debate over Eating Meat*. Ed. Steve F. Sapontzis. Amherst, NY: Prometheus, 2004. 344–58. Print.
———. "The Cemetery Wars: Cemeteries, Biodiversity and the Sacred." *Local-Global: Identity, Security and Community* 3 (2007): 54–71. Print.
———. *The Eye of the Crocodile*. Ed. Lorraine Shannon. Canberra, Australia: Australian National UP, 2012. E-book.
———. *Feminism and the Mastery of Nature*. New York: Routledge, 1993. Print.
———. "Human Vulnerability and the Experience of Being Prey." *Quadrant* 39.3 (1995): 29–34. Print.
Pollan, Michael. "The Intelligent Plant." *The New Yorker*, 23 and 30 Dec. 2013. Web. 17 July 2017.
Preston, Rohan. "Puppet Master Sandy Spieler Wins McKnight Award." *Minneapolis Star Tribune*, 20 June 2014. Web. 18 July 2017.
Regan, Sheila. "Big Spectacle, Low-Tech Magic and Running Around in a Skull Mask: Maren Ward Remembers 20 Years of Barebones Theater." *Twin Cities Daily Planet*, 21 Oct. 2013. Web. 18 July 2017.
Sandilands, Catriona. *The Good-Natured Feminist: Ecofeminism and the Quest for Democracy*. Minneapolis: U of Minnesota P, 1999. Print.
Shiva, Vandana. *Earth Democracy: Justice, Sustainability, and Peace*. Boston: South End, 2005. Print.
Westervelt, Amy. "A Thousand Words." *Sierra* 99.5 (September/October 2014): 32–35, 53. Print.
Wolosky, Shira. "Relational Aesthetics and Feminist Poetics." *New Literary History* 41.3 (2010): 571–91. Print.

CHAPTER 7

BEAUTY AND THE BODY
TOWARD AN ECOFEMINIST AESTHETIC THAT INCLUDES LOVING OUR NAKED SELVES

JANINE DeBAISE

It was a clear June day with sun glinting off canyon walls, and I was floating down the Colorado River on a raft filled with ecocritics. We'd just come from a conference where we'd talked about politics and power and literary theory, and those conversations were still swirling in our heads, but as the river pushed us down through the sculpted rock cliffs that towered above us, all of our talk came down to the same observation: this landscape was beautiful. "It's so beautiful that I've quite run out of superlatives," the professor sitting next to me said. That beauty is why we were there, what drew us to the interdisciplinary conference where we talked about environmental literature and creative writing and science and how to save the world. Love of beauty motivates environmentalists and ecocritics; that is the passion behind what we do.

Project Naked began some time after that raft trip on the Colorado River, when I was at another academic conference, this one held in an impersonal hotel with windows that didn't even open. I snapped a photo of my roommate posing naked in our hotel bathtub and posted it on my blog. We were being silly, really, yet the intimate discussion we were having about our bodies and the concept of beauty was absolutely serious. My blog readers loved the photo. Their comments on the blog post began a conversation about body image that was both playful and thoughtful. Intrigued by what the photo had triggered, I decided to keep the discussion going by taking more photos. Whenever I go to an academic conference, I ask friends and sometimes strangers to pose naked for me so I can post the photo on my blog. Always, someone is willing. The best moment of Project Naked is when a woman, looking for the first time at a naked photo of herself, says in surprise, "I look beautiful."

Humans are drawn to beauty, humans value beauty, and we can't ignore that. It's a powerful motivation. If we are going to heal our relationship with the earth, if we are going to heal the disconnect between ourselves and the places where we live, we need to begin by seeing ourselves as part of nature—and seeing our bodies as beautiful, just the way we see waterfalls and rock cliffs and summer skies as beautiful. Just as the love of beautiful places led to laws that protect national parks, the love of the human body can lead to regulating the amount of toxins that we put into the air we breathe, the water we drink, and the plants we eat. Seeing the human body as beautiful and natural, loving ourselves as we are, can lead to environmental activism that protects the human body. Bell hooks said, "When we love the earth, we are able to love ourselves more fully" (28). But the opposite is also true. When we love our bodies, we more fully love the earth.

Accepting our bodies as beautiful affects the choices we make, as individuals and as communities. If we love our bodies, we care about the environmental issues that have led to higher levels of cancers, asthma, and other health problems. Loving our bodies means being able to talk about a health problem like obesity and work toward finding the source of that problem, which some scientists link to processed foods in the American diet that result from our separation from nature, without fat-shaming women in our culture and without insisting that all women conform to rigid and Photoshopped standards of beauty.

The writer Adrienne Rich said, "It is the body's world / they are trying to destroy forever." The earth that we environmentalists are trying to save, the earth that we admire and celebrate through countless photographs, songs, artwork, and poems, is the world that the human body inhabits. Caring about nature can begin with caring about our own bodies. The naked photo project is about each woman looking at a photo of herself and saying, "I am beautiful." Beauty is something to be claimed by the individual, rather than a judgment decided by an outside (and usually male) gaze. An ecofeminist aesthetic must include body love.

In her essay "The Erotic Landscape," Terry Tempest Williams talks about our fear of the erotic, the natural power of our untamed bodies. She wonders about the "walls we have constructed to keep our true erotic nature tamed" and says that we "continue to distance ourselves from nature sources" (28). Perhaps she is right, and it is fear that makes us uneasy with our naked, wild, beautiful bodies. Too often when I talk to strangers about the naked photo project, they think the important question is whether or not the photos are sexual in nature—as if anything erotic would automatically put the photos in the category of porn. The implication is that the project is socially acceptable so long as the bodies are somehow asexual. What if we just admitted that every human is a sexual animal? What if we just admitted that the human body is intrinsically beautifully and erotic and part of nature?

It may well be significant that this project began in the world of the academic conference, where attendees get little sleep, eat unhealthy food, fuel themselves with caffeine, sit in basement rooms with no outside air, don't go outside for days, and deprive themselves of sensory stimulation. Academics especially are encouraged to focus on their brains, the life of the mind, as if their bodies do not exist. Feminists have sometimes learned to distance themselves from the biological reality of their bodies because, as ecocritic Stacy Alaimo points out in her book *Bodily Natures*, we live in a culture in which biology has been used to set up sexist norms, policies, and laws. Policymakers have used women's bodies to silence and subjugate them. But ignoring our bodies is not the answer, as activist Eve Ensler pointed out in a 2013 interview: "I am not anti-intellectual by any means, but I think we've worshipped the brain at the expense of the heart and the body and the spirit. As a result, a terrible separation and split has happened. Our work now is to embody intelligence. To make us whole and the world whole" (Klein). The reality is that we need to live in our bodies, listen to and respect the needs of our bodies. When a woman sneaks away from a conference to take off her clothes and pose naked, it's a reminder that we are not separate from nature. We are animals who live in our bodies.

Of course, if each individual loves her own body, then by extension, she must love the earth, since we aren't really separate, if you consider the concept that Alaimo calls "trans-corporeality." Our bodies, like our whole selves, are always in flux, always growing and changing, always breathing in air, breathing out gases, eating and excreting, exchanging nutrients and toxins, shaping and being shaped by everything outside of our skin (11). Alaimo describes a "trans-corporeal space, in which the human body can never be disentangled from the material world, a world of biological creatures, ecosystems, and xenobiotic, humanly made substances" (115). Water, air, food, microbes get breathed in, eaten, swallowed, drunk, touched—and then we sweat, pee, and exhale. We excrete water, gases, germs, compost. We eat plants that have grown in the soil, we drink water that has cycled through clouds and streams and oceans, we breathe air that has been inside the lungs of other four-legged creatures.

In her poem "Fire," Joy Harjo collapses the distinctions between humans and their surroundings: "look at me / i am not a separate woman / i am a continuance

/ of blue sky / i am the throat / of the sandia mountains / a night wind woman / who burns / with every breath / she takes" (3). In her poem "Perhaps the World Ends Here," she talks about food as "gifts of the earth" that "are brought and prepared, set on the table," and she makes the connection between our bodies and the food we eat (68). Robin Wall Kimmerer, in her book *Braiding Sweetgrass: Indigenous Wisdom, Scientific Knowledge, and the Teachings of Plants*, writes about strawberries as gifts of the earth, and asks us to acknowledge and respect reciprocity between humans and other species. She says, "Gifts from the earth or from each other establish a particular relationship, an obligation of sorts to give, to receive, and to reciprocate" (25). Both Kimmerer and Harjo emphasize that we are not separate from the earth, but part of it, subject to the cycles and rhythms of nature.

It's the project of ecofeminist writers, activists, and artists to remind all humans, both women and men, that our bodies connect us to the earth, that we cannot ignore the demands and needs of those bodies, that by filling the air, water, and soil with toxins we are poisoning our bodies. Throughout this chapter, I use the feminine pronoun to refer to the participants of the naked photo project, but men have participated as well. The liberal feminism that I grew up with helped move women into the political, economic, and social sphere of men, but that movement further separated women from nature. An important goal of ecofeminism is to remind all humans, women and men and everyone in between, that we are part of nature.

As Paula Gunn Allen has observed, our feelings toward our own bodies cannot be separated from our feelings toward the earth: they are intertwined.

> Each of us reflect, in our attitudes toward our bodies and the bodies of other planetary creatures and plants, our inner attitude toward the planet. And, as we believe, we act. A society that believes that the body is somehow diseased, painful, sinful, or wrong, a people that spends its time trying to deny the body's needs, aims, goals, and processes—whether these be called health or disease—is going to misunderstand the nature of its existence and of the planet's and is going to create social institutions out of those body-denying attitudes that wreak destruction not only on human, plant, and other creaturely bodies but on the body of the Earth herself. (52)

Learning to love our bodies can lead to an ethic of care toward the earth that supports us, toward the kind of partnership ethic that Carolyn Merchant has proposed, an ethic based on relationships and connections, an ethic that "sees the human community and the biotic community in a mutual relationship with each other" (216). Learning to see our bodies as beautiful, actually declaring and claiming our bodies as beautiful rather than allowing outsiders to make that call, is an important step in valuing our bodies and the earth that our bodies inhabit.

My hope is that Project Naked is empowering to the women who pose for me. I've tried hard to make sure each woman is a participant, not a passive subject. She chooses the setting and the pose for the photo. After I take a bunch of photos, I put them on my laptop, we look at them together, and she selects the photo. She chooses whether or not she will allow me to put that photo on my blog. She can ask me to delete the photo or she can choose to keep it to herself. She chooses whether or not to send a link to family or friends. Each woman always retains veto power. At any time, a participant can ask me to take her photo down, and I will. I don't see the naked photo project as my project, really, but rather as a collaboration that I've been entrusted with. It was the readers of my blog who asked for more photos, who volunteered to pose, and who developed a conversation about body image through comments and e-mails.

I am mostly the tripod, holding the camera and pressing the button, helping each woman to take a photo of herself. I don't use real names on my blog, and I don't show faces, to protect the woman's anonymity. Instead, each participant gets to choose her own pseudonym—it seems appropriate that each woman choose her identity. One time when a woman told me that she didn't want her photo taken, that she was not yet ready, I took my clothes off and let her take a photo of me instead. I've posted several naked photos of myself because I think it's important that I be a participant in the project and not just the photographer. One of my rules is that anyone who poses for me has the right to ask me to remove my clothes while I'm taking the photo.

So far, no participant has asked me to take a photo down from my blog. In fact, it seems that posting the photo in a public place is an important element for the women who pose. One woman debated taking her photo down after going through a divorce: she knew that her ex-husband had access to the photo. But in the end, she decided that she wanted to leave the photo up. "It's my body," she said. "He shouldn't control what I do with my body." For women raised in cultures with a high degree of body shaming, the act of posting a photo of our naked, beautiful selves can be empowering.

Digital photography offers an immediacy to our conversations about beauty. Women in our culture are taught to see our bodies in some kind of future tense—when I lose five pounds, after I start going to the gym, after I lose this baby fat, after I start running again. Or in the past tense—when I was younger, before I had children, before that surgery. Our ideal body image is in the past or the future, never right now. When I take a photo of a woman and show her that photo just seconds later, she confronts the image of herself in the present tense, how she looks right now. That's what this project is about, each woman seeing herself as beautiful at this very moment and not in the future at the end of an impossibly difficult self-help project. I think that sense of immediacy—living in the moment—is an important habit for humans living through the current environmental crisis. Appreciating nature isn't something that will only happen in the future, on a vacation to a national park, perhaps, or something that happened long ago, in some golden age, perhaps before the Industrial Revolution. Valuing the beauty of nature means noticing the nature in our lives right now, whether it's the dandelion coming up through a crack in the sidewalk, the moon rising above the city, or the feel of your own muscles as they carry you across the pavement.

Often a woman thinking about posing for Project Naked will say, "You can take a photo of just my legs—I like them." But from the beginning, I've insisted that I want to take a picture of the whole body and not just one part. We live in a culture in which we increasingly think of the body in fragments: a woman is reduced to her butt or her breasts or her legs. A woman will often tell me she likes just one part of her body, often something that somehow fits our culture's convention of beauty. It might take her a while to decide that she likes her whole body and will let me photograph her whole self. But that process is important. We can't separate legs or hair or shoulders from the rest of our bodies.

Saying that only one body part is beautiful is like saying that only the national parks, with their dramatic waterfalls or scenic vistas, are beautiful. When I was a child, it was routine for people who owned summer camps up on the Saint Lawrence River to dynamite marshy areas—or cover the cattails with black plastic to kill them. It's taken changing aesthetic values to convince people of what ecologists knew from the beginning: that marshy areas are beautiful and worth protecting. That we can find beauty in urban parks, in community gardens, in wetlands, in strips of wild.

I don't use Photoshop, either. That's an important rule. Women in their comments on the blog often say things like, "I'm so glad you didn't Photoshop out the stretch marks," or, "I love that I can see the little fold of skin that forms when a woman sits up." Readers have told me that they like seeing how beautiful "normal women" can be. Women get so used to seeing models whose breasts are pushed up and out that when we see breasts in a photograph responding to gravity, sloping naturally, we are surprised—and relieved, because that's what we see when we look in our mirrors. We are so used to seeing Photoshopped images of women that it's a surprise to see the creases or moles or freckles or stretch marks that exist on almost all women. Yet these are the things that make us individual, that make us beautiful.

I want to tell the truth about the human body, with all of the things that make it individual, scars included. It's not just Keats who saw beauty in truth; many nature writers strive to tell the truth about the damage humans have done to the earth even as they celebrate the beauty of wild places. In this age of propaganda, climate change denial, and political spin, the idea of truth seems outdated and old-fashioned, yet it's what we need to move human consciousness toward facing the environmental crisis and taking action.

You might expect that younger women, with bodies that are slim and free of scars, who fit our culture's standards of what a beautiful woman looks like, would be the most comfortable posing naked for me. That has not been the case. Almost all the women I've talked to have confided that they feel more comfortable with their bodies as they get older, even though they are moving away from the dominant culture's standard of beauty. I've learned that the woman with the headful of gray hair is far more likely to pose than the young woman with the clear skin and small waist. Perhaps it's time we saw aging as a natural process, and as beautiful. Perhaps we could begin to value elderly bodies just as we've learned to value old-growth forests and trees with scars on them.

It's been important for me to photograph older women, especially those who have become grandmothers. We live in a culture in which the words "beautiful woman" conjure a woman in her early twenties, with a body that does not bear the imprints left by childbirth, aging, illness, or stress. When I was married, at the age of twenty-three, one of my wedding gifts was a statue of a "granny"—an old woman wearing an apron, with a white bun and spectacles—that had a hollow spot in the back for holding wooden spoons and spatulas. That gift struck me as an ominous warning: this wedding ritual is just the first step on a journey that ends here. The "grandmother" stereotype in our culture is asexual. She is a woman whose body no longer matters, a woman who is valued for her ability to bake cookies and dole out wisdom. My photography deliberately subverts that stereotype. The grandmothers I know are strong, sexy women with beautiful bodies. Our image of beauty can include stretch marks, wrinkles, skin folds, silver hair. I watch my own mother, who in her eighties is a great-grandmother, diving into the Saint Lawrence River, her bare legs propelling her through the icy cold water, her long hair streaming behind her like a mermaid's, and those stereotypes seem ridiculous.

Paula Gunn Allen, in an interview with Joseph Bruchac, said that the reason our culture often tries to degrade or trivialize old women is fear, because old women are powerful: "I think of old women not as grotesque and ugly, but as singular with vibrancy, alive just as the leaves get before they fall. That total brilliance of them. I wish that white women could see that in themselves and in their mothers and grandmothers and in aging women, in general. I wish they could see that incredible brilliance and fire that's so magnificent. Then they would think, 'Well, these are the most beautiful of all.' Of course—because old women are, they are so beautiful" (Bruchac 13). The dominant culture in this country doesn't recognize the beauty and the power of old women, but the naked photo project has made it clear to me that women very much value the marks that time has left on their bodies. These marks are often practically invisible to me (and are almost always invisible in the photo), but they are very important to the woman whose body they mark. Women will tell the stories behind each faint line—surgeries, wounds, pregnancies. The tattoos, of course, are deliberate, but other scars are just as important, each with its own story.

That's perhaps the most important part of this project: the stories. The intimacy between the photographer and the woman undressing for the camera, a deliberately nonsexual intimacy that develops rapidly, is the catalyst that releases the stories embedded in the body, the narratives buried in stretch marks, tattoos, scars. The women I photograph share their stories—about eating disorders, about abortion and rape, about aging and sexual maturity, about religion and spirituality, about abuse and love and loyalty. At conferences, women come up to me and say, "You're the naked photographer, aren't you? I have a story to tell you." Blog readers e-mail me stories about their bodies. Women recount difficult and joyful pregnancies, they joke about menopause, and they are candid about aging. The photo project has initiated conversations about the physical realities of our bodies, about what influences our body image and our ideas about beauty.

The project is about healing, both individual and collective. Most of the women take the time to think about what they want for their pose; almost always, they choose something that has been part of their healing journey, usually some form of self-care. They want to be photographed reading a book, or writing in a journal, or writing on a laptop, or playing the guitar. If you look at my gallery of photos, you can see one woman wading in a mountain lake she's known since childhood and another strolling naked in the surf along a beach she's walked most of her life. One woman sits at her loom, weaving. Others choose yoga poses or they sit cross-legged in a meditation pose. One woman even posed standing outside in a snow bank in a subzero wind to illustrate the storm sweeping through her life.

These stories are embedded in our bodies, just as stories are embedded in the landscape when a people live in the same place for thousands of years. Just as we have come to recognize that the stories indigenous people tell about a landscape can provide traditional ecological knowledge, we need to recognize and value the stories embedded in our bodies. We need to learn to value those stories, listen to those stories. Perhaps those stories can help provide a way forward, a healing.

Women, especially those who have felt invisible in their lives and are on a healing journey, sometimes ask for repeated photos so that they have a record of their emerging selves. For example, one woman told me originally that she would "never pose." That was during the dark time after her divorce from her husband, before she came to terms with her sexuality and came out to friends (and herself) as a lesbian. She did eventually pose, of course—the first time in a whole group of women friends, sitting together on the top of a mountain. The next year, she chose to be sitting in a chair outside, drinking a cup of tea, relaxed on a retreat with her women friends. The next year, she decided to pose with her journal. The next year, she chose to get naked in the woods by a stream during a hike. The year after that, she brought a cowboy hat that she'd bought on an outing with her lover and used it as a fun prop. Last year she danced naked in front of the lake with a lovely scarf—she's a quilt artist and working with fabric has been a creative outlet for many years. The poses she chose reveal elements of her healing journey: a circle of close friends, self-care such as relaxing with a cup of tea on a retreat, writing in a journal, unstructured time in nature, going public as a lesbian, the creative and healing outlet of her art. All of her poses took place outside, despite the weather and the risk of rude remarks from anyone walking past. She wanted the sunlight on her skin, the wind in her hair, and the earth under her feet. That connection with nature has been part of her healing journey.

The naked photo project is about body love, a tiny wedge of resistance in a culture that, especially for women, is permeated with body hate. Every day, women are exposed to a stream of negative messages about their bodies through television commercials, online ads, mainstream movies, video games, magazine ads, and Facebook memes. They are told they need to change their appearance with expensive (and often toxic) cosmetics, buy clothing that hides bulges or folds or what ads call "problem areas," lose weight while at the same time increasing the size of their breasts (a feat that is physically impossible without surgery), dye their hair, bleach their teeth, suck in their stomachs, and shave every body part imaginable. They are expected to hide any sign of aging, as if it weren't a natural and inevitable process. A quick scan of popular websites will show that we have made little progress on this front: more than ever, women are held to rigid and unobtainable standards of Photoshopped beauty.

Of course, beauty—and in this case I mean a particular market-tested standard of physical female beauty—is a commodity in the dominant culture of North America. Without it, how would we sell toothpaste and cars and aftershave? Corporate America exploits the beauty of nature to sell products, and that includes women's bodies. In her essay "Faux Falls," Ginger Strand talks about how Niagara Falls was used to sell the idea of electricity to American consumers. Advertising firms have long known that images of mountain streams and women's bodies can sell beer.

In a culture where the naked body is a commodity, it is only logical that our bodies are controlled by commercial interests rather than by the selves that inhabit those bodies. It's long been acceptable for naked images of women to be used to sell products and the internet is filled with porn, yet more naturalistic photos of naked women are still considered indecent. Facebook has asked women to take down photos of themselves breastfeeding or posing with mastectomy scars. Women have had to fight for the right to breastfeed in public places because some state laws still ban anything that is deemed indecent exposure. When hackers published on the internet nude photos of celebrities—stolen photos that were not meant to be released to the public—the incident was treated as a scandal, as if it were the celebrities and not the hackers who did something wrong (Mendelson). The idea that women have the right to expose their breasts or take naked photos of themselves is alien to us. The American institution of the beauty pageant further asserts the concept of beauty as a competitive hierarchy. Economies function on the hierarchy of some things being more valued, more desired, and therefore worth more currency than others. To see every woman as beautiful would dilute the economic value. An acceptance of all human bodies as beautiful runs counter to the way our culture operates.

Of course, performance artists have long known that getting naked—or even just talking about the naked body—can be an act of resistance. Since 1996, *The Vagina Monologues*, a play written by activist Eve Ensler, has worked to empower women to break taboos and talk about their bodies, and the performances raise money for groups that fight violence against women. For the "Free the Nipple" campaign, a group of young women filmed themselves walking topless in the streets of New York in order to protest female oppression and censorship. As their film observes, sexist laws make it illegal in some states for women to do something as essential and natural as breastfeeding their babies.

American photographer Spencer Tunick convinced nearly six hundred volunteers to pose naked on a shrinking glacier in Switzerland for a Greenpeace campaign to raise awareness about climate change. That photo showed the parallel between the melting glacier and the human body, both made vulnerable by the environmental crisis (Richardson). Naked humans riding bikes are the main event in the World Naked Bike Ride, which began in 2004 as a protest against our dependency on oil. By June of 2014, the naked bike ride in Portland included more than nine thousand people who stripped off their clothes to ride naked through the city. The annual event is still billed as a catalyst for change toward sustainable ways of living and transporting ourselves, but it's also become an event about body awareness and self-image, about each human claiming her own body. Participants realized that choosing to ride naked in the public eye could be a transforming experience on an individual level.

The women who participate in the naked photo project see the photos as a way to celebrate the beauty of their bodies. I think that's a start toward an aesthetic of body love. An awareness of the beauty of our own bodies can lead to a deeper passion for environmental issues. After all, an important role for the nature writer has always been to celebrate the beauty of the natural world in an effort to get people to care about what happens to our planet. Environmental educators, too, have often emphasized the need to get people outdoors to experience the wonders of nature. In his book *Last Child in the Woods*, Richard Louv argues that it's important to simply get children outside, that teaching abstractions about nature disasters is no replacement for a walk in the woods, a chance to touch tree bark or smell pine needles. In a similar vein, David Sobel argues that the movement toward educating schoolchildren about abstract and distant environmental disasters distances them from the natural world and makes them afraid, encouraging them to feel hopeless and disempowered. He argues that what we still need to do is take them outdoors to let them experience the beauty and mystery of nature where they live, kindling their passion for the natural world and ultimately contributing to the development of an environmental ethic. His research shows that most environmentalists attribute their commitment to two things: a wild place they felt connected to as children, and an adult who taught them respect for nature. Says Sobel, "What's important is that children have an opportunity to bond with the natural world, to learn to love it and feel comfortable in it, before being asked to heal its wounds" (186).

I would argue that it is not just children who need time spent in wild places and who need to feel love for the natural world. We all do. And if nature includes our bodies, then learning to love our bodies, learning to see our bodies as beautiful and feel comfortable in our bodies, is an important step that we need to take in our journey as environmentalists. One woman I photographed chose as her site a beach she's come to since she was a child. Now in her fifties, she stripped naked to walk in the surf so I could take her photo. Afterward she said to me, "That felt so good. As children we swim naked or run naked in the rain all the time. But as adults we so often lose that connection."

The naked photo project includes several women posing with *Dark Elegy*, an art installation that features larger-than-life figures of more than seventy-five naked women. The artist, Suse Lowenstein, lost her son in a terrorist attack when an airplane exploded over Lockerbie, Scotland, in 1988. She first did a sculpture of herself, posed in that first moment of grief. Then other mothers and widows, each of whom lost a loved one when the bomb exploded, came to her studio. She talked to each of them, then asked them to remember with their bodies the way they felt when they first heard the news that the plane had crashed. Her sculptures capture that pose, that moment. She made seventy-five figures altogether, all just a little bit bigger than life. Some are screaming, some are pleading, some are begging or praying or falling. Some are reaching out, some are pulling inward, one is curled up like a baby. The figures are real women, with real bodies—breasts and hips and tucks of belly fat—and stripped of their clothing, they could be from any background.

When I visited *Dark Elegy* with friends, one woman asked Lowenstein if she could pose naked with the statues. "I want to hug them," she said. "They're statues, but they're real women too. I can't help wanting to touch them." She stripped off her clothes, leaving them in a pile on the lawn, and walked naked among the statues, touching them, comforting them, even lying down on the ground to grieve with them. When I published the photos on my blog, many of the readers who commented or sent me e-mails used words like "beautiful" and "moving" to describe Lowenstein's statues. Clearly there is beauty in the human body caught in the depths of anguish, perhaps because that feeling resonates with all of us who have grieved.

Dark Elegy was supposed to be installed in Washington, DC, as a monument to all victims of terrorism, an invitation to remember history and work for a peaceful future. The artist herself agreed to fund the project. But then the National Capital Memorial Advisory Commission turned the project down because they were afraid that statues of naked women might be offensive. As of this writing, the art installation is still in the artist's backyard. The dominant culture still subscribes to the idea that the human body in its natural form is something to be controlled, hidden, feared.

Perhaps, like Terry Tempest William said, we are afraid of the power of the wild, erotic human body. Perhaps, too, we are an avoidant culture that doesn't like to face raw emotions or the frightening reality that is the world we live in. Despite the fact that 97 percent of the peer-reviewed science says that climate change is caused by humans (Cook et al.), politicians continue to ignore the facts and pretend it's not happening. The dominant culture seems to be in favor of covering up the truth, covering up human bodies, ignoring deep emotions, and ignoring the environmental crisis that threatens our future as a species on this earth. We need to change that dynamic: we need to uncover the truths about our selves and the planet we live on.

During Project Naked, I've witnessed how powerful it can be when a woman poses naked and claims herself as beautiful rather than waiting to be judged by an outsider. Loving our own bodies can be transformative. Perhaps an ecofeminist aesthetic that includes body love, that values the beauty of the human body and the stories embedded in that body, can help move us toward collective action to improve conditions for our bodies. In Dr. Seuss's book *The Lorax*, the Lorax repeatedly says, "I speak for the trees." The issue of who has the right to speak for plants and wildlife can be complex. But surely we can speak for our own bodies, which are intimately connected to the earth. Speaking up for our bodies means defending the earth that sustains those bodies. Perhaps healing our disconnect from nature can begin with our recognizing the beauty of our own naked bodies.

JANINE DeBAISE is an Instructor in the College of Environmental Science and Forestry at the State University of New York in Syracuse. Her essays and poems have appeared in such publications as *ISLE: Interdisciplinary Studies in Literature and Environment*, *The Fourth River*, *Terrain.org*, and *Hawk & Handsaw*, as well as collections including *Companions in Wonder: Children and Adults Exploring Nature Together*.

WORKS CITED OR CONSULTED

Alaimo, Stacy. *Bodily Natures: Science, Environment, and the Material Self.* Bloomington: Indiana UP, 2010. Print.
Allen, Paula Gunn. "The Woman I Love Is a Planet; the Planet I Love Is a Tree." *Reweaving the World: The Emergence of Ecofeminism.* Ed. Irene Diamond and Gloria Feman Orenstein. San Francisco: Sierra Club Books, 1990. 52–57. Print.
Bruchac, Joseph. "I Climb the Mesas in My Dreams: An Interview with Paula Gunn Allen." *Survival This Way: Interviews with American Indian Poets.* Tucson: U of Arizona P, 1987. 1–21. Print.
Cook, John, et al. "Quantifying the Consensus on Anthropogenic Global Warming in the Scientific Literature." *Environmental Research Letters* 8.2 (2013): n. pag. Web. 8 Nov. 2014.
Dr. Seuss. *The Lorax.* New York: Random House, 1971. Print.
Ensler, Eve. *The Vagina Monologues.* New York: Random House, 1998. Print.
Free the Nipple. Dir. Lina Esco. Disruptive Films, 2014. Web. 20 Sept. 2014.
Harjo, Joy. "Fire." *Sisters of the Earth: Women's Prose and Poetry about Nature.* Ed. Lorraine Anderson. New York: Random House, 1991. 3–4. Print.
———. "Perhaps the World Ends Here." *The Woman Who Fell from the Sky.* New York: Norton, 1994. 68. Print.
hooks, bell. "Touching Earth." *City Wilds: Essays and Stories about Urban Nature.* Ed. Terrell Dixon. Athens: U of Georgia P, 2002. 28–33. Print.
Kimmerer, Robin Wall. *Braiding Sweetgrass: Indigenous Wisdom, Scientific Knowledge, and the Teachings of Plants.* Minneapolis, MN: Milkweed, 2013. Print.
Klein, Michael. "Eve Ensler: Our Work Now Is Embodiment." *Guernica*, 6 Dec. 2013. Web. 20 Sept. 2014.
Louv, Richard. *Last Child in the Woods: Saving Our Children from Nature-Deficit Disorder.* Chapel Hill, NC: Algonquin, 2005. Print.
Lowenstein, Suse. *Dark Elegy.* 1991. Sculpture. Montauk, NY.
Mendelson, Scott. "Jennifer Lawrence Nude Photo Leak Isn't a Scandal. It's a Sex Crime." *Forbes*, 1 Sept. 2014. Web. 20 Sept. 2014.
Merchant, Carolyn. *Earthcare: Women and the Environment.* New York: Routledge, 1995. Print.
Rich, Adrienne. "Contradictions: Tracking Poems, Part 18." *Sisters of the Earth: Women's Prose and Poetry about Nature.* 2nd ed. Ed. Lorraine Anderson. New York: Pantheon, 2003. 375. Print.
Richardson, Ann. "Hundreds Pose Naked on Shrinking Swiss Glacier." *Reuters*, 19 Aug. 2007. Web. 20 Sept. 2014.

Sobel, David. "Beyond Ecophobia." *The Future of Nature: Writing on a Human Ecology from "Orion" Magazine*. Ed. Barry Lopez. Minneapolis, MN: Milkweed, 2007. 181–93. Print.

Strand, Ginger. "Faux Falls." *The Future of Nature: Writing on a Human Ecology from "Orion" Magazine*. Ed. Barry Lopez. Minneapolis, MN: Milkweed, 2007. 131–42. Print.

Williams, Terry Tempest. "The Erotic Landscape." *Literature and the Environment: A Reader on Nature and Culture*. Ed. Lorraine Anderson, Scott Slovic, and John P. O'Grady. Upper Saddle River, NJ: Longman, 1999. 28–30. Print.

CHAPTER 8

DYSTOPIA AND UTOPIA IN A NUCLEAR LANDSCAPE
EMERGING AESTHETICS IN SATOYAMA

YUKI MASAMI

THERE ARE SEVENTEEN nuclear power plants in operation in Japan.[1] None of them are in Tokyo, the nation's capital, which consumes the largest amount of electricity among Japan's forty-seven prefectures. Electric power used there is supplied by the Tokyo Electric Power Company (TEPCO) from its hydro, thermal, and nuclear power stations. TEPCO has three nuclear power plants, two in Fukushima prefecture and one in Niigata prefecture, all of which are pretty far away from Tokyo: the distance between TEPCO's head office in Tokyo and the Fukushima Daiichi Nuclear Power Plant is about 250 kilometers, and from the head office to the Kashiwazaki Kariwa Nuclear Power Plant in Niigata is about 270 kilometers. When the 9.0 magnitude earthquake occurred near the coast of northeastern Japan on March 11, 2011, triggering a powerful tsunami, Fukushima Daiichi had three of its six nuclear reactors melt down, which caused radioactive contamination of water, air, and land, as well as the bodies of humans and animals. Since then, there has been a nuclear exclusion zone in Japan for the first time in its history.

The nuclear meltdown at Fukushima Daiichi continues to severely affect local residents, having forced more than 130,000 people to evacuate and live away from home for countless days, months, years, and possibly decades. Since radioactive contaminants are not contained by political boundaries, drifting and spreading through the air and water, the nuclear incident should not be thought of as a local or regional issue. However, as was clearly demonstrated by Prime Minister Abe in his speech at the 125th Session of the International Olympic Committee on September 7, 2013, Fukushima, at least for the political class, has been located and contextualized as a regional problem. At the very opening of his presentation, Abe said, "Some may have concerns about Fukushima. Let me assure you, the situation is under control. It has never done and will never do any damage to Tokyo" ("Presentation").

There are always political agendas afoot regarding what is at issue and what is under control, and these agendas should be critically examined, analyzed, and discussed by scholars and the general public alike. And literature plays no small role in discussing issues related to the nuclear meltdown at Fukushima Daiichi. As Terry Tempest Williams explores in her *Finding Beauty in a Broken World*, beauty provides an important foothold from which to explore a "just" relationship between humans and their environment. However, beauty has not been discussed as widely and openly as have the social and political problems that caused the meltdown and its aftermath. Beyond the specific case of the megaearthquake, tsunami, and nuclear meltdown in March 2011, there has also been a persistent tendency among academics to shun beauty. As literary critic Elaine Scarry points out, "The banishing of beauty from the humanities" in the last few decades "has been carried out by a set of political complaints against it," with one major argument being "that beauty, by preoccupying our attention, distracts attention from wrong social arrangements," thereby making us inattentive and indifferent to social problems (*On Beauty* 57–58). Scarry claims that the power of beauty lies in its decentering function and its evocation of symmetry, which together lead one to a more just relationship with the other. This observation seems applicable to issues of the environment as well; as Scarry says, "The environmental movement is just directly motivated by an awareness of the beauty of the world" ("Afterword" 272). Scarry's statement suggests something which is often neglected: that is, the powerful exercise of beauty in the promotion of environmental consciousness.

It would seem that beauty has contradictory characteristics: one view is that it diverts our attention from problems, thereby making us indifferent to them, while the other holds that beauty motivates us to see in a less self-centered and more just way. Both aspects of beauty can be recognized in the literary and artistic approaches to issues of Fukushima, and both equally need attention and analysis.

First, in order to see how beauty makes us inattentive to social and political problems, I'd like to examine artistic representations of *satoyama*. Because satoyama is probably a foreign idea to many people, non-Japanese-speaking readers in particular, I would like to provide an explanation of what it is and how it relates to nuclear issues. Generally characterized as mosaic environments of different types of ecosystems, such as forests, agricultural fields, irrigation ponds, and human villages,[2] satoyama can be found throughout Japan, with about 40 percent of the land being categorized as satoyama. *Sato* roughly means "homeplace" and *yama* "mountain," while places near the sea in which people earn their living from the environment and are good stewards as well are called *satoumi*, with *umi* meaning "sea." First appearing in a written document form in the eighteenth century, the term "satoyama" did not attract much attention until the 1970s, when the Japanese forest ecologist Shidei Tsunahide rediscovered the idea of satoyama and suggested its use for its environmental significance (Saito and Shibata 18). "Satoumi" is a much newer term, first used in the 1990s. Often satoyama and satoumi are lumped together as a concept that refers to a place in which human interactions with the environment promote and maintain biodiversity and sustainable living for the community; in this chapter, too, when I use "satoyama," it conceptually includes satoumi as well. The seemingly pastoral environments of satoyama and satoumi are important points of reference when we think about issues of nuclear power, because most of Japan's seventeen nuclear power plants are located in rural areas that are designated as satoyama or satoumi.

Since the 1960s, satoyama areas have been suffering a steady economic and cultural decline due to outmigration to urban centers. In their attempt to revive local economies, rural villages and towns invited the building of industrial plants, including nuclear power plants. Interestingly, both the rediscovery of satoyama and the beginning of commercial nuclear power generation took place in the 1970s. It was a time when the nation was enjoying unprecedented levels of industrialization and modernization, which also caused large-scale environmental destruction and pollution. Cities prospered and rural villages were left behind. The end of Japan's bubble economy in the 1990s coincided with the rise in popularity of the idea of satoyama,[3] which started to register in common vocabulary as a word referring to an iconic landscape of symbiotic, sustainable relationships between humans and their environment. Modern discourse of satoyama is deeply connected to Japan's economic, political, and environmental history.

The 1960s and '70s marked an important point in the history of satoyama and that of nuclear power in Japan. The two seem to have some internal connections, and in order to examine them, I will look at another event which took place at that time: the introduction of a postal code system in Japan. As has often been discussed in terms of environmental justice in the United States (cf. Bullard), a postal code (or, in the United States, zip code) system does mirror political and social power structures. Postal codes were introduced in Japan in 1968 in order to promote the mechanization of mail sorting procedures. Japan's postal codes have seven digits (they first started out with three or five digits), and there are ten different postal code zones, which are numbered starting with 1, going on through to 9, and ending with 0. A postal code zone beginning with 1 is Tokyo, and the very first postal code, 100–0001, is assigned to the Imperial Palace. A postal code area beginning with 2 covers Chiba and Kanagawa, prefectures right next to Tokyo. Then 3 goes to the neighboring prefectures, mostly south and west from Tokyo, and 4, 5, 6, and 7 continue on in this same manner and seem to correspond with the scheduled installation of high-speed train systems. A postal code area beginning with 8 is for the southern island of Kyushu. Japan's southernmost prefecture, Okinawa, has postal codes starting with 9, and this number is also assigned all the way up north to the Hokuriku and Tohoku regions, areas in which the majority of Japan's nuclear power plants are located. Postal codes beginning with 0 apply to the northernmost prefectures.

It is obvious that a postal code zone does not correspond to physical distance from the nation's capital; it implies a political and social distance from it. For instance, compare the postal code of TEPCO's head office in Tokyo with that of TEPCO's Fukushima Daiichi Nuclear Power Plants: they are 100–0011 and 979–1301, respectively. Physically they are only 250 kilometers apart (I say "only" because the distance between Fukushima and Tokyo is much less, for instance, than that between Kyoto and Tokyo, which is about 450 kilometers; for reference, Kyoto's postal codes begin with 6), but the political distance embedded in the postal codes tells of a different reality. It is no surprise that thirteen out of seventeen nuclear power plants are located in places with postal codes beginning with either 8, 9, or 0.[4] Thus a nuclear landscape in satoyama involves an environmental justice issue.

Yet the situation is not as simple as we might think regarding issues of blame, intention, and justice. It is not that rural environments have been exploited unilaterally (cf. Kainuma); rural towns and villages invited, albeit perhaps unwillingly, the nuclear industry as well, counting on grants from the central government and hoping for economic revitalization. Left behind in a wave of urban-centered modernization and industrialization, rural towns and villages likely found it the most realistic choice to join in the nuclear model to survive in a society in which economic growth was considered to be the strongest, if not the only, index of happiness. As an ecocritic, I have no intention of commenting on such sociopolitical situations. What I will do is analyze the double aspects of rural environments called satoyama—satoyama as a home for nuclear power plants and satoyama as an iconic environment of biodiversity and sustainability—and discuss conflicts and possible negotiations between how we perceive and represent satoyama and how we actually treat the environment.

Prior to the nuclear meltdown, Fukushima had long been famous for its production of high-quality rice, meat, vegetables, and fruit. In fact, the prefecture of Fukushima was, and still is, eager to tout itself as satoyama, publicizing itself as a good destination for tourists. Looking at the website run by Fukushima Abukuma chiiki shinkōkai, a prefectural organization focusing on regional development,[5] it is evident that the area that the prefecture proudly presents as satoyama overlaps the area that has been designated as a radioactively contaminated zone since the meltdown at Fukushima Daiichi. Since the mid-1990s, with the rise of environmental consciousness, satoyama and satoumi have registered in the public mind as iconic environments of ecologically sustainable life. Fukushima's public website seems to emphasize such a favorable image of satoyama in its attempt to enhance the prefecture's appeal to the general public, who are unlikely to associate issues of nuclear power with the beautiful image of satoyama and satoumi. Here beauty is politically abused to keep an inconvenient fact invisible.

Having nuclear power plants located in areas that are otherwise perceived as satoyama is not peculiar to Fukushima: the same is true in Fukui, which houses nearly a quarter of the nation's nuclear power plants, as well as in Ishikawa, where I live.[6] Few towns promote themselves as having a nuclear power plant; instead, those towns highlight beautiful images of a bucolic life in satoyama and satoumi. Sociopolitical issues surrounding why they have nuclear power plants seem to be glossed over with such imagery.

As I have briefly mentioned, the image of satoyama as a pastoral place of sustainable living became popular among the general public in the mid-1990s, right after the nation's Great Recession. It was most likely instigated by the stunning photographs of rural landscapes taken by Imamori Mitsuhiko, as well as a series of documentaries on satoyama produced by Japan's public broadcasting organization NHK, in which Imamori took part as visual director.[7] Representative of Imamori's photos is a scene of satoyama that shows a number of small terraced rice fields, dotted with groves which probably provide compost for the rice and vegetable fields in the form of fallen leaves. Though it is not within the frame, a small village is likely nearby. Now that rice farming has increasingly adopted large-scale machine-operated systems, those small terraced rice fields have mostly been abandoned. With lots of curves and few straight lines, this photograph demonstrates a way of living that follows the topography, rather than one which controls it. The kind of landscape that Imamori visually represents is rare in reality, but it operates as a powerful image of "good old Japan," an archetypal depiction of a homeland with well-cared-for rice paddies as well as the forests that surround them. In this way, Imamori's photos—and the NHK documentaries that Imamori helped create—carry the metaphor of a Japan that few, if any, have actually experienced.

The rather idealistic aspect of Imamori's visual representations of satoyama can be attributed to the fact that, while he presents agrarian landscapes of secondary forests, rice paddies, and grasslands, his photos often lack human settlements. In fact a physical satoyama environment necessitates communal work in agriculture and forestry as well as socially and ecologically sustainable village governance. Imamori's stunning photographs of satoyama chronicle the results of the good care by the local people, but such impressive photographs rarely illuminate the communal work that was indispensable in maintaining such lovely satoyama environments. And the communal aspects of satoyama may not be as pretty, for human-human interactions involve not only compassion, empathy, and cooperation but also envy, hatred, and prejudice, all of which concern the conservative nature of a community.[8] Neglect of, or a lack of attention to, the collective aspects of human interactions in satoyama pervades the NHK documentaries as well. To a certain degree being conservative is needed to preserve a peculiar culture, yet a conservative power structure may have been part of the reason people—especially the young—desired to leave their rural homes.

With abundant "beautiful" images of satoyama ecosystems, the impact of Imamori's works and the NHK programs most likely diverts the viewer's attention from sociopolitical issues regarding the decline of satoyama. Not only do these works not pay attention to the human-human relationships of a community, but they focus more on a world of insects, plants, and animals, using highly developed photographic and filming/editing technologies such as zooming and time-lapse, providing an affirming image of satoyama's sound ecosystems and biodiversity. The pastoral representations of satoyama look almost utopian. In fact, the first episode of NHK's satoyama series begins with the narration, "Remember when you were a child," as it invites viewers to look back upon their childhoods while showing boys playing in the water that runs through their community, splashing and shouting out loudly with joy. Given that the majority of contemporary viewers have never had such a bucolic experience in satoyama, it is likely that NHK intends to present satoyama in a way that leads the audience—children and adults alike—toward an imaginary satoyama utopia.

In such beautiful images of satoyama and satoumi, there is no hint that nuclear power plants are located in satoyama/satoumi areas. Imamori's and NHK's highly structured presentations of satoyama make the unattractive reality of economic depression, cultural decline, and now radioactive contamination invisible. And yet representations of satoyama as a beautiful pastoral landscape have some advantages. Because of the fascinating visual images, works such as Imamori's photographs and NHK's high-definition programs help raise individual and societal awareness of satoyama and thus promote collective attention to the rural agrarian environments that were neglected and forgotten in Japan's rapid industrialization and modernization from the mid-twentieth century onward. Without Imamori's visual depictions of rural Japan, perhaps the "satoyama boom" of the mid-1990s wouldn't have occurred.

Still, the idea of satoyama-as-beautiful-landscape that we have seen in Imamori's and NHK's visual representations fails to go beyond an idealization of rural environments and is therefore less likely to enable a critical reconsideration of the modern values that both promoted industrialization and the related economic growth and caused the decline of satoyama, which eventually resulted, albeit involuntarily, in industrial plants, including nuclear power plants. Beauty in the popular representations of satoyama works ambiguously: it brings attention to satoyama while diverting attention from the problems that satoyama suffers from. This ambiguous function of beauty, however, has radically changed since the meltdown at Fukushima Daiichi, which inevitably increased the individual and societal attention paid to the social and political problems of nuclear power plants, at least for the first year or two. Although the aspect of beauty that is thought to make people inattentive is still recognizable, the other aspect—beauty as a catalyst for just relationships—has become more conspicuous since the 3/11 incident.

In order to see how beauty has helped renegotiate human relationships with the environment in a more just way after the incident in Fukushima, it would be helpful to look at Minamata, a city with a population of twenty-six thousand in Kumamoto prefecture, southern Kyushu. It is not so surprising that Fukushima has often been discussed in light of Minamata, a place that has perhaps the most commonly known story in Japan's environmental history. Minamata is home to Minamata disease, a nervous disorder caused by the industrial mercury poisoning of a marine environment, which in turn contaminated the local food chain. Occurring in the 1950s, the Minamata disease incident had long been neglected and still has not received just treatment, partly because the town housed a chemical plant of the Chisso Corporation (the company has been reorganized as the JNC Corporation since 2011), which was practically and symbolically important for Japan's development as a modern industrial nation. Also, as Minamata's postal code (which begins with 8) implies, the disregard of Minamata disease has much to do with the political distance between the town and the nation's capital. In this way, Minamata's sociopolitical relationship with Tokyo is similar to that of Fukushima. In terms of nuclear issues, Fukushima is often compared with Hiroshima, Chernobyl, and Bikini Atoll in the Marshall Islands. But, as has been exemplified by a countless number of scholars and journalists, including Timothy S. George, Lyric Hughes Hale, and Harada Masazumi, to name just a few, when the focus is on geopolitical and ethical problems, Minamata is used as the analytical framework within which to examine the enviro-socio-political issues of Fukushima.

In the literary arena, too, Minamata serves as an important reference point with which to think about Fukushima. Literature necessarily pivots on language, and writers and literary scholars were struggling for a language with which to grasp the 3/11 triple disasters and their aftermath. Takahashi Gen'ichiro, in his collection of essays entitled *Hijōji no kotoba* (Language of emergency), focuses on Ishimure Michiko's 1969 novel about the Minamata disease incident, *Kugai jōdo* (the novel's English translation is titled *Paradise in the Sea of Sorrow: Our Minamata Disease*), which is regarded as a seminal work in Japanese literary environmentalism. Takahashi examines how Ishimure uses language when faced with the unprecedented disaster of the mercury contamination of the sea and the people in southern Kyushu.

Takahashi repeatedly emphasizes the "beauty" of Ishimure's writing. The main theme of *Kugai jōdo* is the world of Minamata disease victims, who suffer not only physical pain but also segregation, neglect, and disregard. In other words, the novel concerns the victims' suffering. Yet *Kugai jōdo* depicts it in such a way that Takahashi cannot help but ask, "How come we feel Ishimure's 'writing' is 'beautiful'? . . . How come we feel beauty in our encounter with the worst tragedy? How come such 'beautiful' writing was born of her encounter with a landscape that makes one want to look away?" (Takahashi 67).

Takahashi cites quite a few long passages from *Kugai jōdo* to show what he calls the "beauty" of Ishimure's writing. Here is a part of one of the passages he quotes, a passage that depicts an elderly man living in a coastal fishing village talking about his grandson, Moku, who has congenital Minamata disease:

> "As long as my old woman and I live, Moku will be well cared for. As long as there is a bit of strength left in us, we'll carry him on our backs to the toilet. We'll continue to change his diapers and stuff food into his mouth for him. Ah, sister, this child is a poor wretch.
>
> "He may be misshapen and dumb, but his soul is unfathomably deep. He is also endowed with good hearing.
>
> "If you talk to him, he can understand everything you say. He can hear well, but can't speak. . . .
>
> "Sister, our Mokutaro is a saint. He never disobeys us. He can't speak, can't use his hands to eat, can't go to the toilet by himself. But he can see, and has unusually sharp hearing. Besides, his soul is deep and mysterious like the ocean. It wouldn't annoy us, on the contrary, we'd prefer him to be naughty and peevish from time to time, but he's awfully considerate: he just sits there, smiling like a Buddha statue, and trying hard not to get on our nerves. His eyes are always sad, and he always seems to be gazing at something we can't see. I'm dying to know what he thinks, what it is that he always gazes at and that is unknown to us." (Ishimure, *Paradise* 192–99)

What this passage presents is not really a description of a Minamata disease victim but the concrete, palpable life of Ezuno Mokutarō, who contracted Minamata disease before he was born. It is not a record of information but a heart-piercing story of a living individual. Perhaps Takahashi finds a powerful beauty in this use of language, the kind of beauty that Elaine Scarry describes as enhancing a reciprocal feeling of aliveness (Scarry, "Afterword" 272).

In addition to Ishimure's *Kugai jōdo*, Takahashi refers to French writer Jean Genet's essay entitled "Four Hours in Chatila" as another example of the "language of emergency," and points out that Genet's "beautiful" writing represents the concrete death of people in a keenly palpable way, rather than illustrating the abstract events of a massacre in a Palestinian camp.

Kugai jōdo is indeed a good point of reference when we think about literature after Fukushima. Radioactive contamination is neither visible nor tangible; consequently, it is not easy to feel the reality of the radioactive contamination. Likewise, the mercury poisoning in Minamata was not obviously visible, and people living in fishing villages continued to catch fish for their everyday meals. Ishimure's approach to the invisible reality of the Minamata disease incident involves a linguistic construction of reality in which victims' individual lives are made palpable. It is not so clear in the English translation, but the original Japanese *Kugai jōdo* reverberates with voices, chants, and prayers, creating a literary soundscape of life in Minamata's fishing villages. Enhanced through such a soundscape is a sense of aliveness, which in turn is crystallized as beauty.

Kawakami Hiromi's *Kamisama 2011* (God bless you 2011) is another example of a literary approach to Fukushima. Contained in this slim book of less than fifty pages are two stories: "Kamisama," which was Kawakami's first work and was originally published in 1993, and "Kamisama 2011," written shortly after the 3/11 incident. The main characters and the setting are the same in each, as is the general plot: the narrator takes a walk with a bear that has recently moved into an apartment down the hall, they have a picnic together on a riverbank in a pastoral satoyama-like countryside, and they walk back to the apartment building together. This story is, of course, fiction, but in a strange way it captures a lived reality of our everyday life, perhaps because of the details regarding the food they eat and the cultural conventions they follow.

By putting the two stories side by side, *Kamisama 2011* illustrates things that have and haven't changed since the meltdown at Fukushima Daiichi. Changes are marked by words such as "plutonium," "strontium," "radiation-protective equipment," and "decontamination," which did not appear in the 1993 version. These are not small changes: the original story depicts a peaceful, pastoral environment in which a human and a bear enjoy a picnic, whereas the 2011 version illustrates their everyday lives in a contaminated environment. And yet the "everyday" aspects have not really changed between the two stories: the narrator and the bear walk, enjoy a picnic, and walk back. Such an unchanging way of daily life stands out against the changed and contaminated environment, showing the strength of everyday life. This in turn intensifies a sense of "aliveness," which, again according to Scarry, is intimately connected to beauty.

In her afterword to *Kamisama 2011*, Kawakami states that the meltdown at Fukushima Daiichi urged her to study nuclear power, and that while doing so she increasingly became angry with herself as she realized that, as an adult and a member of society, she herself was responsible for the meltdown. Kawakami says, "Even as we bear this anger, we will carry forward in our mundane lives. Stubbornly, we refuse to give up, to say the hell with it. For when all is said and done, it is always a joy to be alive, however daunting the circumstances may be." Such an intense affirmation of life is also seen in Yoshimoto Banana's post-Fukushima novel entitled *Suîto hiâfutā* (Sweet hereafter) (2011). Reanimating life through an act of affirmation, works such as *Kamisama 2011* and *Suîto hiâfutā* direct our attention to individual, irreplaceable lives in the post-Fukushima era. The beauty of such writings draws the reader's attention to ordinary, concrete, indispensable life, something that is not necessarily acknowledged fully in social and political discussions of nuclear power and radioactive contamination.

Finally, I would like to briefly discuss one more literary response to the 3/11 incident: Taguchi Randy's collection of novellas entitled *Zōn nite* (In the zone). Unlike Kawakami, whose story takes place in a fictional place, Taguchi writes fiction set in actual locations—such as Fukushima's exclusion zone and the nearby towns, including Minami Souma and Namie—that she herself has frequently visited. (One exception is the fourth novella, entitled "Morumotto" [A guinea pig], in which Taguchi uses a fictional place called Nekozoko, described as an ex-commune for hippies, which is modeled after Bakugenjin-mura, located about twenty kilometers away from Fukushima Daiichi.[9]) Taguchi's choice to use actual place names suggests her attempt to reframe and rewrite contaminated places by bringing the beauty of each place, a beauty rarely talked about and which runs the risk of being forgotten, into discussions of issues such as radiation cleanup. It is not only the apparent pastoral beauty of satoyama we find in these stories, but also beauty engendered in a living ecosystem. This is perhaps most vividly exemplified in the novella entitled "Ushi no rakuen" (A paradise of cows), in which a man from Tokyo who is dying of cancer visits a cattle farm in the exclusion zone to see his friend's cow, which she and her family had to leave behind during their evacuation. The cattle farm is depicted as a hell, with the dead bodies of cows and the accompanying stench. Yet the man is struck by an intense sense of hope when he encounters a spider, symbolizing balance in the world, on the ground overrun with grass.

As the title "A Paradise of Cows" suggests, this novella implies an attempt to recover—or uncover—the beauty of a place that is now designated as an exclusion zone. This area, where people once lived their everyday lives, possesses a sense of place for some and exists only as a prohibited zone for others. The distinction between them may not be as clear as the words suggest. In a somewhat similar way to Andrei Tarkovsky's film *Stalker*, Taguchi's novellas depict the zone as a contested arena of one's values and views of the environment. One thing that is clear, though, is that those places within the exclusion zone would be forgotten if individual and societal memories of them were to fade away. In this sense, literary attempts to restore the beauty of life and place have an important role in resisting collective disregard, indifference, and apathy regarding Fukushima and what it implies in an age of global environmental contamination.

In conclusion, I would like to look again at the ambiguous yet dynamic roles of beauty in cultural and literary representations of satoyama. It might be a mere coincidence, but it is interesting to note that all of the literary works I have discussed as demonstrating an emerging attention to beauty in contaminated environments are set in satoyama-like areas where people used to live in everyday contact and negotiation with the natural environment. Ishimure illustrates how Minamata's inland sea nurtured people in its coastal villages—satoumi—before being poisoned with mercury; Kawakami depicts the strength of everyday life in a countryside that used to be peaceful but now has become apocalyptic due to radioactive contamination; and Taguchi's novellas are set in towns within and near the Fukushima exclusion zone, which once attracted those who hungered for a sustainable life in satoyama. Unlike conventional representations of beautiful satoyama, which aim either to hide the dark reality of depopulation and the economic vulnerability of the countryside or to idealize a past legacy of symbiotic life, writers such as Ishimure, Kawakami, and Taguchi demonstrate the potential of a beauty that transcends the seemingly opposing functions of hiding or idealizing certain social, political, or cultural conditions to help us be aware of the strength of life, or what Kawakami refers to as "a joy to be alive."

YUKI MASAMI is Professor of Literature and the Environment at Kanazawa University in Japan. A prolific scholar of ecocriticism, American literature, and Japanese culture, her recent books include *Foodscapes of Contemporary Japanese Women Authors: An Ecocritical Journey around the Hearth of Modernity* and the coedited volume *Ishimure Michiko's Writing in Ecocritical Perspective: Between Sea and Sky*.

NOTES

Earlier versions of this chapter were presented with different titles at the symposium "Reframing 3.11: Cinema, Media, and Literature after Fukushima" (University of California, Berkeley, 5 Apr. 2014) and an ECOHUM seminar (Mid Sweden University, 16 Dec. 2014), both of which provided me with helpful comments and suggestions for the completion of this work. I would like to thank Professor Dan O'Neill at the University of California, Berkeley, and Professor Steven Hartman at Mid Sweden University, respectively, for providing me with the above-mentioned opportunities, as well as the Scandinavia-Japan Sasakawa Foundation for funding my research at Mid Sweden University.

1. As of September 2010. From *Convention on Nuclear Safety National Report of Japan for the Fifth Review Meeting*, Government of Japan, September 2010, 3. http://www.nsr.go.jp/archive/nsc/NSCenglish/documents/conventions/2011.pdf.

2. There is no single authorized definition of satoyama. The most comprehensive research on this issue defines the term as "landscapes that comprise a mosaic of different ecosystem types including secondary forests, agricultural lands, irrigation ponds, and grasslands, along with human settlements" (Duraiappah et al. 3).

3. This is clearly shown in a chronological table of Japanese environmental history at the end of *Kankyoshi towa nanika*, edited by Yumoto Takakazu.

4. Nine nuclear power plants are located in postal code zones beginning with 9, and there are two each in zones 8 and 0.

5. http://www.abukuma-shinkou.org/top.html.

6. In the case of Ishikawa, refer to the official website of the town of Shika, where a nuclear power plant is located: http://www.town.shika.lg.jp/shikasypher/www/movie/satoyama.html. The website's home page proudly presents Shika as being included in Noto's satoyama and satoumi, which is designated as a site in the Globally Important Agricultural Heritage Systems. According to GIAHS's official website, these are defined as "remarkable land use systems and landscapes which are rich in globally significant biological diversity evolving from the co-adaptation of a community with its environment and its needs and aspirations for sustainable development." Housing nearly a quarter of the nation's nuclear power plants, Fukui provides a list of the prefecture's thirty most important satoyama areas, in which the four locations of nuclear power plants—Tsuruga, Mihama, Oi, and Takahama—are all listed: http://www.fncc.jp/joho_kensaku/syuzo_siryo/satochi_satoyama/sato1.htm.

7. For detailed discussions of Imamori's and NHK's visual representations of satoyama, see Mark Meli's "High-Vision Satoyama" as well as my "Analyzing *Satoyama*" (53–56). I should note that this chapter is a part of my research on representations of satoyama in modern environmental discourse, and my analyses of Imamori and NHK overlap with those in "Analyzing *Satoyama*."

8. The conservative nature of rural communities is not necessarily something that should be criticized. As writers such as Nebuka Makoto and Taguchi Randy point out, local culture and tradition, which are increasingly reevaluated while being threatened in the age of cultural homogenization, would be hard to preserve without a closed, conservative attitude. See Nebuka (3); and Yuki, *Foodscapes* (which includes an interview with Taguchi) (56).

9. I would like to express my thanks to Taguchi Randy, who responded to my e-mail inquiry on 3 June 2015 and confirmed that the fictional village Nekozoko is modeled on Bakugenjin-mura.

WORKS CITED

Bullard, Robert. "New Report Tracks Environmental Justice Movement over Five Decades." *Dr. Robert Bullard*. 9 Feb. 2014. Web. 21 June 2015.

Duraiappah, Anantha Kumar, Koji Nakamura, Kazuhiko Takeuchi, Masataka Watanabe, and Maiko Nishi, eds. *Satoyama-Satoumi Ecosystems and Human Well-Being: Socio-Ecological Production Landscapes of Japan*. Tokyo: United Nations UP, 2012. Print.
Eizoushi satoyama—Hito to shizen ga tomo ni ikiru [Visual poem satoyama—Humans and nature living together]. Tokyo: NHK, 2001. Print.
Eizoushi satoyama II—Inochi o meguru mizube [Visual poem satoyama II—Water garden of life]. Tokyo: NHK, 2004. Print.
George, Timothy S. "Fukushima in Light of Minamata." *The Asia-Pacific Journal: Japan Focus* 10.11 (2012): n. pag. Web. 16 Dec. 2014.
Hale, Lyric Hughes. "From Minamata to Fukushima—The Japanese Nuclear Crisis Isn't Over Yet." *Huffington Post*, 14 Nov. 2011. Web. 16 Dec. 2014.
Harada, Masazumi. "Fukushima genpatsu jiko to Minamata byō no kyōkun" [The nuclear incident in Fukushima and a lesson from Minamata disease]. *Tokyo shimbun*, 8 Sept. 2011. Web. 16 Dec. 2014.
Imamori, Mitsuhiko. *Satoyama: In Harmony with Neighboring Nature*. Tokyo: Shinchosha, 1995. Print.
Ishimure, Michiko. *Kugai jōdo: Waga Minamata-byō* [Paradise in the sea of sorrow]. 1969. Tokyo: Kodansha, 1972. Print.
———. *Paradise in the Sea of Sorrow: Our Minamata Disease*. Trans. Livia Monnet. Ann Arbor: University of Michigan, Center for Japanese Studies, 2003. Print.
Kainuma, Hiroshi. *"Fukushima" ron* [On "Fukushima"]. Tokyo: Seidosha, 2011. Print.
Kawakami, Hiromi. *God Bless You, 2011* [*Kamisama 2011*]. Trans. Ted Goossen and Motoyuki Shibata. *Granta*, 10 Mar. 2012. Web. 16 Dec. 2014.
———. *Kamisama 2011*. Tokyo: Kodansha, 2011. Print.
Meli, Mark. "High-Vision Satoyama: Japanese Agrarian Landscape for Home and Abroad." *Kansai daigaku tozaigakujutu kenkyujo kiyo* 44 (2011): 319–40. Print.
Nebuka, Makoto. *Yama no jinsei: Matagi no mura kara* [A mountain life: From where a traditional hunter lives]. 1991. Tokyo: NHK, 2012. Print.
"Presentation by Prime Minister Shinzo Abe at the 125th Session of the International Olympic Committee (IOC)." Prime Minister of Japan and His Cabinet, Speeches and Statements by the Prime Minister, 7 Sept. 2013. Web. 16 Dec. 2014.
Saito, Osamu, and Hideaki Shibata. "*Satoyama* and *Satoumi*, and Ecosystem Services: A Conceptual Framework." *Satoyama-Satoumi Ecosystems and Human Well-Being: Socio-Ecological Production Landscapes of Japan*. Ed. Anantha Kumar Duraiappah, Koji Nakamura, Kazuhiko Takeuchi, Masataka Watanabe, and Maiko Nishi. Tokyo: United Nations UP, 2012. 17–59. Print.
Scarry, Elaine. "Afterword: An Interview with Elaine Scarry." *Environmental Criticism for the Twenty-First Century*. Ed. Stephanie LeMenager, Teresa Shewry, and Ken Hiltner. New York: Routledge, 2011. 261–74. Print.
———. *On Beauty and Being Just*. Princeton, NJ: Princeton UP, 1999. Print.
Taguchi, Randy. *Zōn nite* [In the zone]. Tokyo: Bungei Shunjū, 2013. Print.
Takahashi, Gen'ichiro. *Hijōji no kotoba: Shisai no atode* [Language of emergency]. Tokyo: Asahi Shinbunsha, 2012. Print.
Williams, Terry Tempest. *Finding Beauty in a Broken World*. New York: Pantheon, 2008. Print.
Yoshimoto, Banana. *Suîto hiâfutā* [Sweet hereafter]. Tokyo: NHK, 2012. Print.

Yuki, Masami. "Analyzing *Satoyama*: A Rural Environment, Landscape, Zone." *POETICA* 80 (2013): 51–63. Print.

———. *Foodscapes of Contemporary Japanese Women Writers: An Ecocritical Journey around the Hearth of Modernity* [*Tabi no hōe*, 2012]. Trans. Michael Berman. New York: Palgrave Macmillan, 2015. Print.

Yumoto, Takakazu, ed. *Kankyōshi towa nanika* [What is environmental history?]. Tokyo: Bun-ichi Sōgō Shuppan, 2011. Print.

CHAPTER 9

KNOW BEAUTY, KNOW JUSTICE
WHY BEAUTY MATTERS IN THE CLASSROOM

SHAUNANNE TANGNEY

I'LL ADMIT IT: when I was in graduate school in the mid-1990s, I drank the Kool-Aid. If it ended in an "-ism," I gobbled it up and spat it back out in my papers, which were warmly received by most, if not all, of my professors. When I graduated, I was one of the happy few who got a job, and I was, perhaps predictably, assigned to teach an Introduction to Literary Criticism course, a course I continue to teach today. I rode a pretty high horse in those early days, but I think I'm considerably more down-to-earth now, nearly two decades later. What seems important to me now is not just to introduce undergraduates to a variety of critical theories, but also to interrogate theory itself. My students and I discuss not only how to write a Marxist or feminist or historicist or ecocritical paper, but also how and why theories like these came to prominence in academia. Furthermore, we discuss the purpose and value of critical theory. I suggest to them that the point isn't necessarily to declare permanent allegiance to any one camp, reminding them that if the only tool they have is a hammer then every problem looks like a nail. I teach at a small university and so I see students over and over again. I remind them that if they've taken a writing class from me, they know me as rather formalist, and if they've taken a literature course from me, they know me as a cultural studies kind of professor, one who usually offers a gumbo of feminism,

Marxism, and place studies in those courses, thus presenting myself as a successful professional who doesn't fly just one flag.

This little professional narrative matters to this chapter, not least because of what I've come to recognize as missing from my own teaching: what we might call aesthetics. While certainly the term "aesthetics" is one with a long and complex history, I'm using it here as simply as I can: a type of study dealing with the nature of beauty, with natural beauty and the representation of beauty in cultural production (art, literature, music, etc.), and with the judgment and appreciation of beauty, or taste. Several of the contributors to this volume and I have been having a conversation about the absence of aesthetics in the classroom for several years now; indeed, that conversation gave rise to a panel at the 2012 Western Literature Association conference, a panel that provided the initial fodder for this volume. In its earliest stages of generation, that panel was titled "No Beauty, No Justice," in keeping with the conference's focus on environmental justice. That title didn't make the final program, but it did inspire (with the help of one of my students, Gretchen Collier) the title for this chapter. For while I recognize the dearth of discussion of aesthetics in my own classrooms, I am not inclined to part ways with what I do in the classroom in terms of race, class, gender, and place. I do not think the concentration on cultural criticism prevents or excludes a discussion of aesthetics. In fact, I will argue here that teaching the cultural criticisms that foreground social justice—feminism, Marxism, ethnic studies, and so on—can be augmented by including aesthetics in the discussion. Beauty is crucial to justice, but it does too often go untheorized, and perhaps more importantly, untaught.

The so-called "race-gender-class orthodoxy" (Ellis 217) of the contemporary literature classroom has been under fire of late, but I find this attack to be something of a straw-man argument. Indeed, theory itself may be the straw man here: there are certainly those who are uncomfortable with the rise of theory and work hard to tear down theory in order to reseat aesthetics, those who believe that cultural criticism has made it impossible to talk about beauty. Like all straw-man propositions, however, it's vulnerable and weak. Theory, cultural criticism especially, does not make aesthetics obsolete; to argue that we must recant cultural criticism in order to bring back aesthetics misrepresents the aims of cultural criticism. Harold Bloom worries that "what are now called 'Departments of English' will be renamed departments of 'Cultural Studies' where *Batman* comics, Mormon theme parks, television, movies, and rock will replace Chaucer, Shakespeare, Milton, Wordsworth, and Wallace Stevens" (226). He suggests that this will happen because professors of literature have become, and turn students into, "amateur political scientists, uninformed sociologists, incompetent anthropologists, mediocre philosophers, and overdetermined cultural historians" (228). The implication is that those who teach literature have abandoned aesthetics, as well as a commitment to what we used to call universal human themes: love and death, truth and beauty. Bloom drives this home when he says, "Either there were aesthetic values, or there are only the overdeterminations of race, class, and gender" (228), clearly a false dilemma.

It seems impossible, indeed foolish, to pretend that *Huckleberry Finn* is not about race, that *The Great Gatsby* is not about class, that *The Age of Innocence* is not about gender. Race, class, and gender are in fact universal consistencies in our lives: we all have, or live in, or express them. In fact, those assumed universals truth and beauty are far more rare than race, class, and gender. To pretend that Twain or Fitzgerald or Wharton were not interested in exploring these issues, to insist that their work is great only if or when it explores truth or beauty, seems to divest those writers of their very humanity, a strange move indeed for those who teach literature.

While Bloom may be the most well-known scholar who bemoans the "resenters of the aesthetic value of literature" (Bloom 225), he is not the only one. In the provocatively titled *Revenge of the Aesthetic: The Place of Literature in Theory Today*, Michael P. Clark takes another look at the cultural criticism–aesthetics debate:

> At times, the new cultural criticism identified literary analysis with political action to such an extent that the critic was portrayed as the modern avatar of Sir Philip Sidney's soldiering poet, intent on well-doing and not merely well-knowing.
>
> What Sidney's poet does well, however, is write poetry, and the reluctance of this newly politicized theory to recognize the specificity of the poetic work in the field of social action marks its most significant and most problematic departure from more traditional defenses of the use of poetry. (4)

Sidney, following Aristotle, celebrates the poet over the historian and the philosopher because the poet sees not only what is, but what should be, and can inspire people to act, and it is this inspirational capability that, in Clark's words, "imbues poetry with its social significance" (4). It may be that we cannot uncouple the assumed universals truth and beauty from the admittedly dogmatic political intent of the new cultural criticism; it may be that they have always been connected. I noted above that it seems unwise to pretend *Huckleberry Finn* isn't about race, *The Great Gatsby* not about class, *The Age of Innocence* not about gender; however, it would be equally unwise to ignore that each of those texts has a great deal to say about truth and beauty and that each of them employs the beautiful (in terms of language, style, and even subject matter) in order to make its so-called political agenda distinctive.

Clark explores the connection between aesthetics and social significance, acknowledging his debt to Murray Krieger. According to Clark, Krieger "has repeatedly and systematically returned both sides of the debate, which he characterizes ... as an 'aesthetic' interest in the work vs. an 'ascetic' emphasis on the world, to their common ground in a textual encounter that joins world and word even while flaunting their difference" (11). The aesthetic and the ascetic share a common ground, and it is literature. There is a hint of New Criticism in Krieger's argument: he suggests the literariness of literature, and he reminds us that literature defamiliarizes us. He also reminds us that literature, not least because of its literariness and defamiliarizing, is difficult, that it presents us with a challenge. These things—literariness, defamiliarization, difficulty—are, following Krieger, aesthetic qualities, aspects of beauty. And yet, Krieger says, these are the very qualities that point us back to the world, that make us reconsider our world and our living in it. Put another way, literature is that which uses beauty (Krieger's aesthetic) to propel readers into living a thoughtful and purposeful life (Krieger's ascetic). Literature, as Clark and many others have noted, is highly artificial; it is a made thing, a construction, and as such, its construction presupposes some utility. Beauty and utility are neither distinct nor mutually exclusive; rather, they are interdependent and together they establish the power of literature.

This is why the claim that the new cultural criticism is turning literature professors and students away from literary study and turning us into (perhaps poor) political scientists, sociologists, anthropologists, philosophers, and cultural historians misses the point. The fact is that literary study—*more* than any other discipline—requires us to face the world and what can be its brutality, ugliness, and sorrow, and prompts us to do something about it. Literature, as Martha C. Nussbaum puts it, is subversive. Literature "tells its readers to notice this and not this, to be active in these and not those ways. It leads them into certain postures of the mind and heart and not others" (357). Literature, more than any other kind of reading, makes us do things. And literature is successfully subversive because of its aesthetic qualities, a claim that Nussbaum makes assertively:

> Good literature is disturbing in a way that history and social science writing frequently are not. Because it summons powerful emotions, it disconcerts and puzzles. It inspires distrust of conventional pieties and exacts a frequently painful confrontation with one's own thoughts and intentions. One may be told many things about people in one's own society and yet keep that knowledge at a distance. Literary works that promote identification and emotional reaction cut through those self-protective stratagems, requiring us to see and to respond to many things that may be difficult to confront—and they make this process palatable by giving us pleasure in the very act of confrontation. (359)

It is the quality of beauty in literature that provokes the identification and emotional reaction that Nussbaum describes. It is the aesthetic quality of literature that forces the difficult confrontations she is mindful of. Put another way, it is the aesthetic quality of literature—it is beauty—that demands social action, that provokes not only discussion of but also action for social justice.

Of course, this argument is not new, or even really mine. It was made quite profoundly in the late 1990s by Elaine Scarry in *On Beauty and Being Just*. In what began as a speech at Yale and became a highly praised book, Scarry lovingly depolarizes the either-or proposition of aesthetics versus cultural criticism on her way to proposing an argument that beauty, in fact, gives rise to justice. In undoing the either-or debate, Scarry has this to say:

> The essentialist who believes beauty remains constant over the centuries and the historicist or social constructionist who believes that even the deepest structures of the soul are susceptible to cultural shaping have no need, when confronting the present puzzle, to quarrel with one another. For either our responses to beauty endure unaltered over centuries, or our responses to beauty are alterable, culturally shaped. And if they are subject to our willful alteration, then we are at liberty to make of beauty what we wish. And surely what we should wish is a world where the vulnerability of a beholder is equal to or greater than the vulnerability of the person beheld, a world where the pleasure-filled tumult of staring is a prelude to acts that will add to the beauty already in the world—acts like making a poem, or a philosophic dialogue, or a divine comedy; or acts like repairing an injury or a social injustice. Either beauty already requires that we do these things (the essentialist view) or we are at liberty to make of beauty the best that can be made—a beauty that will require that we do these things. (74–75)

Her argument is beautiful in its simplicity. It simply doesn't matter whether one takes an aesthete's or a cultural critic's stance on beauty, for the result is the same: both defend the notion that beauty compels action.

Having done away with the notion that the two sides in the debate are irreconcilable, Scarry moves on to a discussion of the ways that "beauty prepares us for justice" (78). She first argues for the universal importance of beauty, noting the long history in Western philosophy of the outward turn:

> Plato's requirement that we move from "eros," in which we are seized by the beauty of one person, to "caritas," in which our care is extended to all people, has parallels in many early aesthetic treatises, as when Boethius is counseled by Lady Philosophy, and later, Dante is counseled by Virgil to listen only to a song whose sensory surface will let one move beyond its own compelling features to a more capacious sphere of objects. The metaphysical plane behind the face or song provided the moral urgency for insisting upon this movement away from the particular to the distributional (or as it was called then, in a word that is often now berated, the universal). (81–82)

The point of beauty, then—making it, studying it, teaching it—is not personal or private or individual; rather, it is universal, it is for the good of the whole. And from this long-held position, Scarry moves on to her final point by quoting John Rawls's statement that beauty is "a symmetry of everyone's relations to one another" (93). Here she argues that "it is the very symmetry of beauty that leads us to, or somehow assists us in discovering, the symmetry that eventually comes into place in the realm of justice" (97), and she reminds us that in any discussion of beauty "the attribute most steadily singled out over the centuries has been 'symmetry'" (96). Some eras have insisted on symmetry above all else, whereas other eras have appreciated departures from and exceptions to it, but the aspect of symmetry, Scarry contends, remains central to the discussion and defense of beauty. Likewise, in the sphere of justice, "symmetry remains key, particularly in accounts of distributive justice and fairness 'as a symmetry of everyone's relations to each other'" (97). We can parse both parts of Scarry's argument in the Golden Rule: "Do unto others as you would have them do unto you." Justice—fairness—is all but self-evident here, and so is symmetry: what is right or good—what is fair or just—for one individual is equally so for any other individual. The sentence itself also has syntactical symmetry: "do unto others" and "do unto you" frame the sentence in both meaning and arrangement. It can be argued that the sentence is beautiful because of its symmetry: it is a well-made sentence, one that rolls off the tongue easily, one that commands attention and thoughtful consideration. Scarry's notion that symmetry pervades our understanding of both beauty and justice is evident in the example of the Golden Rule, as both an abstract code of conduct and an artificial linguistic construct.

At this point in my chapter, having established a strong connection between beauty and social justice, I am forced to return to the fact that while my own courses are often focused on social justice—via cultural criticism—the discussion of beauty rarely arises in my classroom. As I noted earlier, I spend a great deal of time in my classes discussing literature in terms of race, class, gender, and place. I believe literature is a social document and I believe, like Nussbaum, that it is subversive and coercive and provokes discussion of and action toward social justice. But what I find myself almost totally remiss in is a discussion of beauty. However, I've been working to remedy this in several ways. I arrange my Introduction to Literary Criticism course around three questions: why do we read, what do we read, and how do we read. We spend the first two-thirds of the course on the "how we read" question, learning various critical tactics like New Criticism, feminism, Marxism, poststructuralism, ecocriticism, and so on. For the rest of the course, we engage in a discussion of why we read and what we read by studying essays by a variety of literary theorists, such as Helen Vendler, Jane Tompkins, Richard Ohmann, Henry Louis Gates Jr., Harold Bloom, and Janice

Radway. The question of why we read prompts a defense of the study of literature: What is the value of reading? Of pursuing a degree in English? Of having a literate society? The question of what we read prompts a discussion of canonicity and quality: Why is this book and not another considered great? What is the test of greatness? Is great literature timeless or timely? It strikes me now that the debate about beauty—especially as mistakenly waged by confirmed aesthetes or cultural critics—might serve as the perfect connective tissue running through the questions of why, what, and how we read. It's not that the answer to those three questions is "beauty"; rather, it is that discussing the debate about beauty, discussing why there are books titled *Revenge of the Aesthetic*, could help my students to understand how beauty—as a subject, a theme, an obligation—does in fact drive or undergird all the other critical tactics that might seem to ignore it.

Perhaps more significantly, I've added a course called The Literature of the Wild to my course rotation. While on the surface it may look like a fairly typical nature writing course, I have tailored it to include a significant exploration and discussion of beauty. The course is centered on three questions: Does beauty matter? What is the value of the wild(erness)? And how do we become native to a place? I used these three questions to frame the course because they have been crucial to my own exploration of nature writing and ecocriticism, and also to my ongoing work to live more carefully and thoughtfully in the physical world. What my students and I discovered as we worked our way through the semester, and through the three questions, each of which anchored a four- or five-week unit, was that we never stopped discussing beauty. Even when our focus was the wild(erness) or becoming native to a place, we returned to beauty, or, more specifically, found that our discussions and understanding of beauty informed and shaped our discussions and understanding of wild(erness), place, and living in places. For us, the answer to the question "Does beauty matter?" was a resounding yes! Perhaps the most significant example of this is our conclusions regarding aspects or characteristics of beauty. Early in the semester, my students and I made lists of beautiful things, places, events, people, and experiences. These lists comprised things from aerofoil propellers to weeds, laughter to redwood trees, the elderly to tennis courts. After discussing our lists and reading several seminal texts on beauty (Muir, Emerson, Jeffers, Scarry, et al.), we composed another list: aspects or characteristics of beauty. In making this second list, we were moving from being able to spot beauty to being able to understand beauty; we were beginning to answer the question, "Does beauty matter?"

Here is our list:
ASPECTS OR CHARACTERISTICS OF BEAUTY
BEAUTIFUL THINGS RESULT IN OR ARE CHARACTERIZED BY OR INSPIRE . . .

Accomplishment
Belief
Bonding
Calming
Ceremony
Community
Confidence
Continuity
Cooperation
Cultivation
Curiosity
Dangerous
Dedication
Design
Emotional
Emptiness
Experimentation
Fear
Focus
Growth—natural, physical, emotional, mental
Happiness
Ideal
Imagination
Imperfect
Inquiry
Inspirational
Joy
Learning
Liberation
Meaning
Musical
Mystery
Natural
Nostalgic
Painful
Passion
Peaceful
Pleasure
Presence
Quiet
Raw
Relaxation
Ritual
Sedative
Sensuality
Shape—e.g., fractals
Spiritual(ity)
Submission
Symbolism
Symmetry
Teaching
Teamwork
Toxic
Tragic
Tranquility
Transcendent
Triumph
Trust
Uncertainty
Urban
Utility
Value
Wilderness
Wildness
Wisdom
Wonder

Perhaps the best way to think about the items on the list is to make sentences along a pattern where *x* stands for a given word on the list: beauty is *x*; or *x* is beautiful. So beauty is peaceful, beauty is imperfect, beauty is inspirational; on the other side, learning is beautiful, wildness is beautiful, presence is beautiful. Many words work both ways: beauty is liberation; equally, liberation is beautiful; beauty is spiritual; spirituality is beautiful; beauty is pleasure; pleasure is beautiful. I would argue that the list definitively answers the question "Does beauty matter?" because it demonstrates that beauty is directly connected to virtually everything human beings consider important. I could easily retitle the list "What Human Beings Want in Life" and few would take anything off it. In other words, what my students and I discovered, using both directed and guided inquiry, was that beauty matters so much that it practically undergirds our entire lives.

The final "assignment" of the Literature of the Wild course was to take a walk. Several walks, actually. We walked, separately and together, in urban landscapes (downtown, a local park, the mall) and in rural landscapes, significantly the Lake Darling Wildlife Refuge. We challenged ourselves with a single task: *pay attention*. Given our proclivity for lists, we did give ourselves a lot to think about while walking, including:

- What are the significant features of the landscapes or places or ecosystems or human construction? Consider patterns or design, both natural and of human construction—how do they differ? How do they inform one another? What is the effect of pattern?
- Don't forget to listen. What noises do you hear? Are they constant or fleeting? Are they beautiful or not? Are they nonhuman (birds, insects, animals—what else?) or human (cars and trucks, construction, human voices—what else?)?
- Look on more than one level. Look up—to the sky, in the trees, on rooftops; look down—not just at the dirt, but in the dirt, in the bushes and grasses, in the gutters and roadsides.
- How are human and nonhuman residents coexisting—carefully, thoughtfully, and well, or carelessly, thoughtlessly, and poorly? Who is accommodating whom? Who is learning from whom? Who is taking advantage of whom?
- What is your land ethic? Should we care for space and place the same way we care for one another and human communities? How could it be different in the places you have walked through? What would you change? What would you leave the same? What do others need to know about these places?

But our mantra truly was *pay attention*. And we did. Our tramp though the Lake Darling Wildlife Refuge was one of the most educational and moving experiences I have ever had. At one point in the walk we all sat on the ground in complete silence for five minutes. After the period of silence, we each reported what we had experienced, and each of us brought something unique to the discussion. We had all become very good indeed at paying attention.

And paying attention, beauty, and social justice are all connected. Consider Scarry's appraisal of novelist Iris Murdoch's treatment of ethics:

> "Ethics," Murdoch writes, "should not be merely an analysis of ordinary mediocre conduct, it should be a hypothesis about good conduct and about how this can be achieved." How we make choices, how we act, is deeply connected to states of consciousness, and so "anything which alters consciousness in the direction of unselfishness, objectivity and realism is to be connected with

virtue." Murdoch then specifies the single best or most "obvious thing in our surroundings which is an occasion for 'unselfing' and that is what is popularly called beauty." (112–13)

It is not, as Scarry points out, just that we become "self-forgetful" in the presence of beauty, but also "that some more capacious mental act is possible: all the space formerly in the service of protecting, guarding, advancing the self (or its 'prestige') is now free to be in the service of something else" (113). This is a great lesson for the undergraduate—the challenge to become less selfish is in fact the challenge to become more mature—and I am moved by Murdoch's assertion that it is when we are faced with beauty that we are most likely to "unself" ourselves. I would argue that paying attention and unselfing are in fact the same thing—they are, to borrow from Jeffers, to look outward, to the astonishing beauty of things—but they also force us to return to the life that we live and challenge us to make it at once more beautiful and more just.

And people seem to want a world that is both beautiful and just. Scarry concludes *On Beauty and Being Just* by reporting on the results of several questions posed to a significant population regarding beauty. Two of the questions were as follows: "Thinking not of ourselves but of people who will be alive at the end of the twenty-first century: is it your wish for them that they be beauty-loving?" (118), and, "In the near future, human beings can arrange things so that there either will or will not be beautiful sky. Do you wish there to be beautiful sky?" (121). There were no negative responses to these questions, or to any questions regarding beauty, from which Scarry concludes, "People seem to wish there to be beauty even when their own self-interest is not served by it; or perhaps more accurately, people seem to intuit that their own self-interest is served by distant peoples' having the benefit of beauty" (123). Not only do these questions and answers add fodder to the argument that beauty matters, but they also offer a good reason to teach beauty. Given the current schism between those who think higher education is about educating students and those who think it is about assuring careers for those students, these questions and answers seem to provide a way to bridge the great divide. No matter what careers students may pursue, it seems that they will want to do so in a beautiful world. Therefore, it seems critical that in the classroom we continue to engage in dialogue about beauty.

Scarry makes the very intriguing proposition that the classroom is indeed the place for the practical pursuit of beauty: "This willingness continually to revise one's own location in order to place oneself in the path of beauty is the basic impulse underlying education. One submits oneself to other minds (teachers) in order to increase the chance that one will be looking in the right direction when a comet suddenly cuts through a certain patch of sky" (7). We don't often think of education as the placing of oneself in the path of beauty, but it is a provocative idea. Scarry's idea here also connects directly with the *pay attention* mantra from the Literature of the Wild course: teaching and learning are also one continuous practice of paying attention, but we too often forget that they are, as Scarry contends, the placing of ourselves in the path of beauty.

It was evident to me that my students developed a very strong commitment to beauty after the Literature of the Wild course—but what about social justice? The premise of this chapter is that beauty is crucial to justice, and while I've touched on ethics and "unselfing" and maturity, perhaps a stronger connection between beauty and justice is warranted. And, in truth, this is yet another hurdle I have to overcome in my own teaching. I have not abandoned, and cannot imagine abandoning, my cultural criticism focus on social justice. I have found ways to make aesthetics and a serious consideration of beauty either part of or the focus of my course offerings. However, I have yet to fully bring the two together; I have yet to make the strongest connections I can between beauty and justice. Certainly, the students and I in the Literature of the Wild course established a firm grounding in environmental justice—the list of aspects or characteristics of beauty and the challenges we gave ourselves on our walks are evidence of that—and certainly environmental justice is an aspect of social justice writ large. But there is more work for me to do. Recall Elaine Scarry's assertion that symmetry is the central aspect of beauty, and furthermore, that "symmetry remains key, particularly in accounts of distributive justice and fairness 'as a symmetry of everyone's relations to each other'" (97). Given that, it seems that any course I may teach is wide open to a consideration of beauty and justice, for what literary text does not concern itself with our relations with one another (or, equally importantly to beauty and justice, our relations with the nonhuman world)? I'll close by simply saying that I'm up for the challenge, feeling a bit like Chaucer's Clerk: and gladly will I learn and gladly teach.

SHAUNANNE TANGNEY is Professor of English at Minot State University, where she teaches American literature and critical theory. Her scholarly interests focus on the literature of the American West. Her most recent publication is *The Wild That Attracts Us: New Critical Essays on Robinson Jeffers*. She is also a poet, and her work has been published in the United States, Great Britain, and Australia.

NOTES

The author would like to thank the students in her Spring 2014 Literature of the Wild course: Kristina Byer, Gretchen Collier, Chris Lalim, Bryan Lynch, Fernando Montenegro, Molly Schulte, and Nick Taylor. Without their trust, curiosity, intellectual discipline, and camaraderie, my own explorations of and commitment to beauty in the classroom would be nowhere near as far along as they are. These students will remain a lasting touchstone for me as a professor.

WORKS CITED

Bloom, Harold. "Elegiac Conclusion." *Falling into Theory: Conflicting Views on Reading Literature*. 2nd ed. Ed. David C. Richter. Boston: Bedford/St. Martin's, 2000. 225–33. Print.
Clark, Michael P. Introduction. *Revenge of the Aesthetic: The Place of Literature in Theory Today*. Ed. Michael P. Clark. Berkeley: U of California P, 2000. 1–24. Print.
Ellis, John M. *Literature Lost: Social Agendas and the Corruption of the Humanities*. New Haven, CT: Yale UP, 1997. Print.
Nussbaum, Martha C. "The Literary Imagination." *Falling into Theory: Conflicting Views on Reading Literature*. 2nd ed. Ed. David C. Richter. Boston: Bedford/St. Martin's, 2000. 356–65. Print.
Scarry, Elaine. *On Beauty and Being Just*. Princeton, NJ: Princeton UP, 1999. Print.

PART 3
MATERIALITY, TRANSCENDENCE, AND AESTHETICS

CHAPTER 10

NATURE'S COLORS
A PRISMATIC MATERIALITY IN THE NATURAL/CULTURAL REALMS

SERPIL OPPERMANN

> This deep blue sky of southern Anatolia, its violet sea, light and land, has nourished various trees, fruits, flowers, human beings and civilizations. These stories too are the product of these heavenly hands, mountains, grass, coasts, wild rocks, ruins and open seas. I dedicate all the stories to them.
> The Fisherman of Halicarnassus, prologue,
> *A Flower Left to the Aegean Sea*

THE QUOTATION ABOVE from the Turkish writer known as the Fisherman of Halicarnassus (1890–1973),[1] whose work reflects the overwhelming beauty of the Bodrum Peninsula at the juncture of Turkey's Aegean and Mediterranean Seas,[2] epitomizes the new ecocritical discourse labeled by Jeffrey Jerome Cohen as "prismatic ecology." Emphasizing nature's polychromatic richness and vibrancy, prismatic ecology investigates the material vitality of colors in affecting the cognitive, perceptual, aesthetic, ideational, and cultural experiences of human subjects, and the ways in which such experiences are related to the moral appreciation of natural environments. But prismatic ecology also explores the color dynamics that shape the experiences of nonhuman entities—biological, vegetal, and mineral.

Since the world is not perceived only through the human eye, and humans see a color spectrum that other species perceive less or more vividly, prismatic ecology asks us to rethink the world in terms of a hybrid map animated through the multiple interactions of many biological and also abiotic prisms. On this map, where boundaries between species are always permeable, we can tune into the drama and evolution of life to see how connections across species unfold in more ways than one. This way of interpreting the earth (and life itself) enriches the ecological imagination in a vision that recasts the color spectrum perceived by both human and nonhuman eyes. We know that the biosphere is teeming with chromascapes and soundscapes, and that colors, like sounds, are essential to life. So, communicative tonality and polychrome expressions are as much an attribute of all other species as of our own.

In this chapter, I posit that a polychromatic ecological approach proposes a productive theory for "a full-bodied alertness" (Abram 173) to human and nonhuman resonances, hues, rhythms, perceptions, and articulations of the world. The theory that prismatic ecology offers aims to attune us to "the tenor of the world's unfolding" (Abram 173). In fact, "doing theory," as Karen Barad eloquently formulates it, "requires being open to the world's aliveness, allowing oneself to be lured by curiosity, surprise, and wonder. . . . Theories are living and breathing reconfigurings of the world" ("On Touching" 207–8). This lucid definition requires no further elaboration. Instead, I turn to the intriguing maps of coevolution of organisms and colors, perception and imagination, and the hybrid zones where the beautiful and the unpleasant meet each other. This is the prismatic vision, one that contests and transcends the monochromatic language of green ecology by opening to the world's chromatic aliveness. If such colorful vibrancy is rightly understood both in its beautiful radiance and in its dark side, its aesthetic experience transcends the passive appreciation of nature and becomes a multisensorial as well as a cognitive interaction with the material world from the human perspective. Through such interaction, aesthetic experience and ecological perception are coupled with an ethical sensibility that forces us to be responsible subjects.

But creative experience is not something possessed by humans alone: it fashions nonhumans as well as humans. In fact, every nonhuman entity exercises a degree of creative experience emerging out of its multisensorial perception of the environment. Since there are no environments unspoiled by human interference today, including our own bodily natures and the biology of other organisms, then the nature aesthetic must be regrounded not just in human material and perceptual interactions, but in the "response-ability" of all beings, through which the world's chromatic aliveness is made possible. Response-ability, as Barad aptly puts it, signifies "the possibilities of mutual response" ("Interview" 55) in a world of experiential richness where color is a constitutive part of human and nonhuman interactions with the more-than-human environment. Prismatic ecology invests in the aesthetics of colors not only in the sense of their vibrant beauties but in their hazardous luminosity—for instance, the plastic waste that lures many nonhuman species to death, as I will discuss later in the chapter.

Let me pause here to remind the reader that prismatic ecology is not the first theoretical approach to go beyond green. Many nature writers have already been calling attention to the fact that our aesthetic experience of nature is never limited to the color green, but it is important to note that their vision is still configured by more or less "natural" landscapes that are not so appealing, such as swamps and deserts. For instance, in his introduction to *Getting over the Color Green: Contemporary Environmental Literature of the Southwest*, Scott Slovic cites Wallace Stegner to underline this point. To really appreciate the inhuman scale at large, "you have to get over the color green," says Stegner, and Slovic agrees by pointing to "the value of vast sprawls of land devoid of human forms and lacking in the verdant, accommodating color green" (xvii). Slovic's inspiration comes from the allure of the desert aesthetic foregrounded by American nature writers who have been attentive to the ecological values of not-so-aesthetically-beautiful places like arid landscapes. What needs to be developed here, as Slovic claims, is "a tendency to 'appreciate the unappreciated'" (xix).

But at this time of colossal environmental degradation, it is not enough to hold on to the aesthetic justification and apprehension of arid landscapes alone. For doing so would simply reenact the taxonomy of green environmentalism, in a more capacious but still incomplete way. What about the symbolic, discursive, and material aspects of massively polluted places? How are we going to revalue or cope with the environments lost to industrial toxicity, agricultural conquest, and other exploitative human practices? While this perspective may seem counterintuitive to the aesthetics of nature, it calls forth a new ecology beyond green that would critically shed light on aesthetic and ethical responses to a trashed planet where not all the colors are natural. Taking us through the postgreen territories in which other species' responses to the beauty of colors—especially shining through plastic refuse—cause their demise, prismatic ecology asks the crucial question of how our appreciation of nature would change if we were to consider the environment choking under human detritus. Like all life forms, ecosystems, too, are not immune to waste and debris recycling poisonous particles into the air, water, and soil. From this perspective, prismatic vision challenges traditional ways of thinking about our aesthetic appreciation of nature, and offers a postgreen framework for an ecological aesthetic that is inclusive of the nonhuman perceptions and experiences of the more-than-human environments. Our perceptual awareness, like that of nonhumans, is multisensory even if we don't realize how our cells, for example, interact with the food we consume, or the air we breathe, while our eyes may be focused on a green lawn or the vast loneliness of the desert brown.

My chapter, in this context, will discuss both the aesthetic appreciation of beautiful landscapes as exemplified in the narratives of the Fisherman of Halicarnassus, and also the moribund realms of the postnatural that raise questions about moral responsibility in the scenes of waste and rubbish. It is in this more capacious understanding of the global environment that prismatic ecology, I argue, explains human perception and experience of the world, and also considers the nonhuman dimension as part of the environmental interactions. Hence, the beauty and dissonance around us necessitate a rethinking of nature, or more realistically, naturecultures, as offered by the prismatic vision.

Prismatic vision affirms that we are cocreators of a reality that emerges from every prismatic being, not only humans. Every entity, in this vision, is differentially prismatic, producing different compositions of being in the complex ecosystem of interdependent elements. The eye in the prismatic discourse is both a sense organ and a metaphor of coexistence; it is dependent on the world of colors as it cannot create light by itself. Color, therefore, is a direct material engagement with the ontology of the world, a vital tool, like sound, for life navigation. Many animals, such as cuttlefish, various squid species, octopuses, spiders, frogs, and chameleons, change coloration for camouflage by producing biochromes. Clearly, then, color, like agency, is not the property of humanity alone, or even unique to biological organisms. Consider stones that show a change of hues, like alexandrite, which turns from bluish-green to pinkish-purple, or tourmaline, a mineral specimen that can blend multiple colors. Color is in the fabric of lively matter itself in which all atoms quiver with life. It is bound up with creative agency that makes the world alive in generative becoming.

GOING BEYOND GREEN

In the introduction to his edited collection *Prismatic Ecology: Ecotheory beyond Green*, Jeffrey Jerome Cohen argues that the color green "dominates our ecology like no other, as if the color were the only organic hue, a blazon for nature itself" (xix), but nature is polychrome, and green itself "is a composite color that arrives in a multitude of shades" (xx–xxi). Green has also been the favorite color of ecocritical analyses: "Green analysis," Cohen writes, "often focuses on the destabilizing encroachment of industrialized society into wild spaces, the restorative and even ecstatic power of unblemished landscapes, and the companionless dignity of nonhuman creatures. Woodlands, serene waterscapes, sublime vistas, and charismatic megafauna feature prominently. Blending the romantic, the pastoral, the georgic, green ecologies tend to dwell on the innate plenitude that nature offers, mourning its commodification and disruption" (xx).

Challenging this approach that homogenizes nature, prismatic ecology projects an image of a planet of multihued biodiversity and prismatic compositions. This new discourse is informed not only by interaction with natural beauties, the moral sensibilities evoked by them, and the desire to participate in the aesthetic experiences they trigger (as in the case of the Fisherman, who dwelled in the sunlit zones of the Mediterranean and Aegean Seas), but also by dark ecologies embedded in the porous zones of the naturecultures of today's postnatural world. Before I elaborate on the unpleasant prisms, I want to draw attention to how the prismatic approach was anticipated by the Fisherman of Halicarnassus even long before green ecology was underway.

The Fisherman started developing his prismatic discourse in the 1930s when he immersed himself in the turquoise waters of the Mediterranean Sea, which in Turkish we call Akdeniz—the White Sea. In *The Blue Exile* (1961) he explains the reason why it is the White—not the Blue—Sea: "In every cubic meter of the Mediterranean waters there exists more than forty million small creatures. In the spring and summer, they bleach the sea water at night. The whitened waters are called sea-milk" (243). He defines lyrically how miles and miles of seawater turn milky white at night with the volcano of milk erupting from the fish: "The sea like Divine Light! This is the reason," he says, "why the Mediterranean is called White Sea in Turkish" (243). But it is not a static white, because "the sea-milk shines blue and greenish some nights, and glows crimson and orange at others. But most nights it flares up like electric white, turning Akdeniz into a snow sea like the snowy nights of full moons" (246). The swirling life of the sea in the Fisherman's narratives is emphasized as the principal expressive force of existence in its ongoing polychromatic emergence: "The real symbol of motherhood is the sea. . . . It is the sea that is the giant breast that suckles all things alive" (245–46).

The Fisherman witnessed how the sporadic Cyclades islands that form the great archipelago accommodate nature's life-sustaining agencies, and also contain countless stories of human and nonhuman entanglements. The prismatic spectacle of the archipelago is thus a storehouse of polychromatic expressions, a colorful spectrum of life, and a majestic display of natural beauties that enchanted the Fisherman: "That sea, those islands were ten times more beautiful than the wildest imagination can conjure up heaven. Especially that lucent sky, how placid it was so far away! I could hear the sea, the whisper of the vine leaves" (*Blue Exile* 182). The dynamic intensity of Homer's wine-dark sea, the astonishingly blue water, "a sapphire or navy of infinite depth" (qtd. in Williams 75), which he captured so well in his narratives, shaped his ecological imagination. "Bodrum, the Aegean, the Mediterranean all seemed an eternal blue. '*The sea and sky cannot be more blue than they are in Bodrum,*' he wrote. '*Blue explodes, absolute, deafening, infinite.*'" (Williams 80; italics in the original). This wondrous blue is intertwined with the craft of his writing. The blue, in other words, was the metaphoric ink that the Fisherman used to weave his stories: "If that blue is the sea's own, then dip your pen into it and write blue, blue on sheets of white" (qtd. in Williams 74).

Writing this way, the Fisherman demonstrates how ecological sensibility can be made coterminous with narrative art and aesthetics, creating a clear-sighted recognition of connections between the immanent vitality of aquatic habitats and the dynamism of human poetics—and, in a more expansive sense, between nature and culture. Roger Williams cites the story of the journalist Ian Crawford's encounter with the Fisherman in Bodrum, published in *New Scientist* in 1977. Crawford found the Fisherman "lying on his boat in the bay with the tiller between his feet." He was "a handsome old man, who spoke seven or eight languages with commanding fluency, wit and erudition. He talked of Homer as if he had just left him in a pub down the road, of how the hexameter had been born of a dance rhythm formed with the fingers of one hand, and of Pegasus on a petrol station sign blushing from head to toe at being used in an advertisement" (qtd. in Williams 14). This is not too surprising if we consider the Mediterranean "one of the most ancient sites of development of ideas and cultural practices" (Iovino 3), and it is no wonder that this ancient sea had communicated its timeless stories to the Fisherman: "Here was a sense of profoundness enveloping us in its infinity. The great Archipelago, darkening in the turquoise of the evening—*the old sea*—showed me its majestic presence. The sea cracked upon the horizon without warning like a vast blue thundering infinity. It was a deep blue roar.... I felt like watching infinity from the hill I was standing on" (*Blue Exile* 172).

Equally significant as the ecological dimension is the cultural facet of colors in the Bodrum Peninsula. Here, the stories of humans and nonhumans have become so densely interwoven that a rich ecocultural heritage is ever-unfolding. The songs of the gray bottlenose dolphins and the monk seals blend with the spirited *viva voce* of the loggerhead (*Caretta carettas*) and green turtles, fusing with the stories of fishermen, of cypress, lemon, and olive trees, and of donkeys, goats, and other animals, to "create a prismatic constellation of biocultural forces inviting a new interpretation of nature as a polychromatic agency" (Oppermann, "Diffractive Narratives"). In the Fisherman's eloquent words, "In Halicarnassus, all the olives, tangerines, oranges, lemons, palm trees, capers, bananas, figs—in short, all the trees that entitle the fruits to have their parade, take their lessons from this coast's sea-green. They sing their multigreen songs to the emerald green of the Aegean" ("Halicarnassus" 47). As it is spoken on these coasts, Turkish, he continues, is dressed with their colorful songs. Like the folk dances modeled on the white-feathered dancing demoiselle crane, a sacred symbol in Turkish mythology, human culture around here echoes the evolutionary rhythms of interconnected beings, of the sea, and of its elemental forces.

Particularly for the Fisherman, this is the creative affirmation of "choreographies of becoming" (Coole and Frost 10) that forge enduring naturalcultural patterns. He was quite emphatic about such choreography that was born out of the creative materiality, vitality, and expressiveness found in all species, material entities, and forces. Using narrative as a means for "plumbing ecological interpenetration" (Cohen, "Elemental Relations" 55), the Fisherman recounts an ongoing energetic creativity within the folds of these watery zones. In his essay "The Craftsmanship of the Mediterranean Fish," for instance, he explains how the cuttlefish communicates using coloration, which is indispensible to its evolution:

> You all know about the cuttlefish. You know how it leaves a trail of ink behind. You think it colors the sea black to escape its enemies. Not so at all! This rowdy is more cunning than you can imagine. Think that a bluefish, or sea bream, its deadly enemy, is chasing after it. No master chameleon can match the cuttlefish in shape shifting. Now it is intense red, then it suddenly turns deep green. When chased by the bluefish it becomes pitch black. But can it really escape from under the noses of bluefish, sea bream, sea bass, leer fish, and dolphins? It may get caught. But when it realizes the situation, it suddenly turns cotton white and tries to get away. Moving sideways it leaves its ink, explodes it one after the other. Then the enemy sees eight or ten holes of darkness. The cuttlefish has escaped in its sheer whiteness while its follower is snapping at empty darkness. (51–52)

In addition to the cuttlefish (and other marine creatures) in the Mediterranean and Aegean Seas that inspired the stories and songs of sponge divers and fishermen, there are many other examples of how nature fashions the cultural imaginary and social discourses all over Anatolia. The tulip prose in Turkish literature is one such example, dating back to the Tulip Age in the eighteenth-century Ottoman Empire, as it conspicuously reflects the naturalcultural enmeshment, particularly in Istanbul. For Turks the tulip is not just a beautiful flower. The Ottoman seals incorporated the tulip, and today it is inscribed in every ceramic tile, marble artwork, touristic map, and brochure, as well as many other artifacts. Tulips frequently feature in literature as well, as in Buket Uzuner's novel *Istanbullu* (2008): "If Istanbul was a flower, it was most certainly a tulip" (377). Tulips in their multicolored variety simply spotlight the intensity of our entanglements with prismatic ecologies, not only materially, but also narratively.

Colors reveal their secrets in the scope of plastic arts and narratives, and they are also "written into" the physical forms, housing meanings, stories, histories, and memories, like Homer's wine-dark sea that enchanted the Fisherman, or like minerals, rocks, and bodies. "Following colors in their materiality" (Cohen,

"Introduction" xxiii) opens up so many entries into the intricacies of natural-cultural domains. The color spectrum of biological entities and ecosystems is an inextricable part of human aesthetic/symbolic palettes. From the Turkish perspective, the electric blue of the Aegean and the Mediterranean Seas, the lush green of forests saluting the Black Sea, the loneliness of maroons in the Taurus Mountains, the passions of the multicolored tulips of Istanbul, and the spectral white snow on Mount Ararat have all been central agents in constructing the symbolism of the aesthetics and poetics of culture. If "human culture is inextricably enmeshed with vibrant, nonhuman agencies" (Bennett 108), a mutual destiny unfolds with ethical commitments on the part of the human in a shared existence. Knowing this well, and cruising the multihued currents in Bodrum, the Fisherman believed that humans and nonhumans shared a mutual destiny. As he wrote in his essay "Aphrodite of Knidos," "Life is such that the mutually created should love one another. Because if they do something else than love one another, they will be the executioners of one another" (23).

Although Bodrum is nothing like what it was in the Fisherman's lifetime, it still stands out, with its turquoise coasts, as Homer's land of eternal blue, inspiring reverence and aesthetic appreciation, but also deep concern for the region's marine ecosystems as well as its historical and cultural heritage, which are under serious threat today. It is not just the excesses of tourism that threaten the Fisherman's beloved sites; it is pollution caused by oil spills, and tons of refuse flowing into the sea. His warning in the quotation above takes us back to prismatic ecology's inclusion of dissonances lurking within the material-discursive prisms.[3] Dissonances yoke together questions of ontology, epistemology, and ecology to reorient our attention toward border crossings between aesthetic and critical stances, and toward the hybrid zones of the postnatural.

POSTNATURAL DISRUPTIONS

The colors of this world do not always speak of vibrant beauties of nature. Though not totally alien, there is a new world of colorful forces, objects, and substances that are endowed with the power of destruction: synthetic matter, chemicals, toxins, migrating viruses, microbes, pesticides, and plastic in varying densities cohabitate in natural and urban environments everywhere. They all dwell, quite settled, in the most intimate recesses of the earth's bodily natures and are now linking stories of environmental injustice, violence, and catastrophe. And they come in an amazingly multicolored diversity and collectively invade into life. Covered with plastic trash, Kamilo Beach on the Big Island of Hawai'i is famously emblematic of this chromatic phenomenon, with countless plastic objects that come in various sizes, some as small as the beach's grains of sand. The "co-existence of these strangers and their strange iridescence," to quote Timothy Morton ("X-Ray" 312), signals a cyclical conjunction of repression launched by the global human. Kamilo Beach is a beautifully colored lethal zone for seals, seabirds, sea turtles, and many species of fish.[4] Like the albatrosses on Midway Island in the north Pacific Ocean, brought to public attention by Chris Jordan's film *Midway: Message from the Gyre* (2009), they consume macro- and microplastics as attractive food and die. Kamilo's story, like Midway's, is the story of environmental tragedy; it presents the life of *materia color*—beautiful yet dangerous, with plastic twisting itself into the digestive tracts of sea creatures and birds. The beautiful ambience of plastic prism occupying such places explodes into a horrifying choir of death songs at irreversible moments of contact that the nonhuman makes with toxic human products. Clearly, all is not well in nature's colorful expanses. And in the afflictions of the Anthropocene, color is never innocent or benign. It has the power to kill and to cause emotional pain. Anyone who has seen the tragic story of the Laysan albatross on Midway Island, dying amidst colorful plastic objects, can recognize the pernicious influence of color on nonhuman natures. That is why color is not always innocent even if it possesses aesthetic power.

In fact, whether on an island or in the woods, in a city park, or on a mountain, a chorus of muddy-colored impurities have become simultaneous with *natura color*, calling forth a sensory, critical, and moral attentiveness to environmental transformations. As Patricia Yaeger explains, "In a world where molecular garbage has infiltrated earth, water, and air, we cannot encounter the natural untouched or uncontaminated by human remains. Trash becomes nature, and nature becomes trash" (332). Our world is no longer a self-contained, primal, pastoral, or unspoiled Green Eden, but a composite one with "human and nonhuman actors operating in alliance as well as at odds with each other" (Cohen, "Introduction" xxiv). The significance of this composite world is that it triggers a potentially traumatic tension between ecological aesthetics as embedded in the prismatic world and environmental ethics as invoking a sense of great problem in this embeddedness determined by global contamination. If we don't want human pollutants graying out the colors of nature, we need to reconsider the dynamics of our interdependence with the environment in ways that enhance responsiveness and responsibilities. As Bill McKibben notes in his 2006 introduction to his classic book from 1989, *The End of Nature*, "It is the contrast between the pace at which the physical world is changing and the pace at which the human society is reacting that constitutes the key environmental fact of our time" (xv).

Being profoundly altered by the Anthropocene-induced climate change and massive pollution, the earth today is a mesh of humans, biological organisms, and humanly made substances trans-corporeally connected in multifarious and often dangerous relations.[5] One need not go to Kamilo Beach, or to Midway, to decode dark ecology; the biochemistry of our bodies equally discloses such relations, demonstrating how the human "is essentially co-opted, hybridized, and entangled with alien beings, always in negotiations with other agencies, other bodies, and other natures" (Iovino and Oppermann 333). The varieties of dark ecology that emerge in the aftermath of such entanglements are quite distinct, demanding a sustained attention for at least two reasons. First, although dark ecology "possesses aesthetic power," as Cohen observes, "we may well find ourselves in a grey and brown space of stumps, fumes and sludge" ("Elemental Relations" 58). We simply cannot seal out its harmful effects. Second, our enmeshment in dark ecology, which is now part of the ecology colors, invites a reparative stance rather than one that ignores its gray and brown space.

Dark ecology asks us to cultivate a sensibility that attunes us more critically to ourselves and to nonhuman natures mutually caught up in its tornadoes. Importantly, this is not a shift away from aesthetic appreciation of natural beauties, but rather an opening up of a different orientation toward the questions of pollution, toxicity, climate change, and environmental degradation. Dark ecology is a like a wake-up call for a new engagement that extends beyond the allure of beautiful colors. It compels us to recognize the maps of intersections between the beautiful and the perilously colorful elements, because what is at stake is the ecological health of our planet and its naturecultures. It follows that from the blueness of the Mediterranean to the multihued dance of the auroras in the Canadian and Norwegian skies, the chromatic complexity around us presents an amazing diversity and beauty alongside grief and tragedy. As anthropogenic processes continue to produce cascading effects on our ecologies, creating cracks in the aesthetic tableau of global natures, the ugly is bound to coexist with the beautiful, diffuse and discrete as the auroras.

The vistas of sylvan charm found in nature narratives are important, but equally crucial are critical accounts of plastic debris, parasites, chemical refuse, and our daily pollutants, intervening directly in the biosphere, "making decisive contact with humans" (Morton, "X-Ray" 313). Comingling with biological organisms, these corrosive forces and disruptive substances spill onto the planet's life support systems and bodily natures. Consider the oil spills in the Niger Delta, Gulf of Mexico, and off the coast of Rhode Island, or the ongoing ecological devastation caused by the Great Pacific Garbage Patch. The prismatic approach, therefore, wants us not to turn a blind eye to what Cohen calls "multihued contaminations, impurities, hybridity, monstrosity, contagion, interruption, hesitation, enmeshment, refraction, unexpected relations, and wonder" ("Introduction" xxiv). Being attentive to "the topographies of the world's hybridization" (Iovino and Oppermann 334), prismatic ecology in fact clarifies various threads of our coexistence, as well as our dark ecological alterity. Rather than debunking this reality it cultivates a realistic attitude toward it.

With intensifying environmental insecurities, it is obvious that our polychrome world is turning postnatural, like the moribund realms of gray or like the melancholic mindscapes of black. As Levi Bryant concurs, absorbing light and not emitting it, black embodies "melancholy existential connotations" (292). Being nonreflective, though, it "helps us move beyond anthropocentrism" (293). Reminding us of snakes, fish, and insects that "encounter the world through infrared," a spectrum in which the black bodies can be seen, Bryant argues that black is important for understanding the perspectives of many nonhuman beings, because it "invites us to explore the perspectives of *other* entities, investigating how the world is encountered *for them*, thereby overcoming the anthropocentric perspective that focuses on how things are *for us*" (293). So conceived, these postgreen ecologies are segments of prismatic ecology, which navigates on a continuously redrawn map by the forces of *harmonia* and *dissonantia*. In the face of environmental crises, the boundaries between them become more porous, necessitating a more critical assessment of the chromatic magnetism of life. As Simon Estok reminds us, our future "is situated on ground overwrought and overrun with various irreversible invasions (cultural, species), shifting and unstable soils in which profound power struggles continue to play out" (221). Although Estok says this is the future, it is in fact the very ground—the *dissonantia* plane of the postnatural—where our present reality is being redrawn.

"We have entered the gigantic fjord of the next moment of history, without even knowing it" (25), writes Timothy Morton in his essay "At the Edge of the Smoking Pool of Death." This is an apt metaphor for the age of the Anthropocene. The humans are now altering almost every feature of the planet, and these changes occur at a global level, such as the yearly release of 160 million tons of sulfur dioxide into the atmosphere, the massive increase in ocean acidification, and the toxification of the soil through artificial fertilizer applications. As Stefan Helmreich notes, life scientists, for instance, "assess large-scale changes in the ocean by looking at the sea's smallest inhabitants: marine microbes. Such microbes are looped into massive planetary processes" (50). Not too different from the findings of marine biology is the result of research conducted on the phenomenon known as colony collapse disorder (CCD), or the alarmingly rapid rates of disappearing honeybees. Scientists have discovered that neonicotinoids, widely used insecticides that kill bees at an exponential rate, are the direct cause of CCD, and the consequences of the loss of bee populations are grave, as CCD is directly linked to our food chain (Hagopian).[6]

Although we cannot always produce scientific certainties about the complexity of environmental transformations (see Zalasiewicz et al.), we can say with certainty that social, political, and cultural factors have a great impact on these changes that take place from the oceans to the atmosphere. Thus there is no easy alliance in human-nonhuman encounters. If there is "biospheric connectedness" (Heise 62), it is certainly more to the detriment of the nonhumans today than to the "raced, gendered, classed, sexualized humans" (Estok 221), as in the case of the bees and marine life, among others. Therefore, it is important to develop new types of ecological thinking and economic practices and to find better ways of interacting with nonhuman others.

It is in this light that prismatic ecology's insistence on going beyond green should be taken into account. The prismatic lens enables us to explore in a more thoughtful way what Peter Quigley calls "radical forces of nonhuman energy" (10), and what Terre Satterfield and Scott Slovic describe as "the complexity and wonder of all forms of intelligence" (103). These forms are teeming with layers of interesting stories and multiple levels of meaning to be unearthed, and today the storied world is filled with the entanglements of the beautiful and the horrific. As Karen Barad says, "These are entangled tales. Each is diffractively threaded through and enfolded in the other" ("On Touching" 207). While beauty is an indispensable aspect of prismatic ecology, as showcased in the Fisherman's Mediterranean tales, pollution and devastation cast a shadow of skepticism over this vision. Quigley warns against an excessive skepticism in this regard: "If skepticism is taken too far and is an unrelenting end unto itself, one ends up in a paralyzing, corrosive, nihilist, realm of the absurd, looping endlessly on a draining, politically obsessed, hamster wheel" (13).

Fortunately, prismatic ecology would never get onto that wheel, but it will emphasize nature as a hybrid or mixed space housing the biological and the synthetic, the natural and the manufactured, in critical entanglements. As Cohen emphasizes, Latour's term *kakosmos* describes this "tangled, fecund, and irregular pluverse" ("Introduction" xxiii), which prismatic ecology finds useful in broadening the conceptual arguments over the protean meanings of nature. Inherently irresolute, nature's meanings are never culture-free, biology-free, and technology-free, nor are they ever going to be story-free universal truths. William Cronon once said that "nature will *always* be a contested terrain. We will never stop arguing about its meanings" (52). In a horizon like this, the world becomes a prism through which the pure and the impure hybridize, and the dynamics of this hybridity necessitate nonanthropocentric ecologies, so that a more meaningful, less pernicious, and more accountable human participation in the more-than-human world can be made possible.

SERPIL OPPERMANN is Professor of English Language and Literature at Hacettepe University in Ankara, Turkey. She is the current President of EASLCE (the

European Association for the Study of Literature, Culture, and the Environment). Her most recent publications include *Material Ecocriticism* (2014) and *Environmental Humanities: Voices from the Anthropocene* (2017), both edited with Serenella Iovino.

NOTES

1. The Fisherman of Halicarnassus is the pen name of Cevat Şakir Kabaağaçlı, an Ottoman aristocrat and writer who was sentenced to exile for three years in Bodrum in 1925, then a remote fishing village. For a detailed account of his life and works, and a historical sketch of the region, see Williams, *The Fisherman of Halicarnassus*; and for an ecocritical interpretation of his work, see Oppermann, "Enchanted by Akdeniz." His works are included under his real name in the list of works cited. Translations in this chapter are mine.

2. The Bodrum Peninsula is located in southeast Turkey where the Aegean Sea meets the Mediterranean. It is surrounded by thirty-two islands and islets that form a 174-kilometer coastline. Homer described this exceptionally beautiful site as the land of the eternal blue. The town of Bodrum (Halicarnassus in ancient times) was founded by the Carians in the eleventh century BC as a union of six cities. It became the capital of the kingdom of Caria (meaning "steep country") during King Mausolos's rule, in the fourth century BC. The name Bodrum is used by the Turkish cartographer, geographer, and admiral of the Ottoman fleet Piri Reis in his book *Kitab-ı bahriye* (Book of navigation, 1521, 1525), which contains his famous and mysterious map of the world, the oldest and the most accurate world atlas drawn in 1513.

3. Introduced by Karen Barad, the concept of "material-discursive" denotes an integral approach to the relationship between discursive practices and the material world without "collapsing important differences between them" (*Meeting* 25).

4. For a detailed account of the plastic-covered beach, see Martinez.

5. Stacy Alaimo coined the term "trans-corporeality" to explain the transits of material substances and forces within and across bodies. Trans-corporeality emphasizes "the material interconnections of human corporeality with the more-than-human world" (2), she writes, which reveal the "bodily immersion" within "a landscape of interactions" (70).

6. In addition to Hagopian, also see Walia. For those interested in reading the scientific account behind these posts, see Pettis et al. The authors here expose the fact that pesticides and pathogens interact in deadly ways "to have strong negative effects on managed honey bee colonies. Such findings are of great concern given the large numbers and high levels of pesticides found in honey bee colonies. Thus it is crucial to determine how field-relevant combinations and loads of pesticides affect bee health."

WORKS CITED

Abram, David. *Becoming Animal: An Earthly Cosmology*. New York: Vintage, 2010. Print.
Alaimo, Stacy. *Bodily Natures: Science, Environment, and the Material Self*. Bloomington: Indiana UP, 2010. Print.

Barad, Karen. "Interview with Karen Barad." *New Materialism: Interviews and Cartographies.* By Rick Dolphijn and Iris van der Tuin. Ann Arbor, MI: Open Humanities, 2012. 48–70. Print.
———. *Meeting the Universe Halfway: Quantum Physics and the Entanglement of Matter and Meaning.* Durham, NC: Duke UP, 2007. Print.
———. "On Touching—The Inhuman That Therefore I Am." *Differences: A Journal of Feminist Cultural Studies* 23.3 (2012): 206–23. Print.
Bennett, Jane. *Vibrant Matter: A Political Ecology of Things.* Durham, NC: Duke UP, 2010. Print.
Bryant, Levi R. "Black." Cohen, *Prismatic Ecology* 290–310.
Cohen, Jeffrey Jerome. "Elemental Relations." *O-Zone: A Journal of Object-Oriented Studies* 1 (Spring 2014): 53–61. Web. 20 June 2014.
———. "Introduction: Ecology's Rainbow." Cohen, *Prismatic Ecology* xv–xxxv.
———. *Prismatic Ecology: Ecotheory beyond Green.* Ed. Jeffrey Jerome Cohen. Minneapolis: U of Minnesota P, 2013. Print.
Coole, Diana, and Samantha Frost. "Introducing the New Materialisms." *New Materialisms: Ontology, Agency, and Politics.* Ed. Diana Coole and Samantha Frost. Durham, NC: Duke UP, 2010. 1–43. Print.
Cronon, William. "Introduction: In Search Of Nature." *Uncommon Ground: Rethinking the Human Place in Nature.* Ed. William Cronon. New York: Norton, 1996. 23–56. Print.
Estok, Simon, C. "Afterword: Reckoning with Irreversibilities in Biotic and Political Ecologies." *Postcolonial Ecocriticism among Settler-Colonial Nations.* Spec. issue of *Ariel: A Review of International English Literature* 44.4 (October 2014): 219–32. Print.
Hagopian, Joachim. "Death and Extinction of the Bees." *Global Research: Centre for Research on Globalization,* 28 Mar. 2014. Web. 20 July 2014.
Heise, Ursula K. *Sense of Place and Sense of Planet: The Environmental Imagination of the Global.* New York: Oxford UP, 2008. Print.
Helmreich, Stefan. "Human Nature at Sea." *AnthroNow* 2.3 (December 2010): 49–60. Print.
Iovino, Serenella. "Introduction: Mediterranean Ecocriticism, or A Blueprint for Cultural Amphibians." *Mediterranean Ecocriticism.* Spec. issue of *Ecozon@* 4.2 (2013): 1–14. Web. 15 June 2014.
Iovino, Serenella, and Serpil Oppermann. "After Green Ecologies: Prismatic Visions." Cohen, *Prismatic Ecology* 328–36.
Kabaağaçlı, Cevat Şakir (The Fisherman of Halicarnassus). "Aphrodite of Knidos" [Knidos Afroditi]. *A Flower Left to the Aegean Sea* 15–26.
———. *The Blue Exile* [Mavi sürgün]. 1961. Istanbul: Bilgi, 2003. Print.
———. "The Craftsmanship of the Mediterranean Fish" [Akdeniz balıklarının marifetleri]. *The Coolness of the Breeze* [İmbat serinliği]. Istanbul: Bilgi, 2002. 51–53. Print.
———. *A Flower Left to the Aegean Sea* [Egeden Denize bırakılmış bir çiçek]. Istanbul: Bilgi, 1972. Print.
———. "Halicarnassus" [Halikarnas]. *A Flower Left to the Aegean Sea* 43–49.
Martinez, Amanda Rose. "Swirling Seas of Plastic Trash." *Science News for Students,* 22 June 2011. Web. 12 July 2014.
McKibben, Bill. *The End of Nature.* 1989. New York: Random House, 2006. Print.

Morton, Timothy. "At the Edge of the Smoking Pool of Death: Wolves in the Throne Room." *Helvete: A Journal of Black Metal Theory* 1 (Winter 2013): 21–28. Web. 20 June 2014.

———. "X-Ray." Cohen, *Prismatic Ecology* 311–27.

Oppermann, Serpil. "Diffractive Narratives, Prismatic Ecologies: The Fisherman of Halicarnassus." *O-Zone: A Journal of Object-Oriented Studies* 1 (Spring 2014): n. pag. Web. 10 June 2014.

———. "Enchanted by Akdeniz: The Fisherman of Halicarnassus's Narratives of the Mediterranean." *Mediterranean Ecocriticism*. Spec. issue of *Ecozon@* 4.2 (2013): 100–116. Web. 15 June 2014.

Pettis, Jeffery S., et al. "Crop Pollination Exposes Honey Bees to Pesticides Which Alters Their Susceptibility to the Gut Pathogen *Nosema ceranae*." *PLOS/ONE* 8.7 (July 2013): n. pag. Web. 20 Aug. 2014.

Quigley, Peter. *Housing the Environmental Imagination: Politics, Beauty, and Refuge in American Nature Writing*. Newcastle upon Tyne: Cambridge Scholars, 2012. Print.

Satterfield, Terre, and Scott Slovic, eds. *What's Nature Worth? Narrative Expressions of Environmental Values*. Salt Lake City: U of Utah P, 2004. Print.

Slovic, Scott. Introduction. *Getting over the Color Green: Contemporary Environmental Literature of the Southwest*. Ed. Scott Slovic. Tucson: U of Arizona P, 2001. xv–xxviii. Print.

Uzuner, Buket. *Istanbullu*. Trans. Kenneth J. Dakan. Istanbul: Everest, 2008. Print.

Walia, Arjun. "New Harvard Study Proves Why the Bees Are All Disappearing." *Collective Evolution*, 15 May 2014. Web. 20 July 2014.

Williams, Roger. *The Fisherman of Halicarnassus: The Man Who Made Bodrum Famous*. London: Bristol Book P, 2013. Print.

Yaeger, Patricia. "The Death of Nature and the Apotheosis of Trash; or, Rubbish Ecology." *PMLA* 123.2 (March 2008): 321–39. Print.

Zalasiewicz, Jan, et al. "Are We Now Living in the Anthropocene?" *GSA Today* 18.2 (February 2008): 4–8. Web. 21 June 2014.

CHAPTER 11

FROM THE HUMAN TO THE DIVINE
NATURE IN THE WRITINGS OF THE TAMIL POET-SAINTS

CYNTHIA J. MILLER

SACRED LITERATURE IS OFTEN interlaced with illustrations of the ways in which people situate themselves in relation to the natural world—what is conceived of as "nature" or as "culture"; how nature is implicated in human thought and action; whether or not the smudge of human fingerprints may be found in even the densest of landscapes; and how notions of aesthetic and essential beauty are formed and communicated over time. These sorts of processual shifts are particularly apparent in the classic poetry of Tamil speakers, who in India are concentrated largely in the southern state of Tamil Nadu. These sacred verses, authored by ancient poets now considered saints, merge inner and outer worlds, nature and culture, to craft a seamless and subtle beauty that permeates not only the natural environment, but also the emotions, actions, and relationships that take place in it. This chapter explores these various constructions and expressions of beauty in the writings of the Tamil poet-saints, along with the ways in which they have shaped and informed Tamil relationships with the natural world and place-based identities.

Tamil literature is traced back to the Sangam era (which ended by the third century AD), and is considered by some to be "the only language of contemporary

India which is recognizably continuous with a classical past" (Ramanujan, *Interior Landscape* 97). Poetry produced during this era has stood the test of time, and has been celebrated as a major literary achievement of Indian civilization, heralded for its uniqueness, maturity, and artistry: "In their values and stances, [the poems] represent a mature classical poetry: passion is balanced by courtesy, transparency by ironies and nuances of design, impersonality by vivid detail, leanness of line by richness of implication" (Ramanujan, *Interior Landscape* 102). The Tamil tradition developed independently of Sanskrit—the dominant literary tradition of India—and while the latter is often characterized by its sophistication, Tamil poetry may be seen as reflecting the lives, emotions, and experiences of commoners and aristocrats alike, highlighting the "dignity of the common man" (Jesudasan and Jesudasan xiv). Referred to collectively as the Ten Idylls (*Pattuppattu*), these works are unique in the ways in which they draw their inspiration from the everyday—from observation and lived experience of the natural and human-made world—and it is this aspect, specifically, that sets these early writings of the Tamil poet-saints apart from both Sanskrit works and later Tamil literature, which are more devotional in nature.

This literary tradition, then, has reflected, as well as shaped, views, experiences, and constructions of the natural world that are very different from those reflected in works of the Sanskrit-based literary traditions. As a result, a particular way of reflecting on and writing about nature, the environment, and notions of natural beauty has also arisen. Naturalism and romanticism are distinct elements of the age of Tamil literature: some poets, in a manner reminiscent of Wordsworth, paint word pictures of hills, lakes, and rivers; others are more like Scott, crafting descriptions of the natural world so accurate that they would merit the appreciation of botanists; and still others resemble Keats, in their sensuous renderings of color, texture, fragrance, and melody (Varadarajan 2). In each of these poets' works, their affinity for the natural world permeates all other themes, yet no word analogous to "nature" is ever used—rather, the natural world, in all its power and beauty, is intricately interwoven with human existence, creating a seamless whole. Nature, as Francis Turner Palgrave (9) observes, is clothed in the hues of human passion, as in this verse by the poet Narrinai:

> Facing their man's cruelty to us
> their love for us is great
> and they just can't bear it
> Friend,
> those fruit-shedding hills of his
> will weep waterfalls of tears. (*Narrinai* 88)

Similarly, human existence finds its highest expression in the various aspects of nature, such as when a young heroine, adorned with shining gold jewelry, is described as being as grand as the *venkai* with golden blooms, but when in a desolate state without adornment, she is the vine that has shed its flowers (*Narrinai* 206). Thus, in the works of the Tamil poet-saints, the boundaries between inner and outer worlds are subtle and permeable. Nature, as John Campbell Shairp notes, "is always wooing man's spirit in manifold and mysterious ways, to elevate him with its vastness and sublimity, to gladden him with its beauty, to depress him with its bleakness, and to restore him with its calm" (2).

With the passage of time, however, shifts in these aesthetic expressions occurred, following shifts in the wider social, political, and linguistic context of South India. While the depth of human appreciation for nature's splendor remained constant, the vantage point from which it occurred did not.

EARLY TAMIL NATURE WRITING

Between the second century BC and the second century AD, there was a very large output of Tamil literary works, but very few of these—only about thirty thousand lines of poetry—have survived into the present day, and of those, it is almost exclusively the lyric, heroic, and bardic poetry of ancient Tamil that has survived (Nayagam 1–3). Through these remaining works, however, the relationship between people and their environment, culture and nature, social life and landscape, may readily be explored. As M. Varadarajan explains, "They knit together the feelings of man and the beauties of Nature in closest bonds and warmest associations" (3). The ancient poets did not treat nature in isolation but nearly always as a device with which to describe human life in its various dimensions, and chiefly in its deepest, most moving and passionate acts and emotions—those associated with love and war.

While there is little trace of the origins of Tamil literature, evidence exists that a significant literary culture existed well before the third century BC. The earliest extant book of ancient Tamil, the *Tolkaappiyam* (third century BC), codified both the grammar and the literature of the day, as well as made reference to over 250 preexisting works. This volume has provided a wealth of material for the study of the culture and literary conventions of the Tamils in the half millennium preceding the Christian era. The third part of the book, "Porulatikaaram," is the first and fundamental source for the study of nature in ancient Tamil literature, describing the conventions that regulate the classification of Tamil poetry into *akam*, or love poetry, and *puram*, or all that is not love poetry. The landscape, the seasons, the hours appropriate to each aspect and emotion of love, as well as the trees and flowers that are symbolic of different landscapes or climates, are all outlined here—in short, how nature is to be framed as the background of human behavior and emotion. The literary conventions of the age may be seen not only in the graceful blending of human passions with the beauties of nature, but also in the ways that human emotions and actions are elaborated and comprehended through the beauty and power of the natural world. In *puram* poetry (largely the elegiac, panegyric, and heroic), the treatment of nature is mainly objective and manifests itself in similes and metaphors, illustrating power and greatness of purpose; whereas in *akam* poetry, nature is the background and the sympathetic stage for the emotional and aesthetic aspects of love. In Tamil love poetry there exists a highly sympathetic interpretation of nature, whereby nature is brought into relationship with people, furnishing lessons and analogies for human conduct and human aspirations, and is expressed as being in sympathy with or in antagonism to people's lives.

The Ten Idylls, poems largely composed before the second century AD, illustrate many of the literary conventions regarding nature that would be elaborated in the *Tolkaappiyam*, as they describe in great detail the natural beauty, fertility, and resources in the lands of the poets' travels. The interrelationship of culture and nature, lives and landscapes, unfolds in various ways—exemplifying the greatness of a sovereign through the fertility and diversity of the regions found within his kingdom; humanizing deities through their affection for aspects of the landscape; linking human sentiments and the forces of nature. In *Nedunalvādai* (The good long north wind), for example, the poet Nakkirar sets a scene in winter:

> The earth is cold....
> From chilly boughs hang coloured drops of rain....
> When sharp winds blow to chill the very hills....

Even in the king's capital, Madura, the vibrant life of the city has been dulled by the cold, as illustrated by one of the small taken-for-granteds of urban nature:

> The domestic pigeon-cock, red-legged, goes not abroad,
> But stunned and helpless ...
> Shifts constantly his feet upon the perch....

Against this backdrop of gray, rainy winter, the poet begins to spin a tale of love and longing. A stern king, away at battle, visits the wounded, while his gentle queen awaits his return to their home, pining for her absent love. Though miles apart, the couple's deep emotional bond is conveyed by the shared backdrop of the rain—and human nature (interiors) is shown to be inseparable from the natural world (exteriors) as the rain that sets the stage for their actions is also manifested as heartfelt emotion in the queen's tears.

> ... and with the tip
> Of her rosy finger now and then she spills
> The shining tear-drops that in heavy lids
> Collected, roll down fast. (Jesudasan and Jesudasan 30–31)

The graceful detail of each verse exploits the contrasts in the two figures' worlds, building an artistically complex bardic tale of love, war, and the pain of separation. The beauty of the natural world, even the "good long north wind," is ever-present, whether as background, metonym, highlight, or constitutive element in the tale. The worlds of men and nature are inextricably interwoven.

Beyond this, though, these early Tamil notions of beauty—the spectacle of the natural world in all of its many aspects—were not attributed to some unseen entity, but rather located directly in nature, as an essential force. The colors, sounds, textures, and scents of flora and fauna, sky and earth—both dynamic and subtle—surround and infuse human existence. As a result, the worldview of the poet-saints was characterized by sensuality, deep emotion, and rootedness in the present. This orientation, however, would change dramatically with the passage of time.

WRITING THE TAMIL LANDSCAPE

The earth, clothed in the imaginations of the poet-saints, is conceived as being surrounded by the sea, or, as the poet Tolkappiyanar writes, "patu tirai vaiyam" (the earth surrounded by the sea of waves; translation mine). It is adorned by a canopy of blue sky above, and illuminated by the sun and the moon, which move around it daily. Over the past two thousand years, there have been changes in the geographic and territorial configurations of Tamil Nadu, as well as in the climatic conditions of South India in general. Here and there the sea has gained upon the land, or the land has encroached upon the sea; a harbor has been silted up, a river has changed its course or been divided by anicuts, a hill has subsided, the forests have given way to acres of tea, coffee, and rubber. The main aspects of the natural panorama, however, remain unaltered. The physical texture of the South Indian landscape, with its dividing mountains and rivers and its clearly defined contours, not only gave the South of India an occasion for its small kingdoms and smaller chieftaincies, but also formed the basis for the division of poetry on geographical regions—for example, mountain poetry, pasture-land poetry, and seaside poetry. By the time of the *Tolkaappiyam*, Tamil literature had already divided the landscape into five types: the mountains and hills, the pasture-lands, the maritime zones, the agricultural areas, and the forests and seasonally arid lands. According to literary conventions, each one of these five regional landscapes formed the background of poems dealing with definite groups of subjects of love and warfare, and within those categories, each is represented by characteristic flora and fauna, has a seasonal period in which its influence on human impulses and activities is most powerful, and is the realm of particular types of emotions.

For example, in *akam* poetry, a poet wishing to write a poem on love, regarding the union of lovers, nocturnal trysts, first meetings, and so on, had to choose the mountain scenery as the background of his poems, since the hills more than any other region afforded opportunities for clandestine meetings.

> As the deer begin to hide in the bush
> and the millet clusters with ears of grain
> and the mountains grieve as the rains pound and hammer
> look,
> O you, with those big quiet eyes
> your faraway lover
> is back
> old companion of your arms (Ramanujan, *Poems* 80)

The mountainous scenery always signified courtship, and was symbolized by the *kurinci* flower, which covers the hillsides in white blooms once every twelve years. Having located the scene of his poem in the mountains, the poet also needed to observe temporal conventions regarding regions and emotions. Midnight was the hour of choice for secret trysts and conversations. Similarly, he could not choose as his setting any season of the year—of the six seasons of the Tamil year, he had to choose the one that was the coldest, the most rainy, and the most beset with difficulties. These were the times when the mountainous climate was considered to be most itself, and was seen to present the greatest challenges to clandestine lovers, thereby heightening their desire and longing through suspense and struggle. According to Varadarajan, "Rough and frowning steeps, foaming floods, wandering beasts, darkness and cold make up the terrible but dramatically appropriate environment" (8).

Another example of this sort of region-emotion convention—poetics and thematics grounded by topography—may be found in the following passage by Kapilar, one of the foremost poets of the mountain region. A heroine is replying to her lady companion's question about how she will bear the separation from her lover for a short period before marriage. Her reply is that she will console herself by looking at "his" mountain, where they held clandestine meetings, as often as possible—as she does even now when he departs from her after their trysts. In this verse, the poet depicts the passion of the heroine and at the same time paints mountain scenery with rain and peacocks and langurs:

> Just now I had a look at that mountain of his
> where the rain poured in such heavy showers that
> the peacocks screeched in flocks and the grey-faced

langurs with their young ones trembled with fear.
Is my forehead still of the same old state, or
have I found peace in the sight of it? (Caminataiyar 249)

In contrast to the mountains' signification of lovers coming together, each of the other four regions was reserved for lovers in varying degrees of separation. Bucolic pastures served as the ideal location for tales of short separations. The lovers were portrayed under cloudy skies, or at dusk, and the overarching emotional tone was one emphasizing virtue and patience. The maritime region served as the setting for lovers' sense of loss during longer separations; the setting sun and wind off the water highlighted their emotions of pining and sorrow. The dangers of the forest enhanced the mood of sorrow and isolation that resulted from longer separations, and gave form to lovers' many fears and anxieties. And finally, the blazing heat of summer at midday in the fields of the agricultural region served to accentuate the flaring of tempers and jealousy accompanying a lover's infidelity during time apart.

The three key components of *akam*, or love poetry—the emotional experience (*urippourl*), the geographic and temporal setting (*mutalporul*), and the objects of the environment (*karupporul*)—are inextricably joined in the poetic convention of the era, such that one cannot help but signify the other. Tradition has so closely associated the sloping hills and mountains with the adventures of the lover coming to his sweetheart at midnight that the name of the white flower, *kurinci*, is itself enough to evoke the appropriate sentiment in the reader or listener. In this way, a direct interrelationship between nature, emotion, and literature evolved—such that elements of nature (the landscape, flora, climate, and other natural phenomena), which were first simply the setting for human activities, became independently recognizable signifiers of particular human emotions and relationships—blending the inner worlds of poets and their audiences with the exterior world of nature.

Corresponding writing in *puram* mountain poetry was verse symbolic of the initial stages of warfare—forays and raids made for the purpose of cattle stealing. *Veici* is a flower, again indigenous to the mountain region, that came to designate cattle stealing because the Tamil warriors adorned themselves with wreaths and garlands of these red flowers whenever they set out on cattle raids. In fact, each strategic movement or aspect of war had its own particular flower after which the movement was named (Ramanujan, *Poems* 242). The garland was symbolic of the character of the undertakings, and the feelings of those engaged in them. In addition, *puram* poetry of each region included poems praising the chiefs of the respective regions—reflective poems on the transitoriness of life, poems on statecraft, kingship, and nobility—all evoked by regional landscapes with attendant sentiments symbolized by the climate, flora, and other attributes of the natural world.

This early Tamil literature, then, finds human culture visibly intertwined with constructions of the natural world, and nature deeply implicated in people's understanding of their emotional and social worlds. On one hand, the Sangam-era poets wrote about nature as an essential backdrop for the performance of day-to-day life, as this pastoral poem of two lovers' reunion after a short separation illustrates:

> The bees buzz and the frogs croak;
> the pastoral region is cool and fragrant
> with blooms of mullai; the pleasant season
> accosts; and I have returned as promised.
> Be not downcast and dejected. (Caminataiyar 494)

On the other hand, however, human emotions, be they love, aggression, sorrow, jealousy, or pride, are a part of nature—influenced by the power of the natural world in a way that mirrors early notions of the anthropogeography (the influence of geography in determining the character and culture of a people) that is also prevalent in the place-based identities of Tamil speakers. This deep connection between people and place extends beyond "topophilia," or the emotional attachment to place (Tuan), to represent something more complex—a shared essence between the land and its inhabitants, wherein Tamil speakers not only feel the land of their fathers, but are one with it. A man's or woman's character may be understood simply by knowing their birthplace. The Tamil homeland itself has thus been constructed as a "poetic space," to which borders, boundaries, and natural features lend a naturalized form (Smith 35):

> The river comes down to the plains so that the good
> damsels of cool eyes may bathe and play. It mixes
> itself with the honey of the bamboos. . . . The long drawn
> streams coming down in great numbers gather the gems,
> the pearls and gold so much that the waves respond with noise.
> (Rangaswamy 911)

What greater certainty of identity and being "in place" can there be than for human action and emotion to be linked to the natural flows of time and space—to be truly "grounded," one with the land of one's birth and daily existence? The forces of nature are thus given agency in the drama of human existence and the relationships that ensue, though it is still those relationships that hold the spotlight.

IMPACTS OF SANSKRITIZATION

In the face of increasing Sanskrit literary influence from the North of India (350–400 AD), this predominantly secular relationship with nature began to evolve in ways that brought it closer in line with Vedic literature. Where previously the natural world had been viewed through the lens of everyday life, as part and parcel of the essence of the Tamil people, it soon was recast as a manifestation of the divine. The Vedas, a collection of hymns and verses that, according to Western scholars, were mostly likely transcribed around 1500–1200 BC, are traditionally considered to be *śruti*—texts of revealed knowledge—created by the deity Brahmā, from whom all humans have descended. Vedic texts are organized around four canonical collections: the *Rigveda*, the *Yajurveda*, the *Samaveda*, and the *Atharvaveda*. The vast majority of works in this body of Vedic literature are texts reserved for liturgical use, consisting of religious lyrics traditionally recited or sung solely by priests at prayers, religious events, and auspicious occasions. Only one book contains some secular poems. The verses of the *Rigveda*, or the Veda of Mantra or Recited Praise, are mainly those of praise and invocation—ancient prayers for prosperity, longevity, and well-being—as well as poetic accounts of the origins of the world, often considered to be mythological; the verses of the *Yarjurveda* focus on offering, oblation, and sacrifice; the *Samaveda*, or Veda of Holy Songs, is a compilation of sacred verses, chanted during the performance of rituals; and the *Atharvaveda*, the final book of the Vedas, consists of spells and charms, and is of a different character altogether—with hymns that are simpler and more diverse than those of the other Vedas (Radhakrishnan 21–116).

Careful analysis demonstrates a significant process of personification by which natural phenomena develop into gods. Vedic writers, and those following their tradition, generally attributed occurrences in nature to the agency of members of the pantheon of gods inherent in the phenomena. One direct result of investing nature with these divine personas is that Sanskritic writers positioned themselves at a great remove from the natural world. While Vedic-inspired descriptions of mountains, forests, and streams are full of a deep and abiding feeling for them, the intimate relationship with people's lives has been severed. The workings of nature are observed and narrated with astonishment, as things so distant from the realm of culture as to defy comprehension (MacDonell 67). In early Tamil poems, the sun, the "infant sun," the "rising sun," and its morning and evening appearances are elaborately described—the sun is not spoken of as "the eye of the gods" or as the "husband of dawn" until after a sharp literary turn toward Sanskritic conventions. The following vesper verses illustrate the point:

> Borne by swift coursers, he will now unyoke them;
> The speeding chariot he has stayed from going.
> He checks the speed of them that glide like serpents;
> Night has come on by Saavitri's commandment. (Varadarajan 225)

Early Tamil representations of nature were secular, in part because the Tamils of that era did not possess the highly elaborated mythology that the northern

Indian poets possessed. As Sanskritic practices and traditions became powerful sources of social capital in Tamil Nadu and traditional Dravidian practices became marginalized, Tamil social, religious, and literary practices slowly merged with northern Sanskritic traditions. The growing influence of Sanskritic mythology may be seen as early as the Sangam poems on Murukan and Tirumall, which lay the groundwork for a highly theological nature divinized by human beings. Even so, the divinity Murukan was inseparably and exclusively connected with montane nature—riding an elephant, considered the strongest and most powerful of the hill animals; symbolized by the peacock, a bird of the hills; and worshipped with flowers of the mountain region and offerings of the produce of the hill districts, such as millet and honey (Ramanujan, *Poems* 215, 311). As nature became increasingly associated with divinity in both practice and literature, people's inner worlds, which had formerly been interwoven with nature, grew increasingly alienated from the natural world (Varadarajan 1–22). The artifacts and manifestations of nature either embodied or represented a supernatural world in which humans held no part, and temples and shrines increased in number in hills and at riverbanks as bits of material culture that mediated (in nature) between the human and the divine.

By the ninth century AD, the era of the Tamil poet-saints had begun. During this era, the cult of temples and pilgrimages was taking hold as the poet-saints and their hosts of followers moved from village to village, region to region, writing and performing verses describing the local landscapes and natural attributes in praise of Siva and the lesser deities. It is at this point that we may observe the natural world falling almost entirely into the service of the supernatural in the literature (Radhakrishnan 21–62). Most of the Saivite temples were constructed in and around natural scenery of forest areas, mountains, riverbanks, or the shoreline. By the era of the Pallava kings (300–800 AD), Tamil Nadu had become a seat of Sanskrit learning, and the literature reflects a sharp dichotomy between nature, now completely associated with the supernatural pantheon, and human culture. While it is entirely true that such a dichotomy itself is no more than a product of culture, the positioning of people relative to nature in literary texts had changed radically from early times. In the writings of the poet-saints, the world appears animated by God:

> The world is the vessel of the lamp;
> the sea is the oil; the sun is the flame. (Shairp 34)

Within this framework, poets and other writers are positioned as chroniclers of a natural world that is remarkable, yet distant—a natural world set apart from the experiences and emotions of human beings by divine animation and intention. People's imaginative relationship to nature in the works of the poet-saints is as onlookers rather than active participants. And along with that distance depicted in the literature, we may observe that the Tamil sense of place is altered as well—with Tamil Nadu becoming increasingly configured as a sacred landscape, one where contours are defined by shrines and temples and pilgrimage routes, rather than by earlier ecological wisdom focused on the interplay of regional characteristics and human experiences. And along with those shifts in representation, a sharper ideological division between nature and culture has also occurred, with "nature" being reframed as a creation and signifier of the divine, while all else is the product and purview of man.

THE LEGACY OF THE POET-SAINTS

Inasmuch as this movement to a sacred construction of nature was the result of the unfolding of Tamil social and religious systems over time, certain aspects of earlier Tamil nature writing have also persisted to the present day and have had a significant impact on contemporary South Indian Tamil place-based identities. Most notable among these is a deep, abiding appreciation for the beauty of the natural world. From bucolic fields to brilliantly colored birds to powerful storms, the character and details of nature are viewed with a keen eye, and culture—human agency—is informed by those observations and experiences. Aesthetically, practically, and intellectually, the natural world remains interwoven with both the inner and outer worlds of those who inhabit the Tamil homeland, and who see their essence as bound up with its soil, rivers, mountains, and fields. This is not so much apparent in the scholarly texts emerging from Tamil Nadu, which are in large measure focused on the interplay of religion, identity, and ecology (for example, Nelson; Badiner; Bhardwaj; Sen), but it can be seen in popular culture texts, such as dramas and romances, and in the creative nonfiction of authors whose work confronts the impact of modernity on the Tamil landscape.

It is also particularly apparent in the visual texts of contemporary Tamil cinema, where romantic and melodramatic tales frequently play out in natural contexts informed by a received knowledge and appreciation of the natural world that harkens back to the writings of the poet-saints. The inherent beauty of the South Indian landscape provides a spectacular backdrop for the first blush of romantic love, cold rain signifies separation and longing, and mundane dusty roads baked by the sun invoke memories of village life and home—even as scenes of devotion and fantastic images of Krishna and other figures from the Hindu pantheon are intercut with more "worldly" scenes. In all of these texts, the two contrasting constructions of nature—the sacred and the secular—collide and are interwoven. Embedded in them is a conceptualization of nature tied to, and implicated in, human actions and emotions in ways that evoke early Tamil treatments of nature—within the framework of a distanced sacred landscape—creating a sense of disjuncture in both images and messages about the relationship between people and the natural world in which they live, a disjuncture that may, over time, be resolved.

Taking this sort of processual approach to Tamil literature proves valuable on a number of fronts—it allows us to examine shifts in ideas about culture and nature, as well as to consider people's relationships with their environments over time, and the ways in which they are brought closer together as well as the ways in which they are estranged. It also offers a framework for understanding the roots of contemporary conceptualizations of natural beauty among Tamil speakers and in the unique literary and visual traditions that exist in Tamil culture. Early Tamil nature writing began with a sense of intimacy and attentiveness that offers a window into place-relationships not widely existing in Tamil culture today, even though the place-based sentiments inspiring those relationships continue to serve as foundations for Tamil identity. And even as the writings of the poet-saints illustrate and instruct readers in "ways of looking" at the many and varied detailed wonders of the natural world, they also provide insights into the ways that various social systems, religious attitudes, and structures of power and prestige are implicated in people's conceptualizations of nature and its beauty—seldom remaining stagnant, and shifting with the whims of culture and time.

CYNTHIA J. MILLER is a cultural anthropologist specializing in popular culture and visual media. She teaches in the Institute for Liberal Arts at Emerson College, and is the editor or coeditor of numerous scholarly volumes, including the award-winning *Steaming into a Victorian Future: A Steampunk Anthology*; *International Westerns: Re-locating the Frontier*; and *The Laughing Dead: The Horror-Comedy Film from "Bride of Frankenstein" to "Zombieland."* She also serves as the editor of the book series Film and History, and as an editorial board member for the *Journal of Popular Television*.

WORKS CITED

Badiner, Allan Hunt, ed. *Dharma Gaia: A Harvest of Essays in Buddhism and Ecology*. Berkeley: Parallax, 1990. Print.
Bhardwaj, Surinder Mohan. *Hindu Places of Pilgrimage in India: A Study in Cultural Geography*. Berkeley: U of California P, 1973. Print.
Caminataiyar, U., ed. *Kuruntokai*. Madras: Kapir Accukkutam, 1962. Print.
Jesudasan, C., and Hephzibah Jesudasan. *A History of Tamil Literature*. Calcutta: YMCA, 1961. Print.
MacDonell, Arthur Anthony. *A History of Sanskrit Literature*. New York: D. Appleton, 1900. Print.

Narrinai: Text and Translation. Trans. Nilamekam Kantacarnip Pillai. Pondicherry, Tamil Nadu, India: Institut Français de Pondichéry, 2008. Print.
Nayagam, Xavier S. *Landscape and Poetry: A Study of Nature in Classical Tamil Poetry.* Bombay: Asia Publishing House, 1966. Print.
Nelson, Lance E., ed. *Purifying the Earthly Body of God: Religion and Ecology in Hindu India.* Albany, NY: SUNY P, 1998. Print.
Palgrave, Francis Turner. *Landscape in Poetry from Homer to Tennyson.* 1897. Whitefish, MT: Kessinger, 2010. Print.
Radhakrishnan. *Indian Philosophy.* Vol. 1. 2nd ed. New York: Macmillan, 1929. Print.
Ramanujan, A. K. *The Interior Landscape: Classical Tamil Love Poems.* New York: NYRB Poets, 2014. Print.
———. *Poems of Love and War: From the Eight Anthologies and the Ten Long Poems of Classical Tamil.* New York: Columbia UP, 2011. Print.
Rangaswamy, M. A. Dorai. *The Religion and Philosophy of Tevaram.* 2nd ed. Madras: Madras UP, 1990. Print.
Sen, Geeti, ed. *Indigenous Vision: Peoples of India Attitudes to the Environment.* New Delhi: Sage, 1992. Print.
Shairp, John Campbell. *On Poetic Interpretation of Nature.* New York: Hurd and Houghton, 1877. Print.
Smith, Anthony D. *National Identity.* Reno: U of Nevada P, 1991. Print.
Tuan, Yi-Fu. *Topophilia: A Study of Environmental Perceptions, Attitudes, and Values.* Englewood Cliffs, NJ: Prentice Hall, 1974. Print.
Varadarajan, M. *The Treatment of Nature in Sangam Literature.* Tirunelveli: South India Saiva Siddhanta, 1957. Print.

CHAPTER 12

BEAUTY AS IDEOLOGICAL AND MATERIAL TRANSCENDENCE

WERNER BIGELL

> Ein schöner Garten ist ein produktiver Garten
> (A beautiful garden is a productive garden)
> Slogan of the East German
> allotment garden association

"DIGGING IN THE FIELD"

Beauty is a fundamental category of human experience, but although the term is ubiquitous in daily speech, it is rarely used as an analytical term in the humanities because it is suspected of being metaphysical, elitist, and formalist. Beauty has indeed been elitist; the English countryside, for example, is an idealized landscape based on the enclosure of the commons and the eviction of local farmers who did not fit the rustic ideal of the landowners. Kenneth Olwig points out that "rural landscaping created the scenic image of the country community ideal, while helping to undermine the customary law upon which it was based" (640). In his essay "Nature," Ralph Waldo Emerson both venerated nature and showed disdain for those who work in it: "Yet this may show us what discord is between man and nature, for you cannot freely admire a noble landscape, if laborers are digging in the field hard by. The poet finds something ridiculous in his delight, until he is out of the sight of men" (51).

There is a menacing ring in such statements for someone like me who enjoyed digging in the soil as a child, growing up in an allotment garden colony in West Germany.[1] Edible plants have always been more beautiful to me than flowers, and when I heard the East German slogan "A beautiful garden is a productive garden," I realized that I was not alone in this view. But why does it sound odd to associate edibility with beauty? Beauty is not per se an elitist concept. For an elicitation of a vernacular sense of beauty, one can look to those who "are digging in the field," who create, in other words, a landscape corresponding to their sense of beauty.

THEORETICAL CONSIDERATIONS: WHO IS THE BEHOLDER?

While the individualist statement that "beauty is in the eye of the beholder" makes communication about beauty impossible, a formal understanding of beauty, such as the concept of ideal proportions, or the "golden ratio" in art theory, turns beauty into a universal category. Scientific understandings of beauty follow the universal approach, seeing beauty as a process of evolutionary adaptation, quantifiable as pleasure and attraction.[2] Individualist and universal approaches have a certain validity, as there is a universal, biological basis for beauty, and there are individual variations of its perception. What is missing is the level in between, the notion of social or shared beauty, and I will argue for an understanding of beauty as a relational category, an expression of involvement with the human and natural environment. Since such involvement is framed by history, ideology, and religion, there are regular variations of the sense of beauty.

The reason the question "Can you eat it?" is not commonly associated with beauty is found in Kant's dictum of "interested disinterest" as the basis for aesthetic appreciation. The idea of the disinterested observer has played important roles throughout history: during the Enlightenment, for instance, it confirmed individual autonomy of aesthetic perception, and during the Romantic Era it dissociated beauty from mass production. Art and beauty become spheres outside the functionality of scientific exploration and industrial production. While the material world of nature as well as spiritual narratives lose their alterity and are now controlled by humans, art and beauty form what could be called a sphere of pseudoalterity, the idea that art is different from worldly processes. The postmodern paradigm, then, has followed the path of removing alterity from the world, seeing the material world as an opaque sphere only accessible through social construction. To recover beauty, it is necessary to recover its aspects of creative involvement and alterity. Alterity can be understood as a sense of the unconstructed, nonfunctional, oppositional, different, imaginary, utopian, and inhuman aspects of the world. Beauty, then, is found not in a construction of reality but in a common engagement with alterity.

An earlier effort to restore a sense of alterity in an increasingly controlled world was transcendentalism. Emerson saw nature as a medium for the spirit: "Through all its kingdoms, to the suburbs and outskirts of things, it is faithful to the cause whence it had its origin. It always speaks of Spirit. It suggests the absolute. It is a perpetual effect. It is a great shadow pointing always to the sun behind us" (49). The element of transcendentalism that merits reconsideration is not so much spirituality per se as the understanding of alterity in nature; in the words of Emerson, "We are as much strangers in nature, as we are aliens from God" (50). Emerson based alterity on an idealistic understanding of beauty, following the Christian trope of the fall, and he viewed spirit above materiality: "Idealism saith: matter is a phenomenon, not a substance" (49). This idealism venerated nature for its spirituality, not its materiality, and therefore science and the transformation of nature were disdained. Emerson pointed out that "idealism is a hypothesis to account for nature by other principles than those of carpentry and chemistry. Yet, if it only deny the existence of matter, it does not satisfy the demands of the spirit" (49). The problem here is that Emerson and the transcendentalists remained caught in the Christian trope of the fallen material world and the higher spiritual sphere, and alterity was thus reduced to spirituality.

Transcendentalism was a reaching out to something that could not be reached; it was an awareness of the limits of appropriation. If the transcendental attitude is to make sense in the current Western world, it needs to be recontextualized. While the transcendentalists of the nineteenth century reacted to the materialism of the industrial and scientific revolution, today the situation is different. The postmodern Western world has not only lost its spiritual dimension but is also increasingly disconnected from the material world. This is seen in qualms about virtuality and in the fascination with the real and authentic. In addition, the logic of postmodern capitalism has turned the past into a pastiche and sees the future as an extension of the present. History is no longer an insight into the alterity of the past, and utopian imaginaries struggle with ideological fatalism, expressed in Margaret Thatcher's mantra that "there is no alternative." In other words, postmodernity can be seen as a form of cultural autism, disconnected from the alterities of both past and future as well as from spirituality and materiality. If beauty is found in the act of reaching out to what is not me, then the transcendental mechanism is useful, but it needs to be extended: whereas the transcendental dimension traditionally was a spiritual one, it is possible to widen the concept along both a temporal axis (past and future) and an existential one (spirituality and materiality). However, the postmodern prison has open doors, and for many people beauty still is a valid category.

BEAUTY IN THE TRANSCENDENCE OF THE PAST

While neoclassicist buildings still dominate many Western cities, neoclassicism is the last architectural style that consciously and seriously invokes the past. Modernist and postmodernist styles have cut the link to the past, and today an artist copying and borrowing from the past is seen as a mere artisan. However, not all societies have gone through such a radical break with the past. I experienced an orientation toward the past when I taught in the Occupied Palestinian Territory of the West Bank. Here I found it difficult to know which of the texts and films I used in my classes were culturally acceptable and which were offensive. Luckily two of my students, women from conservative families, loved reading, made a point of looking at the assigned material ahead of the plan, and often told me their opinion of the texts before I used them in class. When they told me for the first time, "Teacher, this story is not beautiful," I answered as a Western teacher, explaining that beauty is not necessarily a category of literary evaluation and that literature often challenges established ways of seeing the world.

Later I realized that my answer had been that of a typical past-blind Westerner. I understood then that not only had the students warned me to keep me out of trouble, but they had also disliked aspects of those stories.[3] Their phrase was more than code—it was an expression of a sense of beauty linked to tradition. This does not mean that texts and stories are just reproductions of the past; rather, in this case it meant that the students understood change as a continuous engagement with the past to shape the present, an engagement involving stretching and redefining the boundaries it imposes, not breaking them.

THE FUTURE OF THE PAST: THE BEAUTY OF MODERNIST HOUSING BLOCKS

For most Western Europeans, Soviet-style housing blocks (Plattenbau) are an expression of a dystopian, uniform, and technocratic society that brutalized nature and at best possessed the charm of ruins. However, in my observation, many Eastern Europeans see such buildings more pragmatically, as the convenient places where one lives. While such housing makes environmental sense in terms of transport and energy use and can be seen as an alternative to suburban sprawl, the critique of it is often framed in aesthetic terms. Here I do not argue the environmental case but claim that those blocks can be beautiful.

According to Yi-Fu Tuan, a city consists of two components: the material urbs and the immaterial civitas—that is, the patterns of behavior in a city (320). While the forms of social interaction, civitas, may change quickly, the urbs often preserves expressions of a past civitas. An important aspect of civitas is its ideological dimension. One has to see not only the relation between built form and behavioral patterns but also the underlying ideology that drove the creation of the material form. This means that one cannot aesthetically evaluate a building without seeing what society built it and by which ideology that society was driven.[4]

The urbs is at the same time a memory of the past and an ideological projection into the future. Today's consumer individualism creates an urbs of increasing social segregation and of privatized public space, where train stations and airports become indistinguishable from shopping malls. While in the West housing blocks were schemes for the poor, in Eastern Europe they did not have that connotation but were perceived as a promise of escape from the kommunalka, the cramped communal apartments, or from the drafty, humid, and coal-heated old buildings that frequently had shared toilets and no showers; thus moving was a privilege, not a stigma. Also today these buildings serve their function, and some of the developments, such as the GDR showcase of Berlin Marzahn in Germany, integrate good public transport, installations, parks, and public places. In order to evaluate their social dimension, it is important to consider not individual buildings but the entire urban fabric. Housing blocks were surrounded by parks and allotment garden colonies, and public transport made it possible to reach the dachas, the summer cottages. Because of good transportation and child care facilities, women were able to work.

The rejection of socialist housing is not based on environmental concerns or shortcomings in planning. Boris Groys shows that the rejection of their monotony has ideological reasons, that the "postmodern taste is by no means as tolerant as it seems on first glance" (Groys 150), meaning that the perceived monotony can be seen as an attack on the discourse on diversity and difference: "Communist aesthetics seems to be not different, not diverse, not regional, not colorful enough—and therefore confronts the dominating pluralist, postmodern Western taste with its universalist, uniform Other" (151). Groys points out that the alterity of Communist art and architecture, from a current perspective, lies in the fact that it was not produced by a market (151). But the situation here is not that a heterogeneous present rejects a universalist past. Groys argues that "the postmodern cultural diversity is merely a pseudonym for the universality of capitalist markets" (152). While the aim of the postmodern universality is to "aestheticize one's identity as it is—without any attempt to change it" (152), Communist universalism was based on "historical rupture, on the rejection of diversity and difference in the name of a common cause" (154). This is the root of its ideological alterity.

Much as Emerson perceived the alterity of a spiritual dimension in nature, seeing beauty in housing blocks means seeing their transcendence of the future, their social dimension, visible in the creation of housing, mobility, and recreational space for all. Despite all their shortcomings (including the sometimes poor execution of construction plans, the too-wide and pedestrian-unfriendly streets, and the fatal contradictions of the society constructing those buildings), there is still a glow of future in them. In grammar there is the future perfect tense ("By the time you come home, I will have eaten"), pointing (back) to the past from the perspective of the future; what is needed for the understanding of those housing blocks is a tense that could be called the "future of the past" ("I was going to be a cosmonaut"). Owen Hatherley describes the transcendence of beauty of crumbling modernist blocks in Britain, wondering why they have a "sharp poignancy" for him: "What might be at work here is the common contemporary phenomenon of nostalgia for the future, a longing for the fragments of the half-hearted post-war attempts at building a new society, an attempt that lay in ruins at the time I was born. These remnants of social democracy can, at best, have the effect of critiquing the paucity of ambition and grotesque inequalities of the present" (8). We see here a continuation of the struggle between aristocratic landowners and the farmers on their land, as in cases where "the beautification of an inner-city working class area is achieved by removing its inhabitants" (Hatherley 41).

While the beauty of a wooden house by a lake is easily communicated, finding beauty in socialist housing is an acquired taste. The rough edge of those buildings has a point, as Hatherley explains: "This is what made leftist Modernisms so harsh: the need to assert a counter, to create another culture, something the left is at present utterly unwilling to do, endlessly harping on about 'resistance' without the slightest notion of victory, let alone what culture should exist afterwards" (71). It could be argued that beauty in housing blocks is based not so much on a common ideology, but on seeing the transcendence of the future, for which ideology is the vehicle. A common ideology, in the form of a shared understanding of the world and how it should develop, creates a sense of community.

BEAUTY IN THE CITY: A HOMELESS PERSPECTIVE

In July 2014 I participated in a guided tour through the Berlin experienced by homeless people, organized by the welfare organization GEBEWO—Soziale Dienste—Berlin. Klaus Seilwinder, who had been homeless for eight years and now works for GEBEWO, guided part of the tour, demonstrating the daily routines of homeless people in Berlin and how they perceive and use the city. Besides money for daily survival, security is a main concern. Seilwinder recounted that he always attempted to be invisible to the residents in whose neighborhoods he stayed overnight, to the people who were potential threats, and to the authorities. Invisibility here must not be seen as an aim in itself but as a condition motivated by security. I asked Seilwinder about moments and places of beauty during his homeless years. My intention was not to relativize the hardships of homeless people but to see how someone who moves in the city with different interests perceives beauty.

Seilwinder was at first surprised by the question but then answered enthusiastically, recounting beautiful situations rather than beautiful sights. A beautiful moment for him was during an outdoor classical concert in the city, when he mingled with the "true lovers of music" gathering outside the fence, enjoying the music that could be heard there. Other moments of beauty were acts of spontaneous solidarity, as when he once overslept on a playground and a little girl asked him why he was sleeping outside. He answered truthfully that he had no home, and the girl asked him to wait and went away. The girl then asked her mother to help, and brought coffee and breakfast outside; out of that situation a lasting friendship with the family developed. While accounts of hardship mark a difference between the homeless reality and the housed world, beauty appears to be a dimension that connected Seilwinder to society.

Part of our tour was a visit to Haus Schöneweide, a shelter for men who are resistant to alcohol withdrawal therapy. In 2008 the house was renovated as part of an art project to create a beautiful shelter. The common rooms and garden of the shelter are cozy and well designed and decorated with artwork. When the project was finished, it was criticized as being a reward for homelessness, but this misses the point: the beauty of the house is a connecting element. The goal was not to romanticize life on the street, which leads to physical and psychological disorder. Beauty in this case is best understood as a dynamic of difference and otherness. On the one hand, beauty reduces invisibility and difference by building a bridge to society. On the other hand, this understanding of beauty implies a social imaginary, an "other" transcending utility. Music as a connecting medium and the acts of spontaneous solidarity that Seilwinder experienced when he was homeless are suggestions of this otherness of social imagination, a breaking out of the servility of utility. The next two sections will present further examples of beauty that is visible as landscape.

ORGANIC FARMERS IN THAILAND

In 2012 and 2013 I visited two organic farmers' networks in the Thai province of Isaan—Inpang Community Network and the rice mill cooperative Kut Chum—

with the aim of investigating the relationship between community and landscape. The areas have a history of being Red; a Communist guerilla movement was active there until the 1980s. The cooperatives can be seen as a way of continuing their political struggle through peaceful means. For some time, until it was made illegal by the Central Bank of Thailand, Kut Chum used its own currency (the Bia Kud Chum). The main idea of the networks is to abandon the financially unpredictable and aesthetically predictable monoculture and to become independent of agribusiness. Farmers involved with the networks own their farms and have cooperative structures for the processing (such as a wine and herbal medicine factory) and distribution of their products. The farmers have an experimental attitude, trying out new ways of planting and production, and sharing their experiences in community meetings and workshops. The "edible forest" that farmers create on their farms is variable; one farm may grow rattan, while another develops frog farming, but all farms produce a variety of crops for sale and sustenance. The edible forest is also a way to connect the farmers to their past, as many families used to live in the forest and later experienced the alienating transition to monoculture. Organic farming thus integrates heritage and the future-oriented experimental farming style. I asked the farmers what they felt was beautiful about their farms (both the individual farms and the networks). All of them responded emphatically; below is a collection of their answers.[5]

> Beautiful because the soil is of good quality. This means you can plant rice, get good quality and eat it. Also many trees you can eat. You put something into the soil and get it back and eat it.

> Everyone helps each other. The new generation respects the old. There is solidarity and peace among people. The setting of the houses is not complicated, just square. Each house has its vegetable and food, and food is shared in the Buddhist tradition. Honesty. People come to the house to learn.

> Beauty is diversity. When I was young some species were hard to find, so now I planted them here. They connect me to my childhood.

> Space is needed for sunlight and for being able to see the stars and moon at night. Trees, the greenness of the area. Peacefulness. The combination of big and small trees. Picking up fresh things to eat. When I cook tom yam I can use fish from the pond, and when I walk there I pick up everything on my way (chili, ginger, leaves, lemongrass). That is a cheerful life. The feeling that everything is not in straight lines but plants are mixed, and on different levels. Humans are just one element, not everything is under us.

> Before the beauty of paddy fields was like this: no trees, no grass, no weed, only plain land and rice. Trees then were not beautiful as they kept sunlight from the rice. Now a combination of trees provide shade, coolness, and greenness. It is beautiful to cut grass and weeds to cover the soil with it; when

it decomposes it becomes fertilizer; before it was just killed with herbicides. Monoculture is not beautiful, but diversity is. A rubber plantation is green but not beautiful. Beauty is also what you can pick and eat, a variety of plants that can be sold. Beauty is when people are more involved, such as in the certification process of organic farming.

There are two types of beauty: In one you want to grow lemons, so you have one field with many trees, another plain land and you put fertilizer on everything. You can get much produce fast. The other type of beauty is to leave other trees, which takes longer to get fruit, and your farm needs less maintenance and has a longer lifespan. There is also beauty in the solar panels; sufficiency is important, and we can use them without harm.

Beauty is spending time pruning trees and listening to frogs. The house is built on the water, so it is cool. It is nice walking on wood, better than cement. It is better to sleep outside. In the beginning people said I am crazy, planting trees in a paddy field.[6]

Beauty is when people are united and help each other. When there is plenty of food. The forest is very beautiful because it is cool when you walk to the village. The trees are big and reach straight to the sky. With big trees one can see far in the jungle. The ancient jungle sounded like music.

There is a pattern in the farmers' understanding of beauty. Beauty is not seen as something removed from daily life, but as a dimension of it. Beauty links farmers to the material and spiritual aspects of the natural world, as well as to their past as forest dwellers and to the future, which is seen in the effort of building a community. The sense of community and the variation of production the new lifestyle creates have an aesthetic dimension that also keeps young people from moving to the cities. The association of beauty and food is interesting; eating, for them, is about more than satisfying hunger. It is a link to the material world. In addition, common meals are community-building rituals (the Christian Eucharist is a variation of this theme). The aesthetic appreciation of ecological diversity also means variety on the table. Beauty for the farmers is not linked to the satisfaction of individual needs but transcends the frame of servility to connect—through involvement—to contexts of community, materiality, spirituality, and history. The farmers' sense of beauty is not uncontested. In the garden of a rural school I visited, children learned to plant in straight lines, creating small monocultures in patches lined with cement, learning the agriculture of the state.

THE BEAUTY OF GERMAN ALLOTMENT GARDENS

Since the end of the nineteenth century, allotment garden colonies have existed in Germany. In August 2014 I asked gardeners in the Berlin colony Bornholm 1 about what they found beautiful in their own gardens and in the colony as a whole. Below are excerpts from my notes:

> I can walk around in my beachwear and do not have to dress up. It is important that one can eat the harvest, such as tomatoes and potatoes; bread with tomatoes is very good. In the morning one can have breakfast with sun and singing birds. Here one does not hear any cars. In summer the gardens are cooler than the city.

> In the middle of the city there is a refuge for you alone, that you can shape. You get potatoes from the ground, vegetables, herbs, the ingredients for a meal. You can be alone if you want, on your bench, and you can invite friends. The garden community means that we can meet each other in the common areas. My home is two minutes away by bicycle, so the garden is part of my home. What is not good is that some gardeners treat the garden as a summer residence, only planting lawn. This contradicts the rules of the one-third minimum use of space for edible plants and can jeopardize our legal status as an allotment area; if this status is revoked by the authorities, labeling it as a recreational zone, the lease would go up, making the gardens unaffordable for two-thirds of the tenants.

> It is quiet here. I am a pensioner, and we come here early in the morning. I like that you can grow vegetables that you can eat, but I also like to plant flowers. I hope that we can use the garden for a long time without needing help. Children sometimes say how beautiful everything grows. We have a harmonious community, everything is said directly and there is no quarreling. I can have a beer in the garden without getting dressed, and I like playing cards with my spouse. My grandmother used to say that every human needs a little place.

> I like to use my plot as a real garden; there are always flowers, and there are tomatoes, cucumbers, etc. I can walk into the garden and return with potatoes, tomatoes, herbs, and cucumbers for a meal. My garden makes me partially self-sufficient, with organic food. It is enjoyable to dig out potatoes or to collect tomatoes in the morning. I love sleeping in the garden; it is always a bit cooler than in the city (we live not far away). One knows many people, the colony is like a little village, not as anonymous as in the city or in my apartment house. Sunflowers grow in unexpected places. The garden is a better place for children than the playgrounds, and we show them how things smell, e.g., thyme and lemon balm, and how plants grow.

> One factor is recreation. We grow and harvest, and this is an experience of success. Every season there is something to eat. In our part of the colony we have a good community and cooperation. It is sociable there. One can work with things. For me also flowers belong to a garden, everything should be in harmony, lawn, potatoes, bushes, vegetables. Diversity is important; one should not just have a lawn. Sometimes a neighbor has a nice plant and shares the produce with others.

As with the farmers in Thailand, the answers from the gardeners in Berlin do not focus on visual aspects, but on food, natural diversity, and community. The gardens are described as home (including the dress code), and several gardeners also mentioned that they lived nearby. Gardens and nearby apartment buildings form an urban fabric that offers an alternative to the suburban model. Allotment gardens were designed to create better living conditions for the working class and thus have a utopian dimension; they provide a village-like community with face-to-face contact. Beauty for these gardeners is linked to involvement with the material and social environments, and retreating into the garden paradoxically implies connecting to a larger world. Allotment gardens also keep alive the agricultural memory, which makes them attractive for immigrants who have come from rural areas.

Although the gardeners appear to share a common wish to be creatively involved in nature, their sense of beauty is contested. Those who write about gardens often stereotype the design of allotment gardens as displaying a tacky garden-gnome style, and while allotment gardens are mostly ignored by academics, there are some frontal attacks: "The blessings of industrial mass consumption have reached the allotment gardens: prefabricated huts, garden ponds with automatic wells, as well as the floral splendor from the breeds of the garden supercenter bear witness to the achieved industrial wealth. . . . New extermination techniques are deployed against everything unplanned, unwanted, and not tolerated: snails, weeds, and the seeds that follow new plants. . . . Motorized tools turn friends of the garden into omnipotent rulers of growth and selection" (Kropp 79–80; my translation). The sociologist Cordula Kropp is certainly aware of the malevolence of the terms "selection" and "extermination" in a German context. Her stereotypical depiction bears no resemblance to reality and is blind to the diverse styles found in allotment gardens. It is a current expression of the aristocratic demonization of those who are "digging in the field."

While German allotment gardens have enjoyed a degree of protection since 1919 (Bigell), the case of the Soodevahe garden area in Estonia shows how ethnic and economic conflicts are framed aesthetically. For forty years Soviet (mostly Russian) workers have used the area around the eastern runway of the Tallinn airport for setting up their dachas. However, after Estonian independence they found that what was tolerated during Soviet times was now considered illegal squatting. Many older gardeners who had lived in Estonia most of their lives could not pass the language test that is required to become an Estonian citizen. While Estonia steered a neoliberal economic course, seen in the slick, postmodern, "here I am" style of the new banks, malls, and hotels, the dachas around the airport were seen as an eyesore, particularly since they would be the first impression of Estonia for foreign visitors. The former Estonian prime minister Andrus Ansip stated in a press conference, "For me it is a very desirable decision that the airport of Tallinn starts to expand to these areas where currently there are dachas, plastic [green]houses. When you descend to Tallinn and see this 'splendid' summer cottage area from the air, it is sad. But soon that cottage area will disappear" (Republic of Estonia Government; my translation).

When I visited the area in June 2015, I found that much of the dacha area had recently been bulldozed, in particular the areas along and behind the runway, where the cottages had been converted into piles of shredded wood. The tragedy of the dachas was that they had become too visible to those gazing from airplane windows during this new era, and their diverse and somewhat anarchic beauty, more easily appreciated on foot or by bicycle, was unseen.

While beauty should not be reduced to contestation, it is equally reductive to isolate beauty from contestation, from police batons and bulldozers. Rather, beauty is found in the values, imaginaries, communities, and "alter"-natives behind the contestation, in the encounter with social and material alterity.

Beauty, in the case studies I've presented, has a vernacular and processual meaning, marked by involvement in the social and natural environments. The transcendentalist figure of thought that poses beauty as experienced alterity is still relevant. While traditional transcendentalism understood alterity as spirituality, there is also a material form of transcendence, as well as a social and temporal dimension of transcendence, pointing at a common past and future. In this expanded transcendental frame, the seemingly prosaic act of eating gains new significance as a link to the material world and as a social ritual. The gardens in which food is grown are themselves the afterglow of a social imaginary, as are the housing blocks in which many gardeners live.

A sense of utopian beauty is, with ironic refraction, presented in the Norwegian film Gymnaslærer Pedersen (Comrade Pedersen), which is about a teacher who is drawn into a Maoist group during the 1970s in Norway. One of its leaders speaks about the beauty of plastic flowers: "Now listen, I really don't understand why people want those real ones. Plastic is practical, useful, and cheap. And therefore it is also beautiful. I have plastic flowers in a vase on my living room table. They don't wilt. Perfect for an active Communist. In addition, in a strange way they look like real flowers, but maybe more real than real flowers" (my translation). The beauty of plastic is located neither in the material itself nor in the eye of the individual beholder; instead, it is found in a utopian ideal transcending the object, making it more real than its visible shadow. It would be too easy to write this off as an ironic statement about a misguided generation—after all, it is not clear who is more misguided, the dreamers or the realists.[7] Beauty here is found in collective ideological commitment, in a "we" that is untimely in an individualist age.

Beauty is often reduced to attractiveness, and the romantic attempt to find beauty outside the modern world has been appropriated by tourism. Capitalism has created a transparent world of servility, having no room for a concept of beauty based on alterity. Today Kant's concept of disinterestedness could be interpreted as a rejection of the servility of the aesthetic sense. Beauty negates the absoluteness of the present, suggesting a world behind the mirror, or, in Edward Abbey's words, "that out there is a different world, older and greater and deeper by far than ours, a world which surrounds us and sustains the little world of men as sea and sky surround and sustain a ship" (37). While this different world can be found in Abbey's desert, it also exists in our cities, in the material transcendence of gardens and in utopian dreams of the past cast in concrete, and it exists in rural communities that imagine and create a different future.

Werner Bigell teaches English and intercultural communication at the University of Tromsø (campus Alta) in Norway. His recent publications include *Fear and Fascination: Anti-landscapes between Material Resistance and Material Transcendence* and *Allotment and Community Gardens: Commons in German Cities*. Bigell is currently engaged in collaborative projects with Russian and Thai universities.

NOTES

1. German allotment gardens were created during the industrialization of the nineteenth century, to provide the working class with healthy recreation and healthy food. The gardens are located inside cities, grouped into so-called colonies with their own administrative structures and social activities, and are regulated by federal law and protected from speculation (thus remaining affordable for all social classes). See Bigell.

2. An example is Anjan Chatterjee's book The Aesthetic Brain.

3. I used a collection of travel writings by Arab authors who went to the United States. However, as there are considerable differences among Arab societies and regions when it comes to tradition (the northern West Bank where I taught was, for example, more conservative than the southern part), not all stories were equally acceptable. The students found a story where the author describes a traditional "streaking" race at an American university "not beautiful." When I asked them about another story, which dealt with adultery, they said that it was no problem since "adultery is mentioned in the Koran."

4. I use the term "ideology" without its common negative connotations, following the Merriam-Webster dictionary's definition of it as "visionary theorizing," "a systematic body of concepts especially about human life or culture," "a manner of the content of thinking characteristic of an individual, group, or culture," and "the integrated assertions, theories and aims that constitute a sociopolitical program" (http://www.merriam-webster.com/dictionary/ideology). In the humanities, however, "ideology" is often used in a narrow sense, signifying "an idea I dislike," for example in Terry Eagleton's

definition of it as "a kind of mythology, a realm which has purged itself of ambiguity and alternative possibility" (qtd. in Quigley 51).

5. I used interpreters from the Research and Development Institute of Khon Kaen University and made handwritten notes, later assembling them into complete sentences.

6. Whereas on conventional rice farms the paddies are divided by narrow dykes covered with grass, the organic farmers create larger paddies and larger dykes, planted with a variety of trees and bushes. Thus the values of the farmers create a distinct landscape.

7. The argument here is not meant to pitch plastic against wood, a sense of natural beauty against a modern one. Peter Quigley complains that "relativity theorists insist that there is no base for an undisputed claim for beauty or for ugliness" (11). On the one hand I disagree, as beauty is certainly contested, as I have shown, and the proponents of natural beauty have to explain how they do not replicate the aristocratic bias. On the other hand, the issue here is not an exercise of contestation but of seeing dimensions of alterity.

WORKS CITED

Abbey, Edward. *Desert Solitaire*. 1968. London: Robin Clark, 1992. Print.
Bigell, Werner. "Allotment and Community Gardens: Commons in German Cities." *Spaces In-Between: Cultural and Political Perspectives on Environmental Discourse.* Ed. Sigurd Bergmann and Mark Luccarelli. Leiden: Brill Rodopi, 2015. 102–30. Print.
Chatterjee, Anjan. *The Aesthetic Brain: How We Evolved to Desire Beauty and Enjoy Art.* New York: Oxford UP, 2014. Print.
Emerson, Ralph Waldo. *Selections from Ralph Waldo Emerson*. Ed. Stephen Whicher. Boston: Riverside, 1960. Print.
Groys, Boris. *Art Power*. Cambridge, MA: MIT P, 2008. Print.
Gymnaslærer Pedersen [Comrade Pedersen]. Dir. Hans Petter Moland. Motlys, in cooperation with the Norwegian Film Institute and Sandrew Metronome Norge, 2006. DVD.
Hatherley, Owen. *Militant Modernism*. Winchester: Zero Books, 2008. Print.
Kropp, Cordula. "Gärtner(n) ohne Grenzen: Eine neue Politik des 'Sowohl-als-auch' urbaner Gärten?" *Urban Gardening: Über die Rückkehr der Gärten in die Stadt.* Ed. Christa Müller. Munich: Oekom Verlag, 2011. 76–87. Print.
Olwig, Kenneth R. "Recovering the Substantive Nature of Landscape." *Annals of the Association of American Geographers* 86.4 (Dec. 1996): 630–53. Print.
Quigley, Peter. *Housing the Environmental Imagination: Politics, Beauty and Refuge in American Nature Writing*. Newcastle upon Tyne, UK: Cambridge Scholars, 2012. Print.
Republic of Estonia Government. "Government press conference record" [Valitsuse pressikonverentsi stenogram]. Vabariigi valitsus, 12 May 2011. Web. 26 June 2015.
Tuan, Yi-Fu. "The City as a Moral Universe." *Geographical Review* 78.3 (1988): 316–24. Print.

CHAPTER 13

TOWARD SUSTAINABLE AESTHETICS
THE POETRY OF FOOD, SEX, WATER, ARCHITECTURE, AND BICYCLE RIDING

SCOTT SLOVIC

THE PRACTICE OF SUSTAINABLE AESTHETICS

The term "aesthetics" does not appear as a category of analysis in the fourth edition of *The Princeton Encyclopedia of Poetry and Poetics*, yet few would argue with the idea that poetry is a form of expression that seeks in various ways to elicit an aesthetic response from readers and listeners. We associate the concept of poetry with "beautiful words," words that challenge and torque the mundane flatness of "nonpoetic language." If anything, poetry is often thought to be that which defies quotidian usefulness—it is the linguistic equivalent of the long fingernail in traditional Asian cultures, a symbol of leisure. But there is another side to poetry, of course—and this is true as well of other genres and of literary criticism, too: the practical, down-to-earth emphasis on lived experience and social engagement. In environmental literature and ecocriticism, this practical dimension often becomes paramount. This is true in the trenches of environmental justice literature and scholarship, as evidenced in volumes ranging from *The Environmental Justice Reader* (2002) to *Sharing the Earth: An International Environmental Justice Reader* (2015). It is also increasingly the case in sustainability-oriented environmental writing and scholarship. My purpose here is to demonstrate the possibility of uniting aesthetic and practical readings of a few examples of what Leonard Scigaj, in his 1999 study, called "sustainable poetry," with particular focus on William Stafford's 1964 poem "Maybe Alone on My Bike."

Scigaj established an explicit connection between contemporary poetry and sustainability in his book *Sustainable Poetry: Four American Ecopoets* (in which he offers extended commentary on the work of A. R. Ammons, Wendell Berry, W. S. Merwin, and Gary Snyder). In this project, Scigaj defines the "sustainable poem" as "the verbal record of an interactive encounter in the world of our sensuous experience between the human psyche and nature, where nature retains its autonomy—where nature is not dominated, reduced to immanence, or reduced to a reliably benign aesthetic backdrop for anthropocentric concerns" (80). What seems particularly important in Scigaj's definition—helping to distinguish the "sustainable poem" from the traditional "nature poem"—is the idea of the nonhuman world as autonomous, independent from human wishes and needs. In other words, within a truly sustainable poem, the world exists for its own sake, even though the poem itself must of course come from the mind of a human being. In a sense, then, the writer of a sustainable poem seeks to place him- or herself (and the human species more generally) in a proper ecological relationship with the rest of nature, not making human concerns the central issue of the text. In his introduction to the spring 2012 special issue of *American Literary History* devoted to sustainability in America, Gillen d'Arcy Wood asserts that "sustainability... necessitates a humble acknowledgement of the limits of human knowledge" (3). This stance of humility seems intrinsically related to, even foundational for, a particular aesthetic view of the world, which is also highlighted in Scigaj's earlier work.

In an interview in 1988, one of the featured poets in Scigaj's *Sustainable Poetry*, the Hawai'i-based W. S. Merwin, commented at length on the relation between basic human attitudes toward nature and the tendency of human civilization to exert a callously destructive impact on the planet. Emphasizing the importance of cultivating a "feeling of awe" toward nature, Merwin stated,

> The cause of [my] anger is, I suppose, the feeling of destruction, watching the destruction of things that I care passionately about. If we're so stupid that we choose to destroy each other and ourselves, that's bad enough; but if we destroy the whole life on the planet! And I'm not talking about a big bang; I'm talking about ... the destruction of the seas, the destruction of species after species, the destruction of the forests. These are not replaceable. We can't suddenly decide years down the line that we made a mistake and put it all back. The feeling of awe—something that we seem to be losing—is essential for survival. (qtd. in Scigaj 187)

The poet here makes clear that his purpose in writing poetry in today's world is to forestall the further erosion of this feeling of awe, using poetic language to revivify our relationship to the vast and mysterious and, in some ways, fragile planet. In a sense, this means re-creating through poetry what it feels like when a person perceives some aspect of the world for the first time: an "aha" moment—a sense of delighted discovery. Scigaj observes that this poetic representation of "seeing for the first time" helps to cleanse readers of jaded indifference and "refurbishes our *relational* bond with nature" (186).

Students of the history of aesthetics will recognize Merwin's use of the term "awe" as an invocation of the European tradition of the sublime. Lee Rozelle provides a succinct overview of the relevance of the sublime aesthetic to ecocriticism in his 2006 volume *Ecosublime: Environmental Awe and Terror from New World to Oddworld*, beginning with a discussion of the historical roots of the sublime in the eighteenth-century theories of Immanuel Kant and Edmund Burke. Burke discerns that the sublime occurs when the human observer encounters vast physical space that "has a tendency to fill the mind with that sort of delightful horror, which is the most genuine effect, and the truest test of the sublime" (qtd. in Rozelle 5). Such an experience occurs not only when the human subject encounters the enormity of Mont Blanc, but even when people are merely spurred to step outside of a symbolic, constructed paradigm for understanding nature and into the "material"—the latter being what Rozelle dubs "the sustainable" way of thinking about nature (2). Rozelle states that his book "argues that interactions among living things, water, air, and substrate can exist outside of language and culture, that the landscape garden and the forest are not transposable. This recognition can be sparked by an aesthetic impulse that prompts characters in literary texts to become revived in an increasingly disposable culture. This reintroduction of self and place advances our emotional and behavioral relationships to the outside" (2).

Already in Cheryll Glotfelty's foundational introduction to *The Ecocriticism Reader* (1996) it was evident that scholars in this field resist the idea that "literature float[s] above the material world in some aesthetic ether" (xix), but the advent of "material ecocriticism" during the period of 2008–2014 vividly reinforced the field's commitment to material engagement between subject and object—indeed, the physical inseparability of subject and object. The particular contribution of Rozelle's study is to place this material focus in the context of the tradition of the sublime, with all of its emotional emphasis on terror and awe, and perhaps also joy. The joyful dimension of sublime environmental aesthetics has come into play in recent discussions of the literature of sustainability, such as Daniel J. Philippon's 2012 "Sustainability and the Humanities: An Extensive Pleasure," which highlights Wendell Berry's famous essay "The Pleasures of Eating." Berry claims that "eating with fullest pleasure—pleasure, that is, that does not depend on ignorance—is perhaps the profoundest enactment of our connection with the world" (152), a phrasing that calls our attention to the unusual word "profoundest," a sublimely superlative modifier that celebrates material "connection."

Much of the writing about sustainability reaches out toward environmental scholars and activists and toward the general public in a tone of urgent seriousness, imploring people to consider making fundamental life changes: eating local foods (and eating lower on the food chain—that is, avoiding meat, imported goods, and other resource-intensive products); driving and flying less; building more energy-efficient homes and workplaces; and using fewer natural resources in general. The practical suggestions about lifestyle reform that come from the sustainability movement are intended in a spirit of helpfulness and altruism, but such pronouncements and calls to action tend to strike readers as puritanical and threatening, as they seem to require a diminishment in pleasure, in quality of life—as if we're all now expected to tighten our belts and prepare to go hungry. Because of this apparent message of austerity, many members of the general public are likely to shy away from the language of sustainability in books and magazines and newspapers. The public would rather dream of opportunities for greater success and happiness, even if such dreams call for the use of additional natural resources during a time of ecological decline.

There is a strong tendency for people to ignore ecological reality until they are confronted by absolute and immediate changes in the physical world: lack of drinking water, food shortages, impossibly high fuel prices, unbreathable air, and so on. Years ago, poet and essayist John Daniel observed that stories of environmental crisis on television or in the *New York Times* are unlikely to change human behavior, but the "absence of bread on our tables and the presence of salt in our drinking water" might well prompt such change (165). Judging by sales figures, people would rather read *Fifty Shades of Grey* (125 million copies sold as of 2015) than Alan Weisman's *Countdown: Our Last, Best Hope for a Future on Earth?* (Barnes & Noble.com sales rank 687,088, as of 2015).

AWE-INSPIRING EXAMPLES OF SUSTAINABLE POETRY

What I would like to do in the remainder of this chapter is point to and explicate some awe-inspiring examples of sustainable poetry that explore human perceptions of the world and attempt, along the lines of Merwin's comments above, to resuscitate our capacity for wonder, inspiring readers to seek new consciousness not merely as a way of avoiding ecological destruction but in pursuit of enriched and intensified imaginative lives. I wish to suggest, in a very practical way, that sustainable poetry can help readers appreciate such quotidian lifestyle themes as food, water, architecture, transportation/energy, and ecology/pollution without being off-puttingly negative and discouraging. I believe the inspiring beauty of these poetic texts helps readers and listeners to take to heart various sustainability-related messages.

Gary Snyder's famous poem "Song of the Taste" first appeared in his 1969 collection *Regarding Wave*, during the early years of the modern American environmental movement. American readers had become newly sensitized to serious environmental issues with the publication of Rachel Carson's dark exposé of the dangers of agricultural pesticides in her 1962 book *Silent Spring* and Paul Ehrlich's dire forecasts of hunger and disease resulting from human overpopulation in *The Population Bomb* in 1968, and the first Earth Day event took place on April 22, 1970. Snyder's ecological vision in "Song of the Taste," however, celebrates the essential delight of eating, associating nutrition with sexuality. The poem begins with a heavy emphasis on the verb "eating":

> Eating the living germs of grasses
> Eating the ova of large birds

Snyder works toward a concluding passage that fully conflates eating and kissing:

> Eating each other's seed
>   eating
> ah, each other.
>
> Kissing the lover in the mouth of bread:
>   lip to lip. (169)

The poem bursts forth with the sense of fertility, opening with paired references to grass seed ("germs") and bird eggs ("ova"), implying a commonality between plant life and animal life and suggesting that every living being, plant or animal, is "drawing on life of living," one life building itself out of other lives. But in spite of the sense of joyful abundance in this poem of eating, the form of the text itself does not imply lavish excess, a mindless exploitation of resources beyond what is needed to sustain life. The relatively short lines and the stanzas consisting mostly of couplets and tercets point toward frugality of language and moderation of physical consumption. Joyful and healthy life, the poet seems to say, does not require an orgy of overeating, but rather a conscious, delicate tasting of each seed, each grape, and each "mouth of bread." The phrase "eating / ah, each other" startles readers with the ecological idea that the eater is also destined to be eaten—this is the place of all living creatures in the organic world. The poem's final line, "lip to lip" (in fact the entire last stanza), links the process of eating with the act of kissing (and, implicitly, with the process of sexual contact), but the deliberateness of phrasing implies that this process, to be most mindful, should take place in a disciplined, careful way, not with mindless abandon. Published shortly after the appearance of Ehrlich's jeremiad on overpopulation, Snyder's "Song of the Taste" realistically represents sexuality and the consumption of food as processes that celebrate life while exercising appropriate self-control. In drawing readers' attention so freshly to such ordinary activities as eating and kissing, Snyder seeks to spark the renewal of awe (and careful attention) that Merwin calls for.

Ask contemporary scholars what they consider to be the single most pressing ecological concern in the world today, and many will answer "water." To some extent today's water issues are the result of global, anthropogenic climate change. Concerns about water resources also result from the recognition that human population growth has greatly increased the need for food production, but in many parts of the world there is no longer sufficient water for agriculture and the raising of livestock. In the United States, despite the severity of the drought in western states in recent years, city dwellers are often oblivious to the need to use water consciously. Most people can turn a faucet in their homes and water will immediately appear, as if by magic. It is common for people living in single-family homes to have large green lawns requiring lots of water—this is even true in desert regions.

In teaching my students to read poetry that encourages greater sensitivity to the fundamental preciousness of water, I like to refer to a small work by Native American author Ofelia Zepeda, who comes from the Tohono O'odham tribe in southern Arizona, close to the US-Mexico border. Zepeda was raised in a farming community in the Sonoran Desert. Her poem "B 'o e-a:g maṣ 'ab him g ju:kĭ / It Is Going to Rain" first appeared in her 1997 collection *Jeweḍ 'I-Hoi / Earth Movements*:

> B 'o 'e-a:g maṣ 'ab him g ju:kĭ.
> Ṣag wepo mo pi woho.
> Nañpi koi ta:tk g jeweḍ mat am o i si ka:ckad c pi o i-hoiñad c o ñenḍad.
> Ṣag wepo mo pi woho.
> Nañpi koi ta:tk g da:m ka:cim mat o ge s-wa'usim s-we:ckad.
> Ṣag wepo mo pi woho.
> Nañpi koi ta:tk g hewel mat s-hewogim o 'i-me:
> Ṣag wepo mo pi woho.
> Nañpi koi hewegid g s-wa'us jeweḍ
> mat g hewel 'ab o 'u'ad.
> Ñia, heg hekaj o pi ṣa'i woho matṣ o ju:.
>
> Someone said it is going to rain.
> I think it is not so.
> Because I have not yet felt the earth and the way it holds still

> in anticipation.
> I think it is not so.
> Because I have not yet felt the sky become heavy with moisture of
>   preparation.
> I think it is not so.
> Because I have not yet felt the winds move with their coolness.
> I think it is not so.
> Because I have not yet inhaled the sweet, wet dirt the winds bring.
> So, there is no truth that it will rain. (18–19)

This brief poem treats, in both English and the O'odham language, the mundane, unremarkable subject of whether it will rain or not on a particular day. For the average urban person, especially someone living in a nondesert region, this may seem to be an insignificant issue—if it rains, one might carry an umbrella, and if not, one won't need to think about the umbrella. I don't mean to trivialize the subject of whether or not it will rain, but merely to suggest that rain (or water in general) takes on a special significance, even implying the difference between life and death, for someone who resides in a very dry place and who makes his or her living as a farmer. In Zepeda's poem, an anonymous "someone" has said casually that "it is going to rain"—perhaps this speaker is a weather forecaster on television. He or she seems to be someone who is not part of the community where the poem's speaker, the "I," lives. The speaker then very carefully assesses the prediction of rain against her (or his) own local knowledge of what happens when it is about to rain—the way the earth trembles, the air becomes heavy, the wind cools down, and the air takes on a sweet smell. The poem suggests first and foremost that whether it will rain or not is an extremely important question because water itself is such a precious, life-sustaining phenomenon—it is not a casual question. Even the way the speaker gives four examples of what happens before it rains evokes a feeling of sacredness in Native American poetry because it implies the four cardinal directions (north, east, south, and west)—Native ceremonies often begin with an acknowledgment of these four sacred directions.

Perhaps what makes this an especially interesting example of sustainable poetry is how Zepeda's work so clearly demonstrates the speaker's refined knowledge of her physical environment and her passionate concern for the importance of water/rain. Readers of this poem who really take time to think about it come away with a new sense of what water means, how vital it is to the sustaining of life. In his introduction to *Ecosublime*, Rozelle emphasizes the essential importance of pointing to the reality of physical nature and our connection with it. He writes, "We must unlock the constructionist's cage and remember a wider range of human links to the outside" (2). Rozelle's example is the experience of a snakebite—nearly being bitten while walking near a coiled rattlesnake or seeing a cottonmouth on a pile of leaves near one's arm. But sustainable poetry in the vein of Snyder's "Song of the Taste" and Zepeda's "B 'o e-a:g maṣ 'ab him g ju:kĭ / It Is Going to Rain" highlights a more joyful—and less terrified—engagement with the physicality of nature, even if the works also contain serious messages regarding the frugal use of resources and the extreme preciousness of food and water. In a sense, the "ecosublime" feeling evoked in these two poems is one of appreciative and celebratory awe rather than the more fearful or horrified kind of awe identified by Edmund Burke.

Another major theme in the literature of sustainability is that of green building, with relevant texts ranging from the architectural theory of William McDonough to popular writing about architecture such as Sarah Susanka's *The Not So Big House: A Blueprint for the Way We Really Live* (2001). A particularly striking literary treatment of architecture is a poem by the eccentric, wandering Japanese poet Nanao Sakaki called "Specification for Mr. Nanao Sakaki's House," which appeared in his 1987 collection *Break the Mirror*. Here is a brief passage in which the author's ecological sensibility, his sense of dwelling within the complex and awe-inspiring and *living* planet Earth, is manifest:

> A microcosm—
> Height 100M, radius 100M.
> Bamboo & cedar for framework,
> Lava & clay as basement
> Blue columbine carpet,
> Bougainvillea ceiling.
> Pampas grass roofing;
> Alive, breathing statues as wall—winter wren, golden eagle,
> Sea plankton, spermwhale, dinosaur, salamander,
> Myself, the representative of terrestrial mammals
> Standing in a corner as keyboard;
>   Me, & all the creatures in unison
>   Pulsating heart rhythm
>   Swirling breath melody—a life-proving song—
>   The whole dome sounds bamboo pipe organ. (69–70)

Sakaki's notion of himself as a global citizen, not a resident in a single, specific place or an insular representative of a single culture, or even a single species, gives this poem an expansive sense of belonging. One of the elements of green, or sustainable, architecture is the idea of biomimicry, whereby human buildings imitate the processes and materials found in the natural world. The poet's "house," as imagined in this celebration of planetary inhabitation, is made of "plentiful & easily available" materials, such as dirt and flowers and grass, with various animals (including the poet himself) constituting the "wall" of the dwelling as "breathing statues."

Reading the poem, one realizes that the poet is not thinking of an actual, realistic human dwelling in a specific place, but rather celebrating the possibility that the entire planet might be thought of as our "house." After providing the extraordinary "specification" for his house, the poet concludes his meditation by feeling renewed wanderlust, with his wandering lifestyle indicating a new way of belonging to the world rather than mere rootlessness—"My heart starts burning for an unknown land," he writes at the end of the poem (70). At a time when citizens in many parts of the world are becoming increasingly mobile and may be losing a strong sense of what it means to be truly "at home," Sakaki's poem helps us to understand the physical and psychological aspects of dwelling in and on the Earth.

The three poems by Snyder, Zepeda, and Sakaki demonstrate the use of aestheticized language to stir a renewed sense of awe in readers (and, I suspect, in the poets' own minds) regarding such basic dimensions of human experience as food, sex, water, and architecture. My last examples tease out the "splendor of our life" in the context of another quotidian experience: the daily commute home from work, aided by a transportation machine (the bicycle) exquisitely designed to move from place to place without obstructing our exposure to the material world.

MAYBE ALONE, MAYBE NOT

Among the most important themes in sustainability literature, and perhaps in environmental literature more generally, are energy and transportation. Because of this, I developed a graduate seminar on this topic in 2006 and worked with two of the students in that class to compile the anthology *Currents of the Universal Being: Explorations in the Literature of Energy* (2015). In 2017, we devoted an entire special cluster in the journal *ISLE: Interdisciplinary Studies in Literature and Environment* to the theme of transportation and "the ecologies of mobility" (Withers), including work on bicycle literature. William Stafford's "Maybe Alone on My Bike" (originally published in the *New Yorker* in 1964) is an especially powerful example of energy poetry. I will conclude this chapter by discussing this memorable lyric treatment of the ordinary experience of traveling home, which uses the technology of the bicycle as a means of augmenting and intensifying the speaker's contact with nature and his appreciation of what it means to be present in—and in contact with—the world, rather than using technology in the more typical way, to insulate the human self from worldly engagement. This poem explicitly and keenly expresses the joy of sustainable energy usage (bicycling home rather than driving an automobile), and it demonstrates the visceral sense of awe toward the world that Merwin and Scigaj attribute to the genre of sustainable poetry. Stafford writes,

> I listen, and the mountain lakes
> hear snowflakes come on those winter wings
> only the owls are awake to see,
> their radar gaze and furred ears
> alert. In that stillness a meaning shakes;
>
> And I have thought (maybe alone on my bike, quaintly on a cold
> evening pedaling home) think!—
> the splendor of our life, its current unknown
> as those mountains, the scene no one sees.
>
> Oh citizens of our great amnesty:
> we might have died. We live. Marvels
> coast by, great veers and swoops of air
> so bright the lamps waver in tears,
> and I hear in the chain a chuckle I like to hear. (29)

Recall that Scigaj defines a sustainable poem as "the verbal record of a percept, of the poet's originary perception" (80), and think of how Stafford celebrates the essential perceptibility of the world—and the world's own alertness—that comes to him by way of the act of bicycling alone on a wintry evening. Far from the sense of diminishment that ordinary citizens might associate with the act of biking home after work rather than driving an automobile, the "quaint" (old-fashioned) activity of riding a bike becomes an opportunity to really think, to register, the feeling of "the splendor of our life." The way Stafford says "our life" rather than "our lives" implies that we are all in this life together—that even though he might be alone on his bike, he experiences an overwhelming sense of life's magic that envelops and includes all beings—fellow humans, creatures of flight and sensation like owls, and even "mountain lakes" that come alive in the opening lines of the poem and "hear snowflakes come." Reading this poem makes me want to get on my own bicycle not only in pursuit of ordinary transportation, but in an effort to perceive the "meaning [that] shakes" in the still, cold air through which the pedaling poet moves, and also in an effort to achieve the friendly bond with technology indicated in the poem, which concludes by mentioning with powerful repetition "I hear in the chain a chuckle I like to hear." This work vividly illustrates the kind of language that makes it possible for the general public to take to heart the messages of sustainability.

Perhaps it is inescapable, at this time in history, that ecologically attuned writers will articulate moral arguments in their work, in addition to attempting to revivify "our relational bond with nature" and to re-instill in us the "feeling of awe" toward the world, as Merwin stated his own objective. But even in the sometimes hortatory lines of sustainable poetry, there is, on a deeper level, an effort to help readers explore with innocent wonderment the true meaning of our existence as living animals. In his study of English nature poetry, *The Song of the Earth* (2000), Jonathan Bate asks the fundamental question, "What are poets for?" To which he responds, "They are not exactly philosophers, though they often try to explain the world and humankind's place within it. They are not exactly moralists, for at least since the nineteenth century their primary concern has rarely been to tell us in homiletic fashion how to live. But they are often exceptionally lucid or provocative in their articulation of the relationship between internal and external worlds, between being and dwelling" (251–52).

This is what I've been trying to describe here, suggesting further that the specific category of literature that we might call sustainable poetry celebrates the revelatory aspects of alternative (and often countercultural) lifestyles, making it possible for mainstream readers, currently living highly unsustainable lives of overconsumption, to take difficult messages to heart. Such writing facilitates readers' ability to reimagine what they eat, how they use water, where they live, what kind of transportation they use, and the far-reaching impacts their lives have on the planet. This is what sustainable poetry is for, the goal of its aesthetic design.

Fundamental to the impact of such writing is the degree to which it can impress readers with the value of sensory engagement with the world by evoking such engagement and showing its emotional and psychological resonance through the language of the literary text. Environmental aesthetician Arnold Berleant provides a basis for understanding the relationship between "ideas and beliefs" and "direct experience" in his 1991 study *Art and Engagement*. Berleant writes, "To understand the continuity and integration of experience is to be conscious of these factors as a presence in our actual sensory engagement with the world," and, "Engagement . . . , the central feature of the new aesthetic, stresses the active nature of aesthetic experience and its essential participatory quality" (48). As I've written elsewhere, Stafford's poem celebrates the bicycle as a "technology of contact," one that "mesh[es] the gears of [the poet's] mind with the machine and with nature, [enabling him to belong] to the world by way of technology, not in spite of it" (Slovic). Stafford's son Kim, a poet and essayist like his father, published a moving biography of Stafford in 2002, beginning the book with a poignant story about a time his father took him and his brother, both young boys at the time, to the top of a mountain pass in the Oregon coast range, then sent them off on their bikes, riding to the sea. He concludes the prologue, written after his father's death, with the question, "How long can you feel a hand, steady on your shoulder, after that hand pulls away?" (ix).

Environmental artists represent this hand on the shoulder of the reader. "What do we make of our own ride through the world as we pull away from the 'hand' of the poet, the photographer, and the critic?" I asked in "Technologies of Contact." Stafford uses the phrase "*maybe* alone" (my italics) in the title of his poem, suggesting that neither the speaker of the poem nor any of us is truly alone. "We are all 'on our bikes,'" I wrote, "using words and wheels and other technologies to find our way home, not merely acting upon an inert world but participating in a world of mutual interactions." Appreciating the "sustainable aesthetics" of Stafford's poem, bicycle poetry more broadly, and the larger genre of sustainability literature requires us to acknowledge how representing "engagement" with "direct experience" of the world (to use Berleant's terms [48]) plays a role in stirring our own feelings of awe, as readers and as people living in the world, toward the world itself.

SCOTT SLOVIC is Professor of Literature and Environment, Professor of Natural Resources and Society, and Chair of the English Department at the University of Idaho. He served as founding president of the Association for the Study of Literature and Environment from 1992 to 1995, and since 1995 has edited *ISLE: Interdisciplinary Studies in Literature and Environment*. He is author and editor of many books and articles, including *Seeking Awareness in American Nature Writing* and *Going Away to Think: Engagement, Retreat, and Ecocritical Responsibility*.

WORKS CITED

Adamson, Joni, Mei Mei Evans, and Rachel Stein, eds. *The Environmental Justice Reader: Politics, Poetics, and Pedagogy*. Tucson: U of Arizona P, 2002. Print.
Ammons, Elizabeth, and Modhumita Roy, eds. *Sharing the Earth: An International Environmental Justice Reader*. Athens: U of Georgia P, 2015. Print.
Bate, Jonathan. *The Song of the Earth*. Cambridge, MA: Harvard UP, 2000. Print.
Berleant, Arnold. *Art and Engagement*. Philadelphia: Temple UP, 1991. Print.
Berry, Wendell. "The Pleasures of Eating." *What Are People For?* San Francisco: North Point, 1990. 145–52. Print.
Daniel, John. *The Trail Home: Nature, Imagination, and the American West*. 1992. New York: Pantheon, 1994. Print.
Glotfelty, Cheryll. Introduction. *The Ecocriticism Reader: Landmarks in Literary Ecology*. Ed. Cheryll Glotfelty and Harold Fromm. Athens: U of Georgia P, 1996. xv–xxxvii. Print.
Greene, Roland, Stephen Cushman, Clare Cavanagh, Jahan Ramazani, and Paul Rouzer, eds. *The Princeton Encyclopedia of Poetry and Poetics*. 4th ed. Princeton, NJ: Princeton UP, 2013. Print.
Philippon, Daniel J. "Sustainability and the Humanities: An Extensive Pleasure." *American Literary History* 24.1 (Spring 2012): 163–79. Print.
Rozelle, Lee. *Ecosublime: Environmental Awe and Terror from New World to Oddworld*. Tuscaloosa: U of Alabama P, 2006. Print.
Sakaki, Nanao. "Specification for Mr. Nanao Sakaki's House." *Break the Mirror: The Poems of Nanao Sakaki*. San Francisco: North Point, 1987. 69–70. Print.

Scigaj, Leonard M. *Sustainable Poetry: Four American Ecopoets.* Lexington: UP of Kentucky, 1999. Print.
Slovic, Scott. "Technologies of Contact." *Environmental Humanities*, 1 Oct. 2013. Web. 1 Aug. 2017.
Slovic, Scott, James E. Bishop, and Kyhl Lyndgaard, eds. *Currents of the Universal Being: Explorations in the Literature of Energy.* Lubbock: Texas Tech UP, 2015. Print.
Snyder, Gary. "Song of the Taste." *No Nature: New and Selected Poems.* New York: Pantheon, 1992. 169. Print.
Stafford, Kim. *Early Morning: Remembering My Father, William Stafford.* St. Paul, MN: Graywolf, 2002. Print.
Stafford, William. "Maybe Alone on My Bike." *Smoke's Way: Poems from Limited Editions, 1968–1981.* Port Townsend, WA: Graywolf, 1983. 29. Print.
Withers, Jeremy, ed. "Transportation: The Ecologies of Mobility." Spec. cluster in *ISLE: Interdisciplinary Studies in Literature and Environment* 24.1 (Winter 2017): 66–158. Print.
Wood, Gillen D'Arcy. "What Is Sustainability Studies?" *American Literary History* 24.1 (Spring 2012): 1–15. Print.
Zepeda, Ofelia. "B 'o e-a:g maṣ 'ab him g ju:kĭ / It Is Going to Rain." *Jeweḍ 'I-Hoi / Earth Movements.* Tucson, AZ: Kore, 1997. 18–19. Print.

INDEX

Abbey, Edward, 5, 17, 199
Abram, David, 158
activism, 10, 13
aesthetics of engagement, 11, 15, 36, 43–47
Akam, 175–76, 178, 179
Alaimo, Stacy, 99, 117, 169
Aldama, Frederick Luis, 16
Allen, Paula Gunn, 17, 118, 121
Ammons, A. R., 202
Ansip, Andrus, 197
Aristotle, 48, 80, 82, 84, 145
ASLE Online Bibliography 2000–2010, 1–2, 8

Badiner, Allan Hunt, 183
Baird, Theodore, 48
Bakhtin, Mikhail, 18
Barad, Karen, 99, 158, 168, 169
Barrell, John, 85–86
Bate, Jonathan, 18, 211
Bateson, Gregory, 53
Beckstrom, Maja, 109
Bennett, Jane, 99, 164
Bennett, Tony, 6
Berleant, Arnold, 4, 11–12, 15, 48, 49, 50, 211–12
Berry, Wendell, 5, 67, 202, 203

Bérubé, Michael, 2, 4, 5, 6, 17, 64
Bhardwaj, Surinder Mohan, 183
Bigell, Werner, 15, 197, 199
bioregionalism, 14
Birkerts, Sven, 1
Bloom, Harold, 144–45, 148
Boudreau, Gordon V., 61
Branch, Michael P., 17
Brooker, Ira, 5
Brooks, David, 7, 18
Brooks, Van Wyck, 92
Bruchac, Joseph, 121
Bryant, Levi, 167
Buell, Lawrence, 5, 18, 79, 80, 87
Bullard, Robert, 131
Burke, Edmund, 86, 90, 203, 208
Byerly, Alison, 17

Cafaro, Philip, 60
Cameron, Sharon, 54, 59, 61
Caminataiyar, U., 179, 180
capitalism, 7
Carlson, Allen, 4, 49
Carson, Rachel, 16, 205
Cavell, Stanley, 48
Center for Artistic Activism, 106
Chamovitz, Daniel, 99

215

Chaucer, Geoffrey, 144, 153
Cheng, Xiangzhan, 46, 49
Clark, Michael P., 64, 145–46
Cohen, Jeffrey Jerome, 14, 157, 160–61, 163–64, 165, 166
Collier, Gretchen, 144
Commoner, Barry, 80
Conrad, Joseph, 55
Cook, John, 126
Coole, Diana, 163
Cosgrove, Denis, 81, 83
Crawford, Ian, 162
Critical Theory since 1965, 2
Cronon, William, 13, 79, 87, 168

Daniel, John, 204
Darwin, Charles, 55, 74
DeBaise, Janine, 13–14, 127
Denning, Michael, 12, 65, 66, 67
Descartes, René, 98
Dewey, John, 46
Dickinson, Emily, 12, 54, 61
Diogenes, 60
Donoghue, Denis, 16
Dowie, Mark, 79
Dr. Seuss, *The Lorax*, 126
Drinnon, Richard, 48

Eagleton, Terry, 8, 18, 199
ecocriticism, 1–10, 13, 16, 80, 89, 201
Ecocriticism Reader, The, 1, 17, 18
ecofeminist aesthetics, 13, 97–113, 115–28
Ehrlich, Gretel, 5, 18
Ehrlich, Paul, 205, 206
Eliot, T.S., 24, 38
Elliot, Emory, 3, 17
Ellis, John M., 144
Emerson, Ralph Waldo, 35, 38, 47, 54, 61, 71, 149, 187–88, 189
Ensler, Eve, 117, 124
Environmental Justice Reader, The, 201
Estok, Simon, 8, 112, 167, 168

Felski, Rita, 64, 65, 66, 67, 71, 75
feminism, 7, 98
Feyerabend, Paul, 53, 60
Fifty Shades of Grey, 204

Fish, Stanley, 98
Fisherman of Halicarnassus, The, 157–71
Fitzgerald, F. Scott, 145
Flagg, Ernest, 80
Foerster, Norman, 61
formalism, 6
Foucault, Michel, 89
Freeman, Lauren, "relational autonomy," 98
Freud, Sigmund, 74
Friedman, Marilyn, 98
Frost, Samantha, 163
Frye, Norman, 88
Fukushima Daiichi nuclear facility, 14, 129–30, 133, 135, 137–139

Gaard, Greta, 13, 105, 112
Garrard, Greg, 79
Gates, Jr., Henry Louis, 148
Genet, Jean, 137
George, Timothy S., 135
German allotment gardens, 195–98
German architecture, 15, 190–93
Gifford, Terry, 79
Gilligan, Carol, 98
Gilpin, William, 61, 85, 90
Glotfelty, Cheryll, 18, 203
Graulich, Melody, 72
Groys, Boris, 191

Hagopian, Joachim, 167, 169
Halbritter, Jayme, 107
Hale, Lyric Hughes, 135
Handley, William, 67–68, 72
Harjo, Joy, 117–18
Hartman, Steven, 140
Hatherley, Owen, 192
Heidegger, Martin, 98
Heimstead, Alison, 109
Heise, Ursula, 18, 168
Heller, Chaia, 100
Heller, Scott, 3, 17, 75
Helmreich, Stefan, 167
Hendrick, George, 48
Hipple, Jr., Walter John, 61
Hogan, Patrick Colm, 16
Homer, 162, 164

Hunt, Tim, 10–11, 38
Hunter, Ian, 4
Hyman, Stanley Edgar, 42

Imamori, Matsuhiko, 133–34
Ingalls, Jeremy, 38
In the Heart of the Beast Puppet and Mask Theatre, 102, 103
Iovino, Serenella, 166
Iser, Wolfgang, 98
Ishimure, Michiko, 136–37, 139

Jeffers, Robinson, 5, 10–11, 16, 18, 23–39, 149
Jehlen, Myra, 6–7, 12
Jesudasan, C., 174, 177
Jesudasan, Hephzibah, 174, 177
Jeweler, Donald, 48
Jordan, Chris, 165
Juffer, Jane, 6

Kant, Immanuel, 98, 188, 199, 203
Kapilar, 178
Karman, James, 39
karupporul, 179
Kawakami, Hiromi, 137–39
Keats, John, 120
Kimmerer, Robin Wall, 118
Kinkade, Kathleen, 48
Klein, Michael, 117
Kolbert, Elizabeth, 110
Kolodny, Annette, 79
Krieger, Murray, 145–46
Kropp, Cordula, 197

Lao Tzu, 48
Latour, Bruno, 168
Leddy, Thomas, 49
Leopold, Aldo, 18
Lincoln, Abraham, 42
Linnaeus, Carl, 55
Lopez, Barry, vii, viii
Lorde, Audre, 100, 105–6
Louv, Richard, 125
Lowenstein, Suse, *Dark Elegy*, 125–26
Luccarelli, Mark, 12–13, 14, 92
Lyon, Thomas J., 79, 92

MacDonell, Arthur Anthony, 181
MacGregor, Sherilyn, 105
MacLeish, Archibald, 18
Macy, Joanna, 99
Mandoki, Katya, 48, 49
Marcantonio Raimondi, 81, 83
Marsh, George Perkins, 80
Marx, Karl, 48, 74
Marx, Leo, 92
Marxism, 7, 89
Masazumi, Harada, 135
material feminism, 99, 110
materiality, 13–15, 157–71
Mathews, Freya, 98
Matthiessen, F. O., 61
McCarthy, Cormac, 91
McDonough, William, 208
McKibben, Bill, 165
Meli, Mark, 140
Mendelson, Scott, 124
Merchant, Carolyn, 118
Merwin, W. S., 15, 202–3, 204, 206, 209, 210
Miller, Cynthia J., 15, 184
Milton, John, 38–39, 144
Minamata disease, 14, 135–37
Mitchell, W. J. T., 5, 13
Mokutaro, Ezuno, 136
Morris, David C., vii
Morton, Timothy, 18–19, 165, 166, 167
Muir, John, 9, 149
Mumford, Lewis, 80, 87, 91
Murdoch, Iris, 151–52
mutalporul, 179

Nakkirar, 176
Narrinai, 174–75
Nayagam, Xavier S., 175
Neidjie, Bill, 99
Nearing, Helen and Scott, 8
Nebuka, Makoto, 140
Nehamas, Alexander, 4
Nelson, Lance E., 183
Newton, Isaac, 74
Nickl, Tyler, 12, 75
Nixon, Rob, 18
Nordhaus, Ted, 79
Nussbaum, Martha, 146–47

Oelschlaeger, Max, 18
Ohmann, Richard, 148
Oliver, Mary, 9
Olwig, Kenneth, 187
O'Neill, Dan, 140
Oppermann, Serpil, 14–15, 112, 162, 166, 168–69

Palgrave, Francis, Turner, 174
pastoralism, 6
Pater, Walter, 3
Pearson, Amber, 16
Peck, H. Daniel, 53, 61
pedagogy, 14, 143–54
Perloff, Marjorie, 64, 65, 75
Philippon, Daniel J., 203
Plato, 60, 80, 82
Plumwood, Val, 99–100, 105, 111
Poe, Edgar Allan, 38
Pollan, Michael, 99
Porte, Joel, 61
poststructuralism, 7
Pound, Ezra, 23–24, 29, 34, 36, 38
Price, Uvedale, 85
Princeton Encyclopedia of Poetry and Poetics, The, 201
puram, 175–76, 179

Quigley, Peter, vii, viii, 16–17, 18, 88–89, 168, 199

Radhakrishnan, 181, 182
Radway, Janice, 148–49
Ramanujan, A.K., 174, 179, 182
Raphael, 81–82
Regan, Sheila, 109
Rich, Adrienne, 116
Richardson, Ann, 124
Richardson, Robert D., 55, 60
Roszak, Theodore, 13
Rothenberg, David, 16
Rothman, David, vii
Rozelle, Lee, 203, 207–8
Ruskin, John, 56–57, 86–87, 88, 90

Saito, Osumu, 131
Saito, Yuriko, 49

Sakaki, Nanao, 15, 208–9
Sangamera poets, 180
Sandilands, Catriona, 105
Santayana, George, 91
satoumi, 131, 133, 134
satoyama, 14, 130–35, 138, 139
Satterfield, Terre, 168
Scarry, Elaine, 4, 8, 16, 64, 69, 75, 130, 137, 138, 147–48, 149, 151–53
Scheese, Don, 17–18
Schopenhauer, Arthur, 86
Scigaj, Leonard, 202–3, 209, 210
Scruton, Roger, 7, 16
Sedgewick, Eve, 64
Seilwinder, Klaus, 192–93
Sen, Geeti, 183
Shairp, John Campbell, 175, 182
Sharing the Earth: An International Environmental Justice Reader, 201
Shellenberger, Michael, 79
Shelley, Percy Bysshe, 39
Shibata, Hideaki, 131
Silko, Leslie Marmon, 5
Sidney, Sir Philip, 145
Skinner, B. F., 48
Slovic, Scott, vii, viii, 1, 2, 6, 7, 8, 10, 15, 16, 17, 159, 168, 209, 211–12
Smith, Anthony D., 180
Snyder, Gary, 5, 13, 15, 202, 205–6, 209
Sobel, David, 125
Socrates, 60, 61
Spieler, Sandy, 103, 104
Spinoza, Baruch, 48
spirituality, 15
Stafford, Kim, 211
Stafford, William, 15, 202, 209–12
Starhawk, 109
Stegner, Wallace, 12, 63–76, 159
Steiner, Wendy, 7, 10, 11
Sterne, Jonathan, 5, 12, 72
Stevens, Wallace, 33, 144
Stewart, Frank, 11–12, 60
Strand, Ginger, 123
Strand, Paul, 91
sublime, the, 203
Susanka, Sarah, 208
sustainability, 201–13

Taguchi, Randy, 138–39, 140
Takahashi, Gen'ichiro, 136, 137
Takakazu, Yumoto, 140
Tamil culture, 15, 173–85
Tangney, ShaunAnne, vii, 14, 153
Tarkovsky, Andrei, 139
Templeman, William D., 61
Thai farming, 15, 193–95
Thatcher, Margaret, 189
Thompkins, Jane, 148
Thoreau, Henry David, 5, 11–12, 13, 41–50, 51–62, 87–88, 89
Tolkaappiyam, 175, 176, 177
Tolkappiyanar, 177
Tuan, Yi-Fu, 180, 191
Tunick, Spencer, 124
Turner, Frederick, 2, 17
Twain, Mark, 145

urippourl, 179
Uzuner, Buket, 163

Varadarajan, M., 174, 175, 178, 181, 182
Vedic literature, 181
Vendler, Helen, 148
Vignale, Giovanni, 57, 61

Wagenknecht, Edward, 61
Walia, Arjun, 169
Walls, Laura Dassow, 61
Ward, Susan Burling, 65, 67–75
Warhol, Andy, 78
Weisman, Alan, 204
Westervelt, Amy, 106
Wharton, Edith, 145
Whitman, Walt, 38
Williams, Bryon, 6
Williams, Raymond, 9
Williams, Roger, 162
Williams, Terry Tempest, 5, 9, 116, 126, 130
Wilczek, Frank, 16, 61
Wolff, Janet, 7, 19
Wolosky, Shira, 100
Wood, Gillen d'Arcy, 202
Wordsworth, William, 5, 33, 35, 38–39, 144
World Naked Bike Ride, 124
Worster, Donald, 92

Yaeger, Patricia, 165
Yuki, Masami, 14, 139, 140

Zalasiewicz, Jan, 167–68
Zepeda, Ofelia, 206–8, 209

www.ingramcontent.com/pod-product-compliance
Lightning Source LLC
Chambersburg PA
CBHW030649230426
43665CB00011B/1019